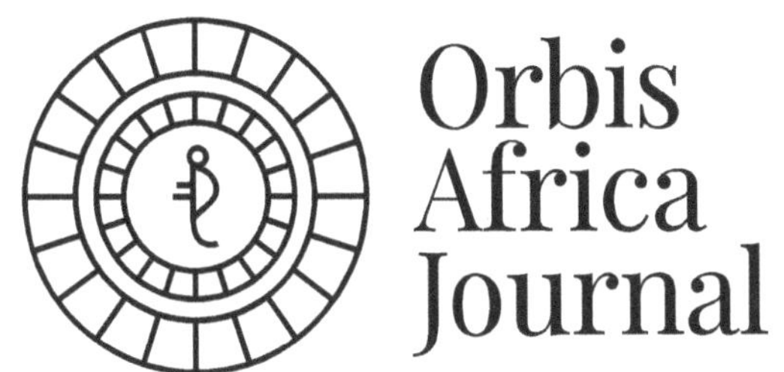

Orbis Africa Journal

VOL. 1

DIASPORIC
AFRICA PRESS

NEW YORK

This journal is a publication of Diasporic Africa Press

New York | www.dafricapress.com

ISBN: 978-1-937306-83-0
ISSN: 3067-1914

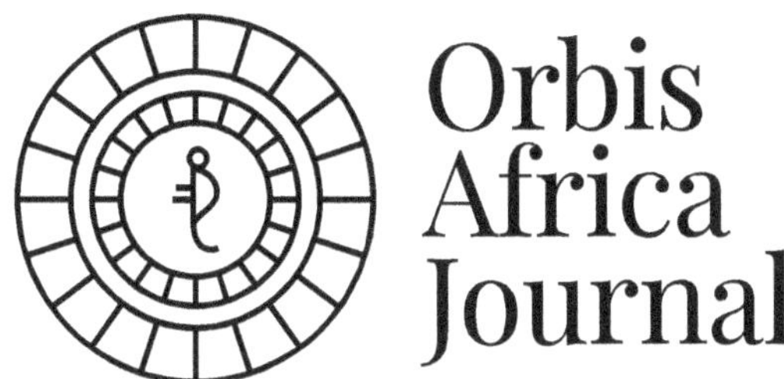

INDIANA UNIVERSITY EDITORS

Bárbaro-Martínez-Ruiz, Associate Professor of Art History and Tanner-Opperman Chair in Honor of Roy Sieber, Indiana University

John H. Hanson, Executive Associate Dean of the College of Arts and Sciences; Professor, Department of History and African Studies Program, Indiana University

Solimar Otero, Director, Latino Studies Program; Professor Folklore and Ethnomusicology and Gender Studies, Indiana University

Rachel Dixon Kabukala, PhD Candidate, Art History & African Studies, Indiana University; Associate Curator of African Art, The Nelson-Atkins Museum of Art

EDITOR & PUBLISHER

Kwasi Konadu, Editor-in-Chief and Director, Diasporic Africa Press

CONSULTING EDITORS

William Beinart, Emeritus Professor, St. Antony's College and the African Studies Centre, University of Oxford

Shadreck Chirikure, Edward Hall Professor of Archaeological Science, Director of RLAHA, British Academy Global Professor, University of Oxford

C. Danny Dawson, Professor in African American and African Diasporic Studies Department, Columbia University

Henry John Drewal, Evjue-Bascom Professor Emeritus of Art History & Afro-American Studies, University of Wisconsin-Madison

Miles Larmer, Director, Center for African Studies; Professor of History, University of Florida

Allen Roberts, Distinguished Professor Emeritus, Department of World Arts and Cultures/Dance, University of California Los Angeles, UCLA

LETTER FROM THE EDITOR

The Orbis Africa Journal is a new publishing platform that aims to foster discussion about the African world and its diaspora. Starting with rock art on the African continent over thirty thousand years ago, our journey extends to creating graphic writing systems in the modern era in the Americas. By recognizing Africa as a central subject across disciplines, we can better understand its foundations and appreciate the unique ways in which the African intellectual legacy intersects with our world. We believe that to understand history, philosophy, art history, archaeology, anthropology, visual culture, and literature from both the recent and distant past, it is essential to study them in relation to Africa. As a platform, the journal will evaluate African contributions and analyze the perspectives of African knowledge on contemporary issues. By doing so, it becomes feasible to use this knowledge to improve our ability to ask better questions about individuals and society.

—Bárbaro Martínez-Ruiz
Editor-in-Chief, *Orbis Africa Journal*
Tanner-Opperman Chair of African Art in Honor of Roy Sieber, Indiana University

CHOKWE CHAIR

Among the many exceptional works of art that can be found in the collection at Indiana University's Eskenazi Museum of Art, the Chokwe throne is one of the most striking. Made by an unrecorded artist during the late 19th or early 20th century and purchased by the Eskenazi Museum of Art from Alan Brandt Inc., NYC in 1976, this piece exemplifies the pinnacle of Chokwe artistic excellence and is rich with symbolism.

This ngundja (ceremonial throne, also called chitwamo) was expertly carved to convey the prestige and authority associated with the Chokwe chiefdom. The throne includes a seat covered in antelope hide and eight stretchers adorned with individual narrative motifs. Each of the eight scenes illustrates an essential attribute of a mwanangana (chief) or depicts a scene in which the leader would be expected to oversee daily life and perhaps intervene. Among the scenes included in this example are two men with firearms pointed at one another in conflict, two men playing music on a slit gong drum (an important part of ceremonies and initiations), and a possible circumcision ceremony, as well as groupings of birds (considered regal animals), bats (a symbol of authority), and monkeys. This iconographic imagery would be immediately understood by the Chokwe people. Also visible in these ceremonial thrones is Chokwe artists' bold appropriation of elements they would have seen in European chairs brought over during the 17th century as part of the Portuguese colonial project.[1] Unlike most seats created on the continent during this period, which were carved from a single piece of wood, the elements of Chokwe thrones are carved independently and then assembled to resemble the peg and pin construction of Portuguese chairs.[2]

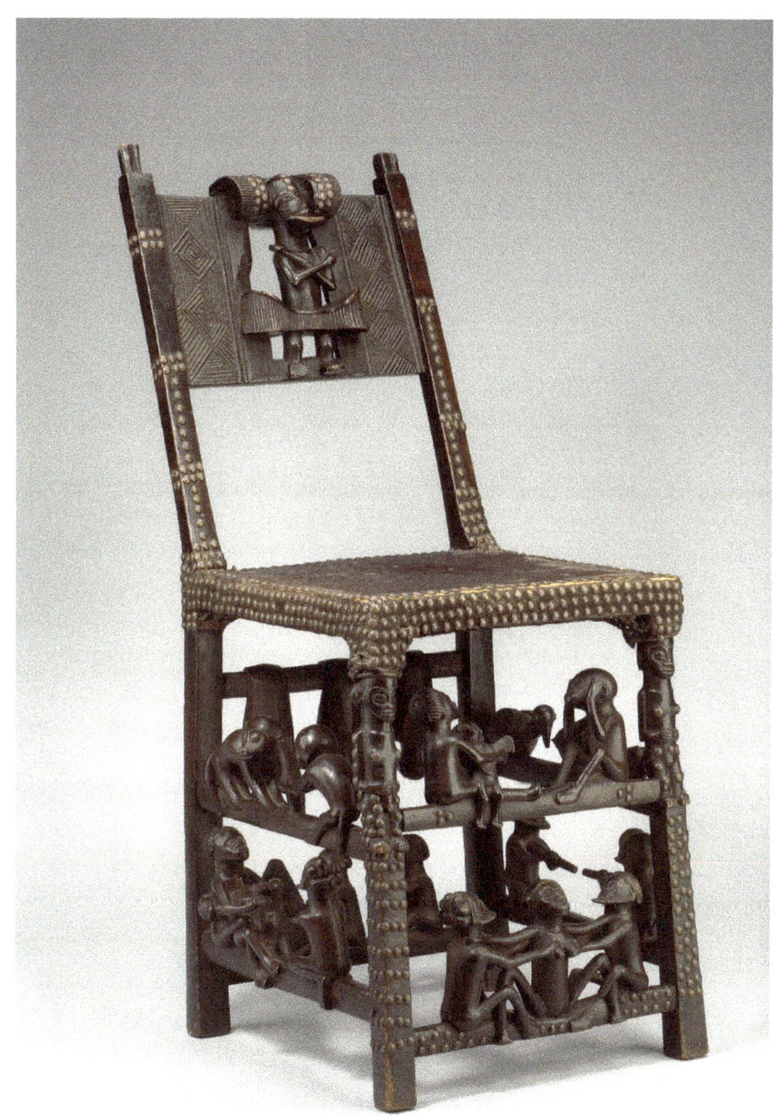

Chokwe
Chief's Chair, 1885–1930
Wood, antelope hide, and brass
31 ¼ in x 12 ¾ in x 13 in.
Eskenazi Museum of Art, Indiana University
76.54
Photo credit: Eskenazi Museum of Art/Kevin Montague

---

1 Marie Louise Bastin, *La sculpture tshokwe*, trans. J. B. Donne (A. et F. Chaffin, 1982), 251.
2 Roy Sieber and Roslyn A. Walker, *African Art in the Cycle of Life* (Smithsonian Press, 1987), 126.

The ngundja is decorated with an abundance of brass tacks found along the apron, the front of the stiles, down the front two legs, and on the lower front stretcher. This expensive, imported ornamental element served as a further symbol of wealth and status. Additional brass tacks punctuate the elaborate winged headdress protruding from either side of the figure featured prominently on the backrest portion of the seat. This figure portrays Chihongo, a male ancestral spirit of the Chokwe, also represented as a masked performer who appears at important ceremonies and signifies the royal ancestry of the mwanangana, as well as wealth and power.[3] Contrary to their European counterparts, which were designed as more overt symbols of prestige and affluence, these royal chairs and their narrative scenes served as a sort of mutual reminder to ruler and subjects about the role and responsibilities of the mwanangana in Chokwe society.

Striking similarities to the ngundja in the collection of the Birmingham Museum of Art (object 2001.104) include the general form, the low-relief carvings of female figures on the front legs, the figure of Chihongo skillfully offset by the accompanying negative space created through openwork carving techniques, delicate geometric patterns found on the chair backs, the choice of depicted scenes on the rungs, and the distinctive stylized appearance of the figures themselves. The extent to which the two works are similar may indicate production at the same studio, if not by the same artist.

— Rachel Dixon Kabukala

BIBLIOGRAPHY

Bastin, Marie Louise. *La sculpture tshokwe.* Translated and adapted by J. B. Donne. A. et F. Chaffin, 1982.

Jordán, Manuel, Marie Louise Bastin, Birmingham Museum of Art (Birmingham, Ala.), Baltimore Museum of Art, and Minneapolis Institute of Arts, eds. *Chokwe! Art and Initiation among the Chokwe and Related Peoples.* Prestel, 1998.

Sieber, Roy, and Roslyn A. Walker. *African Art in the Cycle of Life.* Published for the National Museum of African Art by the Smithsonian Press, 1987.

---

3 Manuel Jordán, et al., *Chokwe! Art and Initiation among the Chokwe and Related Peoples* (Prestel, 1998), 71.

TO TAME OR TO KILL
AFRICAN SPIRITUALITIES IN THE ARCHIVES OF BRAZILIAN SLAVERY

Florencio was bound to the whipping post. He had tried to run away. He was still tethered to it when the others finally returned from the coffee fields after another day of backbreaking work and lay down to rest. It was not yet midnight when a sudden ruckus jolted them awake. A police expedition surrounded their quarters and forced its way in, overturning their few possessions and scattering them across the floor. It found nothing. Outside, the expedition leader spoke to the property owner, Antonio Alves Silva, who had come out of his house. Silva was concerned that his captives were conspiring against him. They belonged to a "society… to which they gave the name 'Pemba'." They wore white caps and carried red sticks to signal their membership to each other. He was chagrinned by their refusal to reveal its purpose even after he beat them repeatedly.

The police arrested twenty-two enslaved women and men and a freedperson. Twelve of them, including all the women, were eventually released. Of the ten remaining, two were *crioulo* (Brazilian-born) and eight were African. Some confessed to the society's existence. They held regular Saturday meetings on the property of another resident, Captain José Barbosa de Lima, whose enslaved, too, belonged to Pemba. Its goal, they said, was to "tame the masters." The expedition rushed to Lima's property that same night around 3am. Drowsy but nonplussed, Lima said that he also knew of the society and believed its intent was, indeed, to tame the masters. He allowed the police to arrest eleven of the

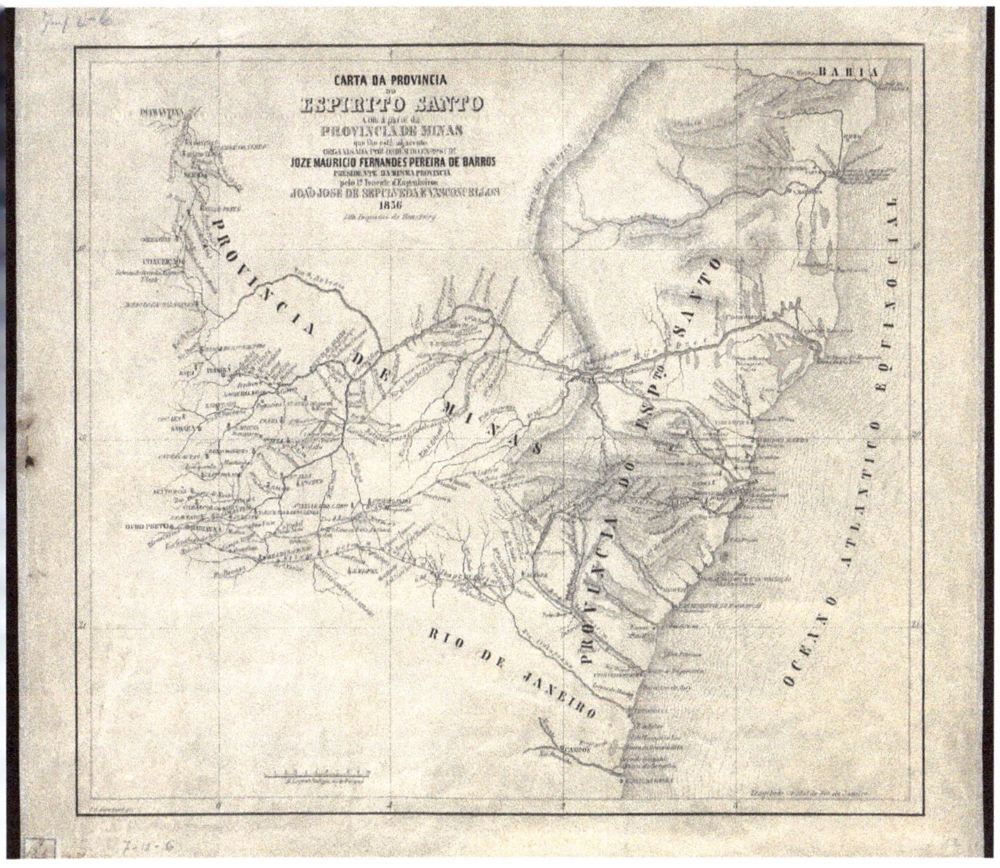

A map of the province of Espírito Santo in 1856. Itapemirim is at the mouth of the eponymous river located in the far south of the province.

CREDIT. Vasconcellos, João Joasé de Sepulveda e. Carta da provincia do Espírito Santo: com parte da provincia de minas que lhe está adjacente (Map of the province of Espírito Santo, with a section of the adjacent province of Minas Gerais). Rio de Janeiro, RJ : Lith. Imperial de Rensbury, 1856. Courtesy of the Biblioteca Nacional, Brazil.

enslaved. Some had fled.[1]

Pemba is a well-known term in the West Central African diaspora in Brazil. Its etymology derives from several languages within, or closely aligned with, the Kongo culture area of West-Central Africa, e.g. Kikongo and Kimbundu. Depending on the language, *pemba*, *mpemba*, or *pembe* signify chalk, the color white, the powders used to make things white, and the spiritual realm of the ancestors. As a color or substance, pemba refers to purification, calm, healing, and initiation into spiritual societies. The term retains tremendous spiritual resonance today, especially in the Afro-Brazilian religions of Umbanda and candomblé Angola.[2]

The historical Pemba in question comes to us in another guise. The arrests took place in the coffee frontier town of Itapemirim, in the Brazilian province of Espírito Santo, on August 25, 1860—ten years after the transatlantic slave to Brazil had been abolished for the second time, but still nearly three decades before slavery itself would be outlawed.[3] Slaveowners and law enforcement together insisted that the enslaved had convened Pemba expressly to mount an insurrection to murder masters and white people. By contrast, its actual initiates did not evoke any violent intent. They described the suffering they endured under their master, and Pemba's rituals to tame him. In later interrogations, they said almost nothing.

Insurrection scares are familiar to scholars of slavery. The conflicting testimonies and silences characterizing many archives of insurrection have often led scholars to one of two conclusions: that the enslaved were concealing their complicity in an actual insurrection plot; or conversely, that the insurrection was an invention of slaveholder paranoia.[4] Both analyses, however, are shaped—and thus limited—by the logic of the archives. To make "was there or wasn't there an insurrection?" the central question traps us in an echo chamber of slaveholder epistemology whose archives were created

---

1   * A previous version of this piece was workshopped at the Slavery & Freedom Working Group at Fordham University. Portions have also been presented at Indiana University and the Schomburg Center for Research in Black Culture. This piece was inspired by numerous conversations and exchanges with Bárbaro Martínez-Ruiz and Ras Michael Brown, and I am deeply grateful to them. I thank Geisa Ribeiro for generously sharing the Limas' inventories and Evelyne Lucena for her research support in Rio de Janeiro. This piece is dedicated to C. Daniel Dawson and in loving memory of Robert Farris Thompson.

Lieutenant Archanjo José de Souza to Chief of Police of Espírito Santo, September 27, 1860, Recurso Crime (Criminal Appeal) 2119/Cx. 193/Gal. C Anno 1860 (RC hereafter), Fl. 26v and Antonio Francisco de Oliveira Sobrinho, Second Lieutenant of Itapemirim to Manoel Pedro Alvares Moreira Villaboim, Chief of Police of Espírito Santo, August 26, 1860, IJ1 733, Arquivo Nacional, Rio de Janeiro (ANRJ hereafter). The freedperson, Mamedio, is neither charged nor questioned, so I presume he fled.

A note on the language: in recent years there has been a significant shift in the language used by scholars of slavery. While I incorporate these shifts where possible, I have maintained words such as "slave" and "master" if that is how they appear in the sources, or they reflect the point of view of the historical character in question. The term "enslaver" is also employed selectively as it does not always reflect the specificity of a person's role, eg as a trafficker, trader, driver, owner, etc., and I hope this article makes clear that I am not replicating their world view or obfuscating power relations.

2   According to the missionary Holman Bentley, *mpemba* is synonymous with *luvemba*, both signifying pipe clay or the marks made with it. W. Holman Bentley, *Dictionary and Grammar of the Kongo Language: English-Kongo Dictionary. Kongo-English Dictionary.* (Baptist Missionary Society and Trübner, 1887), 333. MacGaffey, based on the texts collected by Swedish missionary Karl Laman from Bakongo informants, defines *mpemba* as white clay (p. 65) and cites one source named Matunta who spoke thus of *luhemba*, one of the main medicines (*bilongo*) added to nkisi: "that the eyes of the nkisi and the nganga may be "brightened," which is why, when they are preparing medicines, chalk is always the first." Wyatt MacGaffey, ed., *Art and Healing of the Bakongo Commented by Themselves: Minkisi from the Laman Collection* (Stockholm: Folkens Museum-etnografiska and Indiana University Press, 1991), 5, 65. Anita Jacobson-Widding discusses the many meanings of the color white and its importance in initiation rituals in *Red-White-Black as a Mode of Thought: A Study of Triadic Classification by Colours in the Ritual Symbolism and Cognitive Thought of the Peoples of the Lower Congo* (Uppsala, Sweden: Almqvist & Wiksell, 1979), with a good summary on 216-217.

Martínez-Ruiz notes that Lemba initiates smoke tobacco in a pipe made from luvemba (pl. mpemba) in order to commune with ancestors. Apud Ras Michael Brown, the Lei de Pemba (Law of Pemba) is the basis of Umbanda's spiritual power.

3   An 1815 law banned the slave trade north of the equator (thus prohibiting the trade from the Bight of Benin). The trans-Atlantic slave trade in general was banned in 1831. Both laws were ineffective, and nearly 800,000 illegally enslaved Africans were transported to Brazil after 1831. Overall, Brazil alone received over 5 million enslaved Africans, dwarfing the estimated 252,652 Africans who arrived in the United States. Beatriz Gallotti Mamigonian, *Africanos livres: a abolição do tráfico de escravos para o Brasil* (São Paulo: Companhia das Letras, 2017); for statistics, see http://www.slavevoyages.org/estimates/x9FCRacn, accessed June 12, 2024.

4   Works that have argued that slave insurrections were slaveocratic inventions include Winthrop D Jordan, *Tumult and Silence at Second Creek: An Inquiry Into a Civil War Slave Conspiracy*, 1996; Michael P. Johnson, "Denmark Vesey and His Co-Conspirators," *The William and Mary Quarterly* 58, no. 4 (2001): 915–76, https://doi.org/10.2307/2674506. Johnson argued that historians, driven by their own desires to see a slave insurrection, invented one through careless historical work, thereby becoming "co-conspirators." An important counterperspective can be found in Aisha K. Finch, *Rethinking Slave Rebellion in Cuba: La Escalera and the Insurgencies of 1841-1844* (Chapel Hill: University of North Carolina Press, 2015) in which the author critiques historians who have considered La Escalera of 1844 as an invention by the Spanish colonial government. Finch reconsiders this interpretation by centering Black Cubans' political struggles.

to invent Black criminality and narrate the ultimate triumph of white law and order.[5] In these archives, Black life and politics remain obscure.

Facing such impasses, those of us who study African diasporic lives are accustomed to reading our sources "against the grain" for traces of Black life—by finding, for example, even in a brief fugitive slave ad, hints of affective bonds that enslaved people formed with one another. Yet reading "against the grain" falls short of interrogating the very logic of the archives. We remain trapped in the world they create. I first want to expose and understand this logic by reading the sources "along the archival grain," in Ann Laura Stoler's words.[6] This enables what may initially appear counterintuitive: to resist our own desire to see an insurrection by the enslaved, which was what enslavers and their friends would want us to think.

My intention, of course, isn't to negate the possibility of resistance. Brazilian history overflows with astonishing examples, from Palmares to the Malê revolt, *quilombolas* (maroons) to abolitionists.[7] I want to envision a world beyond resistance, to consider the richness and complexity of African peoples' lives in Brazil that do not only exist in relation to their resistance to enslavement. I will do this by interrogating the possibilities and limitations of documentary archives, which is essential to my own practice as an archival historian. The first part examines the documentary archives of Pemba through the eyes of the slaveocracy—owners, police,

the justice system—to show how they create a story about a coming African slave insurrection. The second part delves deeper into Pemba to explore West Central African, and particularly Kongo, cosmologies as embodied archives of African epistemologies that are entangled with, yet far exceed, the archives of slavery.

THE BEGINNINGS

Silva grabbed the lash as soon as he discovered that his captives had been stealing from him under cover of night. He always administered the lash himself to remind them of his mastery. He was likely enraged when some of his captives fled and returned the following day, accompanied by his neighboring slaveowner, José Barbosa de Lima, who urged him to forgive them.[8]

That same day, Silva and his wife started to notice things. She saw the captives with a white cloth that was wrapped around their heads and hung down their backs. Sometimes he noticed them surreptitiously wearing a certain cap. A few days later, one of the enslaved, also named Antonio and a carpenter, confirmed their suspicions that something was afoot. He informed Silva's wife that the others were involved in a secret "club" they called the Pemba society.[9] Because he refused their invitation, however, Antonio didn't know its purpose. It was only when he learned that Silva's wife was planning to marry him to another captive that he decided to tell her. She had unknowingly chosen Pemba initiates as the couple's godparents, but Antonio did not want to be associated with any individuals from "that brotherhood."[10]

To force a confession about Pemba, Silva again grabbed the lash. They remained silent. He whipped them

<hr>

5   On the archives of slavery and narration, see Yuko Miki, "In the Trail of the Ship: Narrating the Archives of Illegal Slavery," *Social Text* 37, no. 1 (138) (March 1, 2019): 87–105, https://doi.org/10.1215/01642472-7286276; Stephanie E. Smallwood, "The Politics of the Archive and History's Accountability to the Enslaved," *History of the Present* 6, no. 2 (2016): 117–32, https://doi.org/DOI: 10.5406/historypresent.6.2.0117.

6   Ann Laura Stoler, *Along the Archival Grain: Epistemic Anxieties and Colonial Common Sense* (Princeton, N.J.: Princeton University Press, 2009).

7   The literature is voluminous. Examples include Keila Grinberg, *Liberata, a lei da ambiguidade: as ações de liberdade da Corte de Apelação do Rio de Janeiro no século XIX* (Relume Dumara, 1994); João José Reis, *Rebelião escrava no Brasil: a história do levante dos malês em 1835* ([São Paulo, Brazil]: Companhia das Letras, 2003); Flávio dos Santos Gomes, *Histórias de quilombolas: mocambos e comunidades de senzalas no Rio de Janeiro, século XIX* (São Paulo: Companhia das Letras, 2006); Silvia Hunold Lara, *Palmares e Cucaú: o aprendizado da dominação* (São Paulo, Brazil: EdUSP, 2021); João José Reis and Flávio dos Santos Gomes, eds., *Revoltas escravas no Brasil* (São Paulo, Brazil: Companhia das Letras, 2021).

8   Florencio, tied to the whipping post, stated that they had "stolen his money." Record of Questions asked to Florencio Crioulo, August 28, 1860, RC Fl. 129-130, ANRJ. It was common for the enslaved expecting punishment to seek out a freedperson to be their patron (*padrinho*) and protect them.

9   Record of Questions asked to Lieutenant Antonio José Alves da Silva (Antonio Alves Silva for short) by Lieutenant and Sublieutenant of Itapemirim, August 27, 1860, RC Fl. 29-34; Fl. 60-120-124, ANRJ.

10   Record of Questions asked to Antonio Crioulo Carpinteiro by Police Lieutenant, August 29, 1860, RC, Fl. 136-138, ANRJ.

more. One of them named Bento finally affirmed that Pemba was meant to last for six months (*era por seis meses*)—it was March of 1860—but still did not reveal its purpose. Silva was unable to get any of his captives to speak, so he punished them more. They still refused. He continued drawing blood until one unspecified day, after administering a "last punishment," a group of women and men, their backs tattered by the lash, approached him in the fields. Kneeling down on the ground before him, they supplicated him for forgiveness. Forgiveness for what? he asked. For Pemba, they replied. What was going to happen in six months? "It was the blacks' greed (*cobiça de negro*) and bad advice they received," they said evasively. Silva forgave all except two who had fled and saw no more trouble from those who remained.

They had not acted alone. Pemba members included several men owned by his neighbor, Lima, among them a West African named Narcizo Mina who was one of the alleged leaders. The other, Fructuozo, belonged to a resident in the nearby town of Cachoeiro known as Dona Anna, possibly Silva's cousin. Some other enslaved and freed people from the area were also believed to take part in Pemba.[11]

ITAPEMIRIM, 1860

Pemba came to light in a comparatively little-known region of Brazil. Silva and Lima resided upriver from the coastal town of Itapemirim in southern Espírito Santo, a narrow province on the Atlantic coast framed by Bahia to the north, Rio de Janeiro to the south, and Minas Gerais to the west. They each owned properties located in the province's southern end. Silva's property, Barra Seca, and Lima's, called Boa Vista, were located across from each other on the Itapemirim River.[12] Further upriver was the town of Cachoeiro de Itapemirim, which had swiftly grown into the economic center of the province. The two men also owned properties there, called Poço Grande and Bananal.[13]

Espírito Santo was sparsely populated in spite of its prime location on the Atlantic littoral. The dense, towering forest was home to Indigenous groups who had tenaciously fended off settlement for much of the colonial period. Settlers around Itapemirim were particularly wary of the Puri Indians who dominated the territory.[14] From the mid-eighteenth century, Crown policy had also discouraged the settlement of the area stretching from southern Bahia through Espírito Santo in order to prevent the smuggling of gold and precious minerals from Minas Gerais to the coast. Spared the ravages of colonization that had assailed communities along much of the seaboard, the region became a refuge for Indigenous populations, maroons, and the poor. But it did not last. With the decline of mining yields by the end of the eighteenth century, settlers coveting new economic opportunities began claiming these once "forbidden lands," unleashing a staggering cycle of anti-Indigenous violence that was eagerly abetted by the Crown. The violence intensified after independence (1822) and endured well into the later nineteenth century as increasing swaths of the Espírito Santo's territory fell prey to the ambitions and violence of farmers, squatters, and speculators who streamed in with their enslaved workforce to claim the land for themselves.[15]

Itapemirim's first large landholdings focused on sugar cultivation. However, as settlers from Rio de Janeiro, Minas Gerais, and São Paulo moved in, by the mid-nineteenth century coffee replaced sugar as the driving economic force in the southern part of the province. Demand for enslaved labor grew in the 1850s, and by 1861, a year after the arrests of the Pemba initiates, the enslaved population in this part of the province had

---

11 Antonio Alves Silva; Record of Questions asked to Florencio by Police Lieutenant, August 28, 1860, RC Fl. 127-131, ANRJ.

12 https://bdlb.bn.gov.br/acervo/handle/20.500.12156.3/31594

13 The properties are mentioned repeatedly in RC, ANRJ.

14 Maximilian Wied-Neuwied, *Travels in Brazil in 1815, 1816, and 1817* (London: Sir Richard Phillips & Co., 1820), 74–82.Indigenous cannibalism rumors increased when there were intensified conflicts with settlers.

15 According to Geisa Ribeiro, the vast majority of Espirito Santo's enslaved population were those born in Brazil or Africans who had already been present for a while who followed their masters with the coffee frontier. Geisa Lourenço Ribeiro, "Enlaces e desenlaces: família escrava e reprodução endógena no Espírito Santo (1790-1871)" (M.A. Thesis, Vitória, ES, UFES, 2012), 110. For the indigenous history of the region in the late colonial and postcolonial peridos, see Hal Langfur, *The Forbidden Lands: Colonial Identity, Frontier Violence, and the Persistence of Brazil's Eastern Indians, 1750-1830* (Stanford: Stanford University Press, 2006); Yuko Miki, *Frontiers of Citizenship: A Black and Indigenous History of Postcolonial Brazil*, Afro-Latin America (New York and Cambridge: Cambridge University Press, 2018).

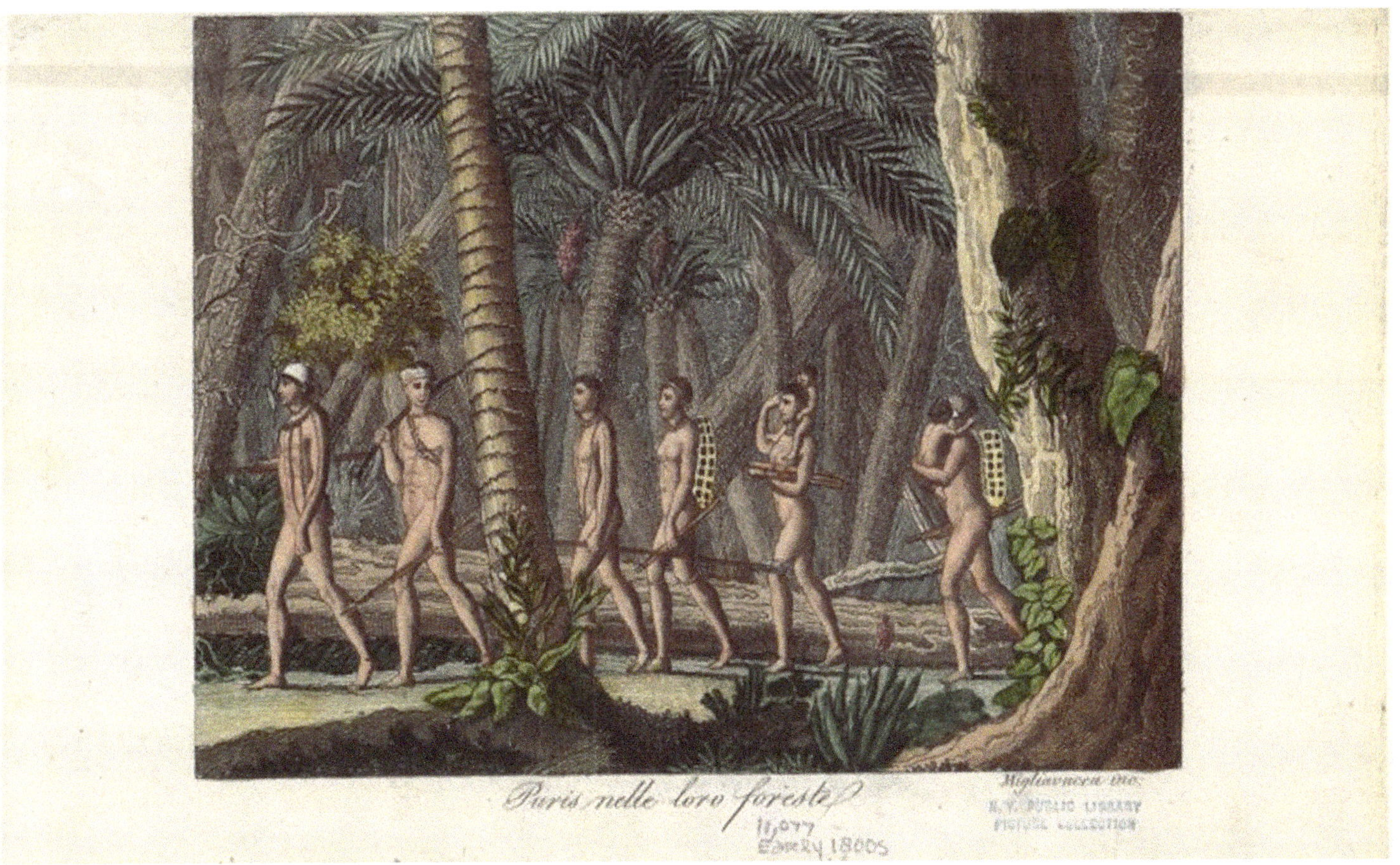

The coffee frontier towns of Itapemirim and Cachoeiro de Itapemirim were built in the Atlantic forest in an area that had long been dominated by the Puri Indigenous people. The expansion of African-based slavery into indigenous territory and the resulting anti-indigenous violence are foundational to understanding Brazil's postcolonial history.

CREDIT: Migliavacca, Innocente. Puris nelle loro foreste. The Miriam and Ira D. Wallach Division of Art, Prints and Photographs: Picture Collection, The New York Public Library.

surpassed that of the provincial capital, Vitória. The same year, nearly a quarter of all enslaved people in Espírito Santo lived in Itapemirim. While the numbers are miniscule compared to the large plantation regions of Rio de Janeiro and São Paulo, in the world in which the Pemba members lived, 49% (4,315) of Itapemirim's population—the highest figure it would reach—and 60% (3,379) of Cachoeiro de Itapemirim's population was enslaved. Cachoeiro's enslaved population would continue to grow rapidly, to 7,482 by 1872, in contrast to decreasing numbers in the rest of Brazil.[16] Meanwhile, although initially an interior parish of Itapemirim proper, Cachoeiro's growing economic might as the center of the province's coffee cultivation led to its becoming an independent *vila* in 1864.[17] Pemba's alleged other leader, Fructuozo, and a suspected member who was later released, Luiz Cabra, were also from Cachoeiro,

attesting to the geographic distances that Pemba's initiates spanned.

Itapemirim maintained a large enslaved African workforce in contrast to the majority of the province's enslaved population, which was Brazilian-born by the nineteenth century. Based on post-mortem inventories between 1850 and 1871, Geisa Ribeiro has concluded that the southern region had a much higher percentage of Africans (26.2%) than the capital region (9.7%) relative to their respective enslaved populations.[18] The actual numbers may have been much higher, since many inventories intentionally obfuscated enslaved people's origins to conceal their illegal captivity if they were among the over 800,000 Africans brought to Brazil after the transatlantic slave trade had already been abolished in 1831. With Espírito Santo's long coastline making it a perfect disembarkation point for illegal slavers, it is likely that some of these Africans ended up in Itapemirim, a

---

16 Laryssa da Silva Machado, "Retratos da escravidão em Itapemirim, ES: uma análise das famílias escravas enre 1831-1888" (M.A. Thesis, Vitória, ES, UFES, 2019), 45; Vilma Paraíso Ferreira de Almada, *Escravismo e transição: o Espírito Santo (1850-1888)* (Rio de Janeiro-RJ-Brasil: Graal, 1984), 114–15.

17 Machado, "Retratos da escravidão," 81.

18 Ribeiro, "Enlaces e desenlaces," 119.

newly settled region where enslaved labor was scarce.[19]

Their origins pique our curiosity. The records are noticeably vague, mostly annotating them, if they did at all, only as "African" or "*de nação*." Ribeiro has shown that West Central Africans predominated, headed by "Angola" and "Congo," "Benguela," "Cabinda," "Cassange," and lesser numbers of "Moçambique," "Minas," "Moange," and "Macua."[20] Laryssa Machado has noted that of the very limited number of Africans whose origins are annotated, 25% were Mina (Upper Guinea Coast) and 21% were Angola, followed by the southern Angolan region of Benguela (14%).[21] These findings generally correlate with the origins of the suspected Pemba initiates we will see later. As with much of the African population of the Center-South, those from West Central Africa predominated. This was Itapemirim in 1860—where the coffee frontier brought African-based slavery into Indigenous territory—when Pemba entered the archives.

SEDUCTIONS OF THE ARCHIVE

Rare is the historian who can resist an insurrection. Leafing through towers of delicate archival documents for hours and days, the sudden appearance of a report warning of an impending insurrection by enslaved people, or even a suggestive rumor, makes our pulse quicken. For although we know that the resistance to captivity took many forms, insurrections still occupy that special place in our minds as the most thrilling example of Black radical politics. Add to that a possible link to an African "secret society," and we feel like we've hit the jackpot.

Or so we think. But there's a catch: the archives might be seducing us. Our desire to see an insurrection could lead us to accept, without question, what the documents say. To proceed with caution, I want to trace the archives' logics or "grain." Accounting for the

obfuscations, unreliable testimonies, and sometimes blatant abuses of power reveals how the archives' authors (police, law enforcement, slaveowners) likely invented a slave insurrection. I am not claiming that all insurrections are invented, but rather am taking this example of Pemba to invite a critical reexamination of the archives. Nor am I denying Black people's antislavery politics. On the contrary, a reexamination allows us to destabilize the slaveholders' limited intellectual world that could only conceive of Black politics and personhood in terms of a threat to their supremacy— the very limitation that engendered these archives in the first place.

By exposing the inventions contained within documentary archives, my goal is to explore how cosmologies of West Central African (and particularly those of Kongo) peoples are embodied archives that can both work together with, and critique, documentary archives. I want to follow the late Maria Elena Martínez's invitation to consider "how the relationship of the two 'archives'—one that stores documents and other historical fragments, and the one that stores human memory—is at the heart of all connections to the past."[22]

Expanding our definition of the archives may also propose a (speculative) response to the conundrum that writing about enslaved lives entails, which Saidiya Hartman called "critical fabulation." A form of "impossible writing which attempts to say that which resists being said," critical fabulation "is a history of an unrecoverable past…it is a history written with and against the archive." If Hartman confronted how her own writing was "unable to exceed the limits of the sayable dictated by the [documentary] archive," the Pemba participants invite us to explore a rich cosmological and spiritual world within and beyond the paper archive, a world shaped by, yet hardly reducible to, slavery.[23] Through Pemba, we explore the possibilities offered by an archive of African

---

19　Rafaela Domingos Lago, "Sob os olhos de Deus e dos homens: escravos e parentesco ritual na província do Espírito Santo (1831-1888)" (M.A. Thesis, Vitória, ES, UFES, 2013), 46–49; Machado, "Retratos da escravidão," 87–94.

20　Ribeiro, "Enlaces e desenlaces," 119.

21　Machado, "Retratos da escravidão," 114–15.

22　María Elena Martínez, "Archives, Bodies, and Imagination: The Case of Juana Aguilar and Queer Approaches to History, Sexuality, and Politics," *Radical History Review* 2014, no. 120 (October 1, 2014): 159–82, https://doi.org/10.1215/01636545-2703787.

23　Saidiya Hartman, "Venus in Two Acts," *Small Axe* 12, no. 2 (July 17, 2008): 12, https://doi.org/doi.org/10.1215/-12-2-1.

epistemologies that is entangled with, yet exceeds, the archives of slavery.

INSINUATION

Pemba's archives are puzzling from the beginning. Antonio Alves Silva learned about Pemba in March 1860 but would wait nearly five months to share the news. The only explanation he gave to the perplexed police was that he wanted to "be sure." His August 5 letter to his neighbor became the first official record of a suspected insurrection. *"We are in a war declared by our slaves*, whose plan was slated to take place in six months that would be coming now, in September," he warned João Marques Pereira. "Don't tell them anything so we can be prepared." He had "stopped punishing [his slaves] because they asked for forgiveness for this tremendous crime that we cannot know about." As for what this alleged crime was, he only stated that it was "what I thought" and warned his fellow slaveowner, "I don't know if yours are involved." Silva singled out Fructuozo, a captive of his cousin Anna, as the "one who went around inviting our people" and that "there were a great number of Cangaré or Pemba" members. Describing the society's undetected spread, he urged that it needed to be stopped before its plan could be realized.[24]

The letter is strikingly vague. Silva never explicitly mentions an insurrection nor divulges any details about this ominous "war" with an unspecified "plan." What he did was tap into his community's alleged familiarity with West Central African-based societies, using them as a dog whistle. By associating Pemba with Cangaré (or Cangerê), he was referring to another Kongo-based society that was discovered in Vassouras in adjacent Rio de Janeiro province in 1848. Although unnamed, their meetings were called "Cangere" and shared some similar practices with Pemba. Official records claimed that the goal of Cangere, which allegedly existed throughout Rio de Janeiro province, was to "kill their masters, of whatever sex or age." Members also intended to kill the "administrators and other free

people employed on the estates, including those slaves who wished to remain faithful to their masters." Those with knowledge of 1848 may have understood Silva's evocation of "Cangaré or Pemba" as a code for violent slave insurrection.[25]

Cangaré would remain embedded in people's awareness in 1861, when insurrection rumors circulating in the Rio de Janeiro municipalities of Valença and Barra Mansa alluded to "well-known nocturnal gatherings named *cangerês*," in which some "opportunists" took advantage of "undisciplined slaves" and "despicable, vagrant, ignorant free men" who came together to "celebrate certain ceremonies and deceitful, vulgar rites."[26] Those seeking to affirm Pemba's insurrectionary intent would soon make their own connections with other societies in the region. As the investigation proceeded, these questionable aspects of Silva's letter would be brushed aside, his letter elevated into a key piece of evidence.

It is worth nothing that practicing African-based religions *per se* was not a crime in nineteenth-century Brazil, unlike in the colonial era when they were subjected to inquisitorial and other ecclesiastical and civil laws. At best, African-based religions existed in a legal gray area and were subject to sporadic local laws. Until the middle of the century, according to João Reis,

---

24 Letter by Antonio Alves Silva to João Marques Pereira, Itapemirim, August 5, 1860, RC Fl. 86-87.

25 Report of Select Committee of the Provincial Assembly of Rio de Janeiro (Secret), July 8, 1848, Inclosure 20 in No. 44. British Parliamentary Papers (BPP hereafter) Slave Trade Class B, 1 April 1850-31 March 1851, p. 88-89. Slenes discusses this case in greater detail, including its organizational structure, but does not specifically mention the term Cangere. Robert W. Slenes, "A árvore de Nsanda transplantada: cultos Kongo de afilição e identidade escrava no sudeste brasileiro (século XIX)," in *Trabalho livre, trabalho escravo: Brasil e Europa, séculos XVIII e XIX*, ed. Douglas C. Libby and Júnia Ferreira Furtado (São Paulo, Brazil: Annablume, 2006), 301–3. He also identifies the location as Vassouras, which was not mentioned in the BPP papers or the original manuscript in the National Archives FO84/802.

26 Gomes, *Histórias de quilombolas*, 209. Gomes also cites Macedo Soares, who in his 1889 *Dicionário brasilerio de lingua portuguesa* defined "cangerê" thus: "Every Friday night [a sorcerer who was magician, witch and healer] conducted cabbalistic meetings where, before a mutilated image of Saint Anthony with a severed nose and hands, the followers of his prodigious art writhed and engaged in extravagant dances, which they called Cangerê." The adherents also looked at their reflections in "small round mirrors which they held in their hands." See n. 122, 356. "Cangerê" is also the name of a samba from the late 1910s and 1920s written by Francisco Antônio da Rocha; the translator states that "In Brazil, *cangarê* (or *canjerê, canjira, canjirê*), deriving from a Kikongo/Kimbundu term meaning to bless or open roads by way of magic, refers especially to Afro-Brazilian witchcraft, witchcraft sessions, and spells." Carlos Sandroni, *A Respectable Spell: Transformations of Samba in Rio de Janeiro* (Champaign: University of Illinois Press, 2021), 169, 246 n. 6.

batuques (social and/or religious gatherings of enslaved and freed people) were sometimes prohibited for their alleged potential to foment revolts. Subsequently, authorities saw them more as causes of public disorder and drunkenness and an impediment to Brazil's civilizatory progress.[27] Therefore, the only way for Silva and his peers in law enforcement to suppress Pemba was by connecting it with a legally defined crime.

Meanwhile, Silva's foot-dragging continued. After penning his letter of August 5, the slaveowner waited nineteen more days to notify others. Although he suggested that a police force might be needed, he never affirmed anything beyond the existence of "slave societies." He contacted his neighbor across the river, José Barboza de Lima, because he wished "what happened on his property not to happen to others" and to that end "had punished his slaves and wished others to punish their own."[28] The news soon reached the local Justice of the Law, João Lima e Castro, who ordered the expedition of August 25. Silva believed that the judge had given the order "in such a way that made [the expedition commander] suspect a slave uprising against him." Again, Silva's testimony is entirely insinuation; he avoided any mention of insurrection, even though he did not contest, and thereby indirectly encouraged, other witnesses' claims that one was in the works.

The Itapemirim police's thirty-person expedition arrived at Silva's property around 11pm on the night of August 25, ready to find a cache of weapons hidden in the captives' quarters.[29] All they found instead were the enslaved asleep after a long day of backbreaking work. The one exception was a young male named Florencio, whom Silva had tied to the whipping post. He was caught trying to flee from an impending sale and had been among the Pemba initiates who had kneeled before Silva in March to beg for forgiveness. The raid on his property over, Silva gave the expedition leader, second lieutenant Antonio de Oliveira, eight helmets and a red stick belonging the society's members. Silva

vehemently denied others' claims that he had been too afraid of the enslaved to come out of his house, going to great pains to present himself as a feared master. The mere thought of being tamed by the enslaved must have enraged him.[30]

Silva's neighbor and master of most of the other arrested Pemba initiates, José Barboza de Lima, was a man of some local social standing. The recent Justice of the Law owned 65 women and men including several multigenerational families.[31] He was also very recently widowed. His second wife, Dona Joaquina Margarida, had died just six days before the expedition, on August 19, leaving behind the couple's five-year-old daughter.[32] Less than a year before, Lima had been charged with trying to reduce a free woman into captivity and of falsifying the documents of a slave sale.[33] Why Silva's captives chose Lima to be their protector, and how this man with a questionable record regarding his treatment of the enslaved would come to clash with the police and justice system over their innocence, remains to be seen.

CONNECTION

Not even a day had passed when Silva's insinuated insurrection assumed the guise of fact. A formal investigation had yet to take place. "It is certain that a slave insurrection was in order," Justice of the Law Castro warned the Espírito Santo provincial president on August 26. "It began in the district of Campos and spread to various points, but especially Itapemirim." He deliberately referred to Campos, the adjacent municipality in Rio de Janeiro, to amplify Pemba's supposed threat. All over Itapemirim, "many groups of armed slaves had appeared, led by assassins from the municipality of Campos," and a "large number of slaves from different fazendas of this municipality [were] in favor of insurrection." Giving urgency to the matter,

---

27 João José Reis, *Domingos Sodré, um sacerdote africano : escravidão, liberdade e candomblé na Bahia do século XIX* (São Paulo: Companhia das Letras, 2008), 142–43.

28 Antonio Alves Silva Questions, RC Fl. 52 and 122, AN.

29 Nor did they find any religious items that often raised suspicion, such as *minkisi* amulets.

30 Oliveira to Villaboim; Sublieutenant Antonio Francisco de Oliveira Sobrinho to Lieutenant Arcanjo José de Souza, August 27, 1860, RC Fl. 27-29; Antonio Alves Silva Questions, RC Fl. 122-123, AN.

31 *Correio Mercantil* November 20,1857 ed. 317 p. 2. Lima was still mentioned as the Justice of the Law in *Correio Mercantil* December 21, 1857 ed. 348 and February 3, 1858 ed. 32.

32 Ribeiro, "Enlaces e desenlaces," 167.

33 *Correio Mercantil*, October 29, 1859 ed. 296 p. 1-2. The article is clearly written by a foe.

the "first victims to fall to the first attacks are already chosen…This shall happen in September." Later police investigations would pinpoint September 7, Brazilian Independence Day.

Like Silva, Judge Castro made claims riddled with peculiarities. Brushing aside the expedition leader's report of a "society which [the enslaved] named Pemba," Castro stated that the members "belong to a society they called 'Assembly' with a hidden goal, which they are forbidden to reveal with an oath which they swore under penalty of death."[34] This sentence was identical *verbatim* to another, completely separate report written on the same day by a completely different person, the Justice of the Law of Campos to the president of Espírito Santo, as cited by the historian Flávio Gomes.[35] I cannot yet explain how two different letters, written on the same day to the same recipient by two different individuals in two different towns, contain the exact same language. But it's possible that one man authored both letters, or the two judges were in communication and had developed a very specific language to present the threat of African-based organizations.[36] Their language was echoed by one of the witnesses who claimed that these societies had a "statute" by which he meant "the complex of ceremonies that the blacks practiced in their meetings they call Assembly" which would unite them "in the first shout of insurrection."[37] Priest João Philippe Pinheiro was another witness who began connecting several terms in circulation, alleging that the "slaves had declared war against their masters, and the doctrine followed by the society called Pemba is the same as the one called Cangaré in Campos."[38]

The expedition leader, Antonio Oliveira, refrained from suggesting an insurrection but noted the ominous potential of the large enslaved population, "perhaps in excess of eight thousand," joining forces across the region.[39]

By associating Pemba with Cangeré/Cangarê, Campos, and Assembly, and mentioning similar insurrection rumors, these police reports and witness testimonies amplified Pemba's threat. They conjure a classic slave insurrection born from slaveholder fears: thousands of the enslaved armed and united in clandestine alliance, with their owners as the chosen victims. Together, the slaveholders' statements weave an ominous world where African-based "secret societies" threatened their very existence.

CONFIRMATION

The police and Judge Castro questioned fifteen of the suspected Pemba initiates between late August and early September 1860. None mentioned insurrection. By late September, twelve were released, including all six women. One of Silva's captives, the African Narcizo Benguela (different from Narcizo Mina, the Pemba leader), died in prison. Meanwhile, Judge Castro was promoted to interim Police Chief of Espírito Santo, the top posting in the province, while apparently maintaining his former job, becoming both the chief investigator and judge.[40]

In early October Castro summoned eight witnesses and five "referred" witnesses[41]—all free men—to his own home to make statements. At stake was Pemba's connection to specific crimes included in the Criminal Code. Castro focused on the crime of insurrection (Article 113), committed when "twenty or more slaves

---

34 João da Costa Lima e Castro, Justice of the Law of Itapemirim to Antonio Alvez de Souza Carvalho, President of Espírito Santo province, August 26, 1860, IJ1 733, AN.

35 Gomes, *Histórias de quilombolas*, 206. In n. 122 (p.356) Gomes cites AN IJ1 869, Oficios de presidents de província (RJ), Ofício do juiz de direito do município de Campos enviado ao president da província do Espírito Santo, 26 August 1860. Gomes and fellow historian Maria Helena Machado are currently co-authoring a book on the wider world of Pemba and other West Central African societies in this region, which we eagerly await – we hope they can answer our question and more.

36 Although Gomes' citation does not give a name, the *Almanak Laemmert* of 1860 lists a "Manoel Felippe Monteiro" as the Justice of the Law of the city of Campos dos Goycatazes on p. 291.

37 Testimony of Joaquim José Gomes de Silva Vito, October 3, 1860 (?), RC Fl.53-59, ANRJ.

38 Referred Testimony of Father João Philippe Pinheiro, October 3, 1860 (?), RC Fl.70-78, ANRJ.

39 Oliveira to Villaboim.

40 The Africans' interrogations in October (*auto de perguntas*) for example begin by mentioning "Dr. João da Costa Lima and Castro Interim Police Chief of the Province…" and then refer to him as "by the same judge the interrogation went thus."

41 *Testemunha referida* is a witness mentioned by another person and is heard upon request of the litigant or the magistrate ex officio. https:// enciclopediajuridica.pucsp.br/verbete/446/edicao-1/prova-testemunhal, accessed June 14, 2024.

gathered to obtain liberty through the use of force," and the crime of "illicit gatherings" (Article 285), which occurred when three or more people gathered with the "intention of mutually helping to commit a crime, or to illegally deprive somebody of the enjoyment or exercise of some right or duty." Article 286 was the crime of practicing the acts mentioned in Art. 285 with a penalty of twenty to 200 *mil reis* and other costs. He also evoked the Law of 6 June 1831, according to which those covered by Article 285 were sentenced to three to nine months of imprisonment. The law also prohibited any nocturnal gathering of five or more persons in the streets, squares, and roads "without a just and recognized intent," the violation of which also carried a jail sentence.[42] Clearly, Castro's intent was to criminalize the Pemba initiates' act of getting together. His leading questions accordingly follow the language of the Criminal Code, such as "Isn't it true that the slaves were intending to stage an insurrection in order to obtain liberty through force?" and "Were the slaves gathering with the intention to commit some sort of crime?"

These witness testimonies have little substance. The very recipient of Silva's August 5 letter warning of a "war declared by our slaves," João Marques Pereira, was unsure whether there was an insurrection and stated that none of the slaveowners had been talking about it.[43] But even confident witnesses also relied almost entirely on hearsay, with statements such as: "It's generally said that the Pemba existed...and their goal was to kill whites and tame masters" or "having heard, and also read the interrogations of some of the accused, I can affirm the existence of a blacks' society called Pemba in imitation of another in Valença with the same statutes and emblems whose goal, through the apparent goal of taming masters, can't but have a hostile intention towards whites."[44] Even as the questions became more leading, e.g. "Was there an insurrection planned on September 7 by a society called Pemba?" one witness could only respond that "I heard there was a society to tame masters, and others

said that it was to kill whites." His response blends the Africans' claim to tame and the masters' obsession with murderous intent.

Ventriloquistic testimony also imputed information to Silva that was absent from the slaveowner's own vague statements.[45] One claimed that Silva himself had stated that his slaves wanted to join others to rise up and "put an end to the masters."[46] Expedition member Alexandrino Pereira testified that two of Silva's slaves came to ask for his forgiveness for having "joined with others to have an uprising on September 7 and kill the whites to be free." Parroting the Criminal Code, he claimed that the slaves had "come together with the intention of helping each other to commit a crime, and that crime was to kill the whites." However, even he admitted that the expedition did not find any weapons. Still another witness claimed that Pemba's goal was the "same that Silva himself thought, and that thought was... to sacrifice the masters," the evidence of which was Silva's vague August 5 letter which "not only affirms the existence of this dangerous society but also deduces its hostile intent."[47] The expedition leader, Antonio Oliveira, had reported that Silva had told him that the enslaved had refused to divulge Pemba's purpose under penalty of death. Silva himself had made no such claims.

The case against Pemba rested upon extremely tenuous evidence. Castro barely accounted for the suspected Pemba initiates' own statements. He eventually dropped the insurrection charge, but on October 20, found the Pemba initiates guilty of crimes set forth in Art. 286 and the law of 6 June 1831, sentencing the initiates to both a financial penalty and three to nine months of imprisonment.

The case soon took a curious turn. José Barbosa de Lima, owner of many of the accused Pemba members, appealed the sentence on November 2. Himself a former Justice of the Law, he criticized discrepancies in the witness testimonies about Pemba's meeting place

---

42 For the text of this law and the other articles, see the Brazilian Criminal Code.

43 Testimony of João Marques Pereira, September 4, 1860 and October 3 (?), 1860, RC Fl. 158-159 and RC Fl. 43-44, ANRJ.

44 Father Pinheiro, RC Fl. 71-72; Joaqum da Silva Vito, RC Fl. 54, ANRJ.

45 Pereira.

46 Testimony of Captain Francisco Gomes Bittencourt, RC Fl. 62, ANRJ.

47 Joaqum da Silva Vito, RC Fl. 55-56, ANRJ.

(some said Lima's property, Bananal; others mentioned Silva's Poço Grande property, a league away); their lack of any concrete evidence and total reliance on hearsay and rumor; and that the only source claiming Lima's own slaves belonged to Pemba was Silva's slave Florencio, who was tied to the whipping post. How could there be an insurrection, Lima asked, when the slaves were found in their quarters, "peaceful and unarmed"? Referring to their testimonies, he argued that while they had gathered to dance and used spells to lessen their masters' anger, committing violence was never their intent. Since the accused hadn't done anything, he also raised Art. 288, according to which "those who withdrew from the illicit gathering before having committed any act of violence will not incur any punishment." The best defense of the Pemba initiates thus came from one of their owners, a major slaveholder in his own right.[48]

Judge Castro remained unmoved. Six days later, he forcefully dismissed Lima's appeal. "There was a society of blacks created in this municipality called Pemba in imitation of others that have existed in other municipalities with the same hostile ends, whose consequences have been ominous to the public order," he thundered. "*There is no doubt* that the appellants associated with Pemba met in various locations of this district in large number with the criminal intent of realizing an insidious plan." The members were "connected to a common cause and obeyed a center," and the witness testimonies and documents, especially Silva's notorious letter, left no room for doubt about their guilt.

Castro credited the police with preventing the insurrection, adding that "although this society's goals were secret and it was prohibited to reveal them under oath and penalty of death, nobody can doubt that it was the masters' massacre." Tellingly, his evidence was its very absence. Because the members concealed Pemba's existence and its intent, the judge argued, "our material is more than enough to subject the appellants to their penalty." The rumors that much of the testimonies relied on were "not unfounded" since they had

"frightened the souls of many people and families in this town." Fear was truth.[49]

This is the grain of Pemba's archives. The justice system muscled unreliable witness testimonies and missing evidence into a single story about Pemba as a violent "secret society" fomenting an insurrection to kill whites. These records narrate the triumph of law and order over Black violence, of free white men reestablishing their supremacy over Africans who dared to challenge them.

Is this the end? We may feel disappointed, even though we are doing a historian's due diligence. However, concluding here reinscribes white male enslavers as the protagonists. It's still all about them. We venture no further than their limited intellectual world that only understands Pemba as a threat to their power. The Africans and their spiritual lives remain opaque. I want to push beyond the "limits of the sayable dictated by the archive," to explore West Central African epistemologies within and beyond the documentary record.[50] The Pemba initiates and what they did share, in spite of many silences, may guide us on another path.

THE INITIATES

Slivers of the Pemba initiates' portraits emerge across several documents. According to their testimonies, the society in Itapemirim was likely established first among Lima's captives, with Silva's captives initiated later. Here are the twenty-one individuals sentenced by Judge Castro on October 20,1860:

Owner: José Barbosa de Lima (11 total)[51]

- Antonio Mina

- Narcizo Mina, one of Pemba's leaders (known as

---

48 José Barbosa de Lima Statement of Appeal, November 2, 1860, RC Fl. 11-23, ANRJ.

49 Judge Castro, Dismissal of José Barboza de Lima's Appeal, November 8, 1860, RC Fl. 173-179, ANRJ.

50 Hartman, "Venus in Two Acts," 12.

51 "Inventory of Joaquina Margarida da Silva Lima" (Cachoeiro do Itapemirim, July 28, 1864), Maço 1, Cartório do 5o Ofício de Cachoeiro de Itapemirim; "Inventory of José Barboza de Lima" (Cachoeiro do Itapemirim, July 15, 1867), Maço 2, Cartório do 5o Ofício de Cachoeiro de Itapemirim, courtesy of Geisa Ribeiro. See Ribeiro, "Enlaces e desenlaces."

Tata Abranda Mundo)[52]

- José São Thomé
- Paulo Cabinda
- João Congo
- Agostinho Congo
- Thomaz Moange
- José Moange
- Caspar (Gaspar) Moange
- Adão Angola
- Joaquim Benguela[53]

Owner: Antonio José Alves Silva (10 total)

- Luis Mocambiqui
- Gabriel Cabinda
- Antonio Cabinda
- Juvencio Angola
- Domingos Angola
- Ricardo Angola
- Joaquim Benguela
- Agostinho Benguela
- Florencio Crioulo (Brazilian-born)
- Ignacio Crioulo (same)
- Narcizo Benguela (had died in prison by September 27, 1860)

Two aspects immediately stand out. They are all men, and predominantly African. Although women also participated in Pemba, the police released the six owned by Silva, including two Africans (Rufina, Emilia) and one Brazilian-born *crioula*, Joana. All eleven men owned by Lima and eight of the ten owned by Silva are African. These could mean a number of things but may indicate the police's own presumptions about insurrections as male affairs and these societies as predominantly

serving the African-born.[54] In addition to the twenty-one individuals listed here, Luiz Cabra (a person of Black and Indigenous heritage) from Campos, and Dionizio, belonging to a woman from Cachoeiro, were released for lack of evidence. The police were unable to locate Pemba's suspected co-leader, Fructuozo, and a freedperson named Mamedio.

The Africans' "nations" provide an intriguing if slippery insight into their backgrounds. Many scholars have shown the highly problematic nature of reading these ethnonyms, such as Nagô, Jejê, Congo and so forth, as indicators of origin or ethnicity. Many of these "nations" were forged in the context of the transatlantic slave trade and often imposed by slave traders onto the enslaved. Some labels, such as Benguela and Cabinda, are actually names of Angolan ports where the Africans were likely embarked. But since the Pemba initiates identified themselves with these ethnonyms in their interrogations, we can understand them as general indicators of geographic origins.[55] Thus fifteen were West Central African, many from around the capital of Luanda and further north towards Kikongo-speaking territory along the Lower Congo River (Angola, Moange, Congo, Cabinda), others from the Kimbundu-speaking region of southern Angola (Benguela). One was southeastern African (Moçambique), and three hailed

---

52 Married to Umbelina. Had 2 children.

53 Possibly married to Veridiana and father of three. Inherited by Lima's daughter after his death.

---

54 Finch, *Rethinking Slave Rebellion in Cuba*, Ch. 5.

55 See for example João José Reis, "'The Revolution of the Ganhadores': Urban Labour, Ethnicity and the African Strike of 1857 in Bahia, Brazil," *Journal of Latin American Studies* 29, no. 2 (1997): 355–93; Michael A. Gomez, *Exchanging Our Country Marks: The Transformation of African Identities in the Colonial and Antebellum South* (Chapel Hill: University of North Carolina Press, 1998); Paul E. Lovejoy, "Ethnic Designations of the Slave Trade and the Reconstruction of the History of Trans-Atlantic Slavery," in *Trans-Atlantic Dimensions of Ethnicity in the African Diaspora*, ed. Paul E. Lovejoy and David V. Trotman (London and New York: Continuum, 2003), 9–42; Gwendolyn Midlo Hall, *Slavery and African Ethnicities in the Americas: Restoring the Links* (Chapel Hill: University of North Carolina Press, 2005); Juliana Barreto Farias et al., *No labirinto das naçoes: africanos e identidades no Rio de Janeiro, século XIX* (Rio de Janeiro: Arquivo Nacional, 2005); Katrina H. B. Keefer, "Scarification and Identity in the Liberated Africans Department Register, 1814-1815," *Canadian Journal of African Studies* 47, no. 3 (2013): 537–53; David Maxwell, "Freed Slaves, Missionaries, and Respectability: The Expansion of the Christian Frontier from Angola to Belgian Congo," *The Journal of African History* 54, no. 1 (March 2013): 79–102, https://doi.org/10.1017/S0021853713000030; Daniel B Domingues da Silva, *The Atlantic Slave Trade from West Central Africa, 1780-1867* (Cambridge [England]; New York: Cambridge University Press, 2017); Aldair Rodrigues, "African Body Marks, Stereotypes and Racialization in Eighteenth-Century Brazil," *Slavery & Abolition* 42, no. 2 (April 3, 2021): 315–44, https://doi.org/10.1080/0144039X.2020.1814055.

from the Bight of Benin in West Africa and nearby islands (Mina and São Tomé).[56]

While the predominance of West Central Africans corresponds to the demography of enslaved Africans in Itapemirim, the presence of Africans from elsewhere and the Brazilian-born destabilizes the direct connection between a person's origins and spiritual affiliations. Their collective initiation into Pemba signals the forging of spiritual families welcoming people of diverse origins. Initiates probably held multiple spiritual affiliations as was common among Africans and in the diaspora. The practice was lost on the police, however, who asked Joana, "Why did you, a *crioula*, join these idiocies?"[57]

Joana's experience hints at the society's intergenerational resonance. José Barboza de Lima and his wife's inventory records show that all of the enslaved implicated in Pemba were African men ranging from their mid-30s to late 40s (the ages are approximations due to the lack of accurate records. He also owned six other Africans who were not arrested). Many of the Limas' forty-eight crioulo captives spared arrest were the Africans' children and grandchildren. Caspar (Gaspar) Moange was married to Maria, an African woman also owned by Lima. Maria was disabled, perhaps due to punishments or harsh work conditions. Since Caspar had been on Lima's property for about twenty years, he may have arrived in Brazil as a teenager around 1840 in the illegal slave trade. At the time of Lima's death a few years later in 1867, both Caspar and Maria were around forty-four, with six children and four grandchildren, all born into slavery.[58] African women and men continued to share their spiritual and cosmological knowledge across generations, even as slavery continued to shape the lives of their Brazilian-born children.[59]

IN THEIR WORDS

The Pemba initiates danced between speech and silence. They were masterfully evasive, sometimes verging on being coy. Florencio explained that the white hat the initiates wore "was fashion."[60] For Thomas Moange, they were for dancing the *jongo*. Luiz Cabra said he was wearing a hat of many colors "because I had a headache." Narcizo Mina initially discussed some of Pemba's practices but later told Castro that he had never heard of Pemba and "didn't know what it means." Florencio would later tell Castro that in spite of his previous statement otherwise, "nobody was in Pemba."[61]

What is Pemba? Did you belong in the Pemba society? What did you do in your meetings? When those being interrogated did respond to the police's questions (giving only monosyllabic responses later to Judge Castro), it wasn't in order to enlighten their captors with the richness and complexity of their spiritual lives. They knew their audience was neither capable of nor interested in understanding Pemba's significance to them. Still, the information they shared, however fragmentary, allows the Pemba initiates' embodied archives to bleed into the official documentary archive, giving us glimpses into their spiritual world. I'll first discuss what the initiates said, subsequently considering them within the overlapping contexts of slavery and Kongo cosmology.

Pemba "means 'ash' in the blacks' language," said Luis Moçambique, who also noted that the initiates carried a stick in their mouths. He insisted he wasn't an initiate himself, having known another man who dabbled in such groups and was whipped by his master.[62] The women Joana, Rufina, and Emília, and Antonio crioulo were among the recent initiates. They described their

---

56 Roquinaldo Ferreira has shown that the illegal slave trade definitively shifted to regions north of Luanda in the 1840s. Roquinaldo Ferreira, "The Suppression of the Slave Trade and Slave Departures from Angola, 1830s-1860s," in *Extending the Frontiers: Essays on the New Transatlantic Slave Trade Database*, ed. David Eltis and David Richardson (New Haven, CT: Yale University Press, 2008), 324–25.

57 Record of Questions asked to Joana, August 26, 1860, RC Fl.142, ANRJ.

58 "Inventory of Joaquina Margarida da Silva Lima"; "Inventory of José Barboza de Lima", both courtesy of Geisa Ribeiro; *O Estandarte*, April 28, 1872.

59 On the strength of enslaved families residing on the same plantation, see

Robert W. Slenes, *Na senzala, uma flor: esperanças e recordações na formação da família escrava : Brasil Sudeste, século XIX* (Rio de Janeiro, RJ, Brasil: Editora Nova Fronteira, 1999); Mary Ann Mahony, "Creativity under Constraint: Enslaved Afro-Brazilian Families in Brazil's Cacao Area, 1870–1890," *Journal of Social History* 41, no. 3 (2008): 633–66. For enslaved families in Itapemirim, see Ribeiro, "Enlaces e desenlaces"; Machado, "Retratos da escravidão."

60 Florencio Crioulo Interrogation, October 15, 1860, RC Fl. 94, ANRJ.

61 Narcizo Mina Interrogation, October 16, 1860 RC Fl.106; Florencio Crioulo Interrogation.

62 Luis Moçambique Interrogation, October 15, 1860, RC Fl. 87, ANRJ.

"baptism" in which Narcizo Mina drew crosses on their arms with a "whitish thing that looked like ash (*uma coisa branquinha que parecia cinza*)."[63] Narcizo Mina himself referred to a "powder called pemba that is mixed with ash to make crosses on the hand." Pemba's other leader, Fructuozo, held some ash in his hand which he blew into the air.[64] They initiates then passed under Narcizo Mina's legs and shook themselves, the initiation complete when he pulled them up.[65]

Saint Anthony also figured prominently in their gatherings. Florencio recalled that "Narcizo [Mina] had a [figure of] Saint Anthony that he carried into the fields where he and his companions got together." The master, as the members alluded to him, would lay a mat on the ground upon which he placed a cloth and candles on each corner. He then made the initiates "kneel and pray, asking Saint Anthony to free them from snakes and from captivity."[66] Another Narcizo of Benguela, who would shortly die in prison, mentioned that "as the day faded, [Narcizo Mina] laid a mat on the ground and placed the Saint Anthony atop it."[67] Although he did not mention Saint Anthony, Luiz Moçambique did see "a cloth laid out and a can of tobacco on it."[68] Narcizo Mina himself acknowledged that he had a figure of Saint Anthony to whom he prayed on the fazenda grounds and at home, including when they performed the jongo. However, he had sold the saint's statue because Silva's captives were "being idiots."[69]

Several also mentioned dancing the jongo, a West Central African-based music and dance still commonly performed in the rural African-descendant communities or *quilombos* of Rio de Janeiro and São Paulo and

today recognized as a Brazilian Cultural Patrimony.[70] Pemba members "got together to dance the *jongo*," Luis Moçambique explained, "because our master didn't let them do it in the house." The dances took place in Lima's fields "next to the marsh." According to Florencio, it was after the prayers that the *"gira mom jongo* would begin," for which the participants had to pay 2,000 mil réis or whatever they could, and 3,000 mil réis for couples. The money was collected by another captive of Lima's named Pedro, who then gave it to Narcizo to pay his "Dad" (*Papai*). Pedro and Narcizo ominously told Florencio that those who danced the jongo without paying would die. Jongo was performed in a circle in a call-and-response format, and had the lyrics to the songs been preserved, they would have been a marvelous record.[71]

TAMING MASTERS: PEMBA AND SLAVERY

These statements offer a sense of what the Pemba initiates did in their gatherings, but little more. I want to return to how they described Pemba's purpose: to tame (*amansar*) the masters. This expression lays bare the quotidian violence that shaped their lives. Silva responded to any sign of disobedience with beatings and the lash. He also repeatedly beat the suspected Pemba members to force a confession. Silva recounted his own acts of brutality with a chilling indifference; terror was mundane. Although it was the enslaved who stood accused of intending to murder masters and whites, the only concrete evidence of violence in this entire case is Silva's.

Pemba was "a way to tame their master and mistress so

---

63 Joana questions, Fl. 141v.

64 Luis Moçambique Questions, August 28, 1860, RC Fl.126, ANRJ. A similar ritual opens candomblé Angola ceremonies. Gomez and Symanski have also noted the presence and importance of white clay in the material culture of enslaved populations of West Central African origin in Brazil's Paraíba Valley. Luís Cláudio P. Symanski and Flávio dos Santos Gomes, "Iron Cosmology, Slavery, and Social Control: The Materiality of Rebellion in the Coffee Plantations of the Paraíba Valley, Southeastern Brazil," *Journal of African Diaspora Archaeology and Heritage* 5, no. 2 (May 3, 2016): 189–90, https://doi.org/10.1080/21619441.2016.1204794.

65 Record of Questions asked to Rufina, August 29, 1860, RC Fl.132, ANRJ.

66 Record of Questions asked to Florencio Crioulo, August 28, 1860, RC Fl. 129-130, ANRJ. See also n.33 above.

67 Narcizo Benguela questions, August 31, 1860, RC Fl. 150v, ANRJ.

68 Luis Moçambique Interrogation.

69 Narcizo Mina questions.

---

70 In the nineteenth century, jongo was more commonly known as *batuque* and *caxambu*. Hebe Maria Mattos de Mattos and Martha Abreu, "Jongo, registros de uma história," in *Memória do jongo: as gravaçõcoes históricas de Stanley J. Stein, Vassouras, 1949*, ed. Silvia Hunold Lara and Gustavo Pacheco (Rio de Janeiro: Folha Seca, 2007), 69, 73.

71 Luis Moçambique, Narcizo Mina, and Florencio Crioulo questions. For similar rituals, see Slenes' descriptions in "Arbore Nsanda Transplantada" and his essay in the aforementioned volume in which he analyzes the lyrics to jongos recorded by the late Stanley Stein. Robert W. Slenes, "'Eu venho de muito longe, eu venho cavando': jongueiros cumba na senzala centro-africana," in *Memória do jongo: as gravaçõcoes históricas de Stanley J. Stein, Vassouras, 1949*, ed. Silvia Hunold Lara and Gustavo Pacheco (Rio de Janeiro: Folha Seca, 2007), 109–56.

they wouldn't beat them," initiates told Antonio crioulo. Florencio heard that Pemba "makes the masters tame." Narcizo Benguela stated that it was a way for the master not to be angry (*bravo*), and others similarly spoke of Pemba as a way to control rage (*zanga*). Rufina denied that they were planning to "do something to the whites to be free," stating only that Silva was to be tamed by late September. Initiates were given a small red stick to carry in their mouths to protect them from threats to their physical and spiritual safety. Narcizo Mina himself was evasive, however. "I don't know anything about taming masters," he demurred, claiming that Pemba's purpose was to heal snake bites.[72]

What impressed Silva's captives was the living example of their violence-prone neighbor, José Barboza de Lima. Lima's captives, who had priorly initiated themselves into Pemba, told Florencio that Silva "would be tame just like Senhor Lima." Joana was informed that "when her master came to watch them [work]," Silva "wouldn't beat them and would return home."[73] This was why Silva's captives chose Lima as their protector after they were caught stealing the coffee, and why he likely became his own captives' most vocal defender before the police and legal system. Was Lima simply a slaveowner trying to reclaim his property? That would be the materialist explanation, but it doesn't explain his total lack of alarm when the police raided his property asking about Pemba and taming masters, and just six days after his wife passed away.

That said, this case may have never entered the documentary archive had Silva been tamed. As we recall, several of the enslaved including Antonio, Narcizo Benguela, Florencio, and Rufina, had gone down on their knees asking for Silva's forgiveness a few months earlier. Their reasons are extremely poignant: "because his master knew everything but continued punishing them"; "Pemba didn't work; the beatings continued"; "the beatings were a lot and [it] didn't work"; "the beatings were a lot and the society didn't do anything

to stop it."[74] We cannot say why Pemba didn't work on Silva, but we can hear the profound despair resounding in their words. For Florencio, even the sliver of solace he could seek in his family and community was endangered by Silva's decision to sell him. Betrayal, fear, despair, resignation, anger—emotions must have swirled within Florencio as he was tied to the whipping post, the hide slashing into his back and exposing the raw flesh beneath. Their words vividly capture the brutality that enveloped the lives of Africans and crioulos, women and men, elders and children. We must bear witness to their suffering.[75]

BEYOND BRAZILIAN SLAVERY

Herein lies the conundrum. On one hand we see how the enslaved suffered under the violence of slavery and drew upon African spiritual practices to cope and resist. "Taming masters" (*amansar senhor*) was in fact a common refrain in Brazilian slave society since the colonial era. The idea of using health and healing practices to weaken seigneurial power had African and non-African origins. Examples abound of enslaved people employing their religious-medicinal knowledge to create concoctions with the power to debilitate or even poison their masters. For instance, in the Cangeré insurrection rumor in Vassouras discussed previously, authorities were alarmed by "large portions of poisonous minerals and vegetables" possessed by the "Tatés" (fathers/leaders), given the "facilities which they had of offering drink to some of their masters." One herb used to these ends, the Guinea hen weed, Is In fact known as "master tamer."[76]

Curandeiros or healers who held such knowledge were often accused of witchcraft, particularly when they created Kongo-based *minkisi* or power objects that contained medicines (*bilongo*) consisting of mpemba, seeds, sticks, stones, bones, and other substances.[77]

---

72 Record of Questions asked to Rufina, RC Fl. 133, ANRJ. Antonio crioulo, Florencio crioulo, Narcizo Benguela, Narcizo Mina questions.

73 Joana questions.

74 Antonio crioulo, Narcizo Benguela, Florencio crioulo, Rufina questions.

75 We wonder why Pemba "did not work" for Silva. Sometimes they just didn't.

76 Report of Select Committee, 89. In Portuguese, the herb is called *amansa-senhor*. Reis, *Domingos Sodré, um sacerdote africano*, 147–59; on Guinea herb, 152.

77 MacGaffey notes that although there is no good translation for *nkisi* (pl. *minkisi*), "in Kongo thought a nkisi is a personalized force from the invisible and of the dead; this force has chosen, or been induced, to submit itself to

That is probably why the police interrogated Dionizio, a freedman from Cachoeiro who denied any connection to Pemba, about the mysterious powder and a braid of human hair in his possession. They both belonged to a slaveowner named Dona Anna, he explained, adding that the "powder was made from the skin of the *surucucu*," a highly venomous snake, "which served as a medicine." We wonder what it was for. He had no idea why Dona Anna had the braid of hair.[78] The concept of "taming masters" shows how African spiritual-medicinal practices could, by containing a slaveholder's power and his prerogative to terrorize the bodies and souls of the enslaved, destabilize the very foundation of enslaver-enslaved relations. Taming was no gentle business, either—consider how one tames a wild horse or deescalates a fight.[79]

And yet, without diminishing it in any way, I cannot shake the sense that there is something fundamentally limited in concluding that Pemba's purpose was just that: to tame the violence of slavery. This reduces Pemba to the slaveholders' epistemological world, once again. I initially approached Pemba as the archives presented it, as an African religion in Brazilian slave society with possible insurrection links. However, I need to remind myself that African spiritualities are not reducible to African people's encounter with slavery. While they undoubtedly informed people's resistance, we need to accept them as full, complex expressions of spirituality and selfhood that cannot be defined only in relation to slavery. For this reason I do not equate African spiritualities in themselves with resistance.[80]

The challenge I face is that much of Pemba remains opaque.[81] Perhaps I too am "unable to exceed the limits of the sayable dictated by the archive," because as an uninitiated person, I can only fleetingly glimpse Pemba's cosmological world through the documentary archive. But we can't keep treading on the same path. We need to travel beyond the usual archival confines into the world of Kongo cosmology.

Pemba, I posit, was based on an initiation society from the Lower Congo called Lemba. Kongo scholar Bunseki Fu-Kiau called Lemba the "science of governance" and the "science of power." It taught initiates to become important leaders and governors of people.[82] According to anthropologists John Janzen and Wyatt MacGaffey, at its height, Lemba was considered to be an "extraordinary institution, the most important of the consecrated medicines (*min'kisi*)." Initiates referred to Lemba as a medicine of the village, of the family and its perpetuation, of fertility, of governance, and one integrating people, villages, and markets. Lemba and similar societies were "ritual complexes intended to bring about improvements in the well-being of individuals and groups, curing disease, identifying and punishing wrongdoers, averting misfortune, and favoring fertility and prosperity." Initiates included many elite merchant families connected to one another through Lemba's extensive market and trade network, which included slave trading.[83]

Regarding the connection between the two, I refrain from the continuity-versus-creolization debate, on which

---

some degree of human control effected through ritual performances" by the *nganga* or initiated expert. MacGaffey, *Art and Healing of the Bakongo*, 4. For a minkisi in Kongo and the diaspora, see Robert Farris Thompson, *Flash of the Spirit: African and Afro-American Art and Philosophy*, 1st Vintage Books ed (New York: Vintage Books, 1984), 117–31.

78 Record of Questions asked to Dionizio, August 31, 1860, RC Fl. 151-153, ANRJ. *Surucucu* is the Tupi name for Lachesis muta or Bushmaster snake.

79 Ras Michael Brown also notes that the word "Kanga," the root for "Cangarê," means to tie or bind, which also suggests taming by force. On enslaved people in Brazil and spiritual-medical knowledge, see for example Laura de Mello e Souza, *O Diabo e a Terra de Santa Cruz* (São Paulo, Brazil: Companhia das Letras, 1986); Reis, *Domingos Sodré, um sacerdote africano*; Gabriela dos Reis Sampaio, *Juca Rosa: um pai-de-santo na corte imperial* (Rio de Janeiro: Arquivo Nacional, 2009); James H. Sweet, *Domingos Álvares, African Healing, and the Intellectual History of the Atlantic World* (Chapel Hill: University of North Carolina Press, 2011).

80 I find this study an interesting counterpoint to Aisha Finch's aforementioned work; in her final chapter, Finch draws a compelling connection between Kongo-based Palo and insurrection, especially given the ubiquity of power

objects like gunpowder and minkisi. Interestingly, however, no direct connection is made in this case between, for example, mpemba or the red sticks and insurrection. Finch, *Rethinking Slave Rebellion in Cuba*, Ch. 7. Other well-known examples connecting African-based spirituality and insurrection include the Haitian Revolution, which began with the mythic Bois-Cayman ceremony led by the Vodun priest Boukman, and the Malê Revolt in Bahia, Brazil, led by Muslim West Africans.

81 I'll discuss opacity more in a little bit.

82 K. K. Bunseki Fu-Kiau, *Le Mukongo et le monde qui l'entourait: Cosmogonie Kôngo*, trans. C. Zamenga-Batukezanga (Kinshasa: Office National de la Recherche et Développement, 1969), 122.

83 Wyatt MacGaffey, *Kongo Political Culture: The Conceptual Challenge of the Particular* (Bloomington, IN: Indiana University Press, 2000), 14; John M Janzen, *Lemba, 1650-1930: A Drum of Affliction in Africa and the New World* (New York: Garland, 1982), 4–5.

enough has been said.[84] It's doubtful that the Pemba initiates in Brazil all belonged to Lemba, an elite society with a rigorous initiation process. What I do suggest is that—based on several elements discussed by the Pemba initiates, such as the initiation rituals and specific forms of worship—Lemba and other Kongo-inspired practices were the spiritual, ritual, and cosmological foundation for Pemba and what informed the initiates connection to their world and to each other.

Narcizo Mina was Pemba's central figure. Enslaved in West Africa and trafficked to Brazil, he eventually married an African woman, Umbelina, also owned by Lima, with whom he had a son and a daughter. His authority was evident in his title, *Tata Abranda Mundo*, or Father Softens-the-World. Narcizo himself explained that "'Tata' means Father, and 'Abranda Mundo' is from here." Many leaders of West Central African-based societies in Brazil were known by the Kimbundu and Kikongo title of "Tata" or Father, sometimes followed by a Portuguese name.[85] Narcizo had a spiritual "Dad" (*Papai*) who may have initiated him. Being West African, it is impressive that he was recognized by West Central Africans as the leader of a Kongo-based society that he first encountered in Brazil. He reminds us that African spiritualities were not exclusive to people of the same origins but held a wise resonance that transcended ethnicity.[86]

It was thus Narcizo who, along with the missing Fructuozo, performed the rites of initiation. He drew a cross on the womens' arms with pemba (*faz cruz no braço*).[87] This was not just any mark, but a *dikenga*—a Kongo cosmogram ubiquitous in the Kongo region and the diaspora that "represents the conception of all living beings in the universe." As Bárbaro Martínez-Ruiz explains, "dikenga is itself believed and understood to

be the energy of the universe, the force of all existence and creation."[88] The varieties of dikenga all share four cardinal points in the shape of a cross. It's possible that what was drawn on the Pemba initiates resembled a dikenga known as a Lemba *yowa*, which was most often used in initiation rituals and contained influences of the Christian cross. The dikenga showed the two worlds of the Kongo universe as two mountains separated by the ocean or *kalunga*, where all life begins and ends. The top half represents the world of the living, and the bottom half, the world of the dead or the ancestors. The land of the ancestors is called *Mpemba*, represented in ritual settings with white ash or clay.

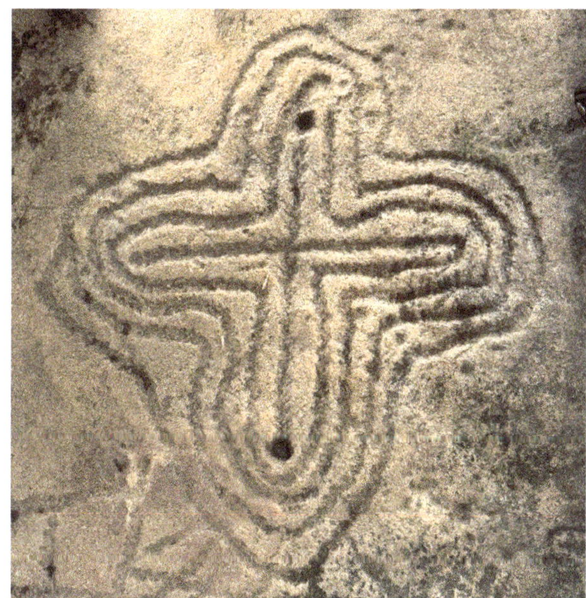

The four points of the dikenga cosmogram represent a "segment of the broader transition between various stages of life" otherwise known as the "four moments of the sun." Beginning at the bottom, the cosmogram follows a counterclockwise direction tracing the movement of the sun, a manifestation of Nzambi Mpungu or God. These were the sun of perfection, the sun of vitality, the sun of warning, and the sun of death and change. Through this journey the community

---

84 For the interested, a good starting point may be Sidney W. Mintz and Richard Price, *The Birth of African-American Culture: An Anthropolgial Perspective* (Boston: Beacon Press, 1992); Thompson, *Flash of the Spirit*.

85 Narcizo Mina, August 30, 1860, Fl. 144. Slenes, "A árvore de Nsanda transplantada," 294, 297, 303; Gomes, *Histórias de quilombolas*, 207–8. The court records state his title as "Tapa" and later "Tala," likely a mistake for Tata, especially since Narcizo himself explained that it meant "Father."

86 Florencio mentions Narcizo's "Papai." Fl. 129.

87 Contemporary initiations of the Umbanda religion also entail a "crossing" or cruzamento that marks crosses on key points of the body.

88 Barbaro Martínez-Ruiz, *Kongo Graphic Writing and Other Narratives of the Sign* (Philadelphia: Temple University Press, 2013), 68.

accumulated, interpreted, and transmitted knowledge.[89] When one died in this world, one transmitted a society's accumulated knowledge to the younger generation and was reborn in Mpemba, and the cycle continued. In Kongo thought, dying is not the end; it allows life to flow and regenerate power to create a new state of being.[90]

The colors that prominently feature in the sources now gain new meaning. Many Kongo societies painted bodies white with mpemba during initiation, the white indicating that members have acquired the relevant knowledge and intelligence.[91] By marking their limbs with mpemba and covering their head with white cloth, Pemba members similarly became ritually white and consecrated by Nzambi Mpungu, the Supreme Being. White combined with red is especially potent. The Pemba initiates wore white caps and kerchiefs on their heads and carried red sticks as protection from malevolence. The two are complementary colors: white the color of *mpemba* or *luvemba* (white clay), symbolizing power, purity, justice, light, and health; red the color of *tukula* powder, symbolizing danger, power, fire, anger, blood, and above all, violent transitions and transformations. Both represent sanctity, one absolute, the other feared. During Lemba initiation, the neophyte's body is smeared with white and red to show God's consecration of him and His almighty power that could not be seen by mortals.[92] People and things painted in red and white are also protected from witchcraft and cured of diseases caused by it.[93]

After a dikenga was drawn, Pemba initiates passed under Narcizo's legs, then "shook." Another Kongo-based religion, Cabula, as practiced in northern Espírito Santo province, had a similar ritual of rebirth in which the initiate "passed beneath the legs of the chief three times to show their faith, humility, and obedience to their new Father (*Pai*)."[94] The practice closely resembled

the first of six phases of initiation into Lemba in which, after the neophyte was anointed with white and red pigments, the nganga or lead practitioner took hold of his student, bounced him three times, then made him pass under his legs, also three times.[95]

As were many spiritual leaders, Narcizo was also a healer with medicinal knowledge. Pemba members told new initiates like Joana and Emilia that, beyond taming masters, Pemba would free them of witchcraft, malevolence, and snakes. Narcizo and his companions had learned snakebite cures from a "freed African from Minas." Snakes and snakebites recur in the testimonies, and it's worth noting that in lower Congo, witches and wizards (*ndoki*) could assume the form of a snake. Perhaps the red and white donned by the Pemba participants also protected them from the malevolence the snakes embodied.[96] The said freed African also instructed the men to collect payments, since otherwise the cures would be worthless. It was normal for healers to be paid for their services. Narcizo shared the payments with his Pemba "brothers of the table" (*irmãos de mesa*), or "those who learned the prayer and were now in charge of ensuring that the others from the same brotherhood don't drink *cachaça*, cause trouble, and gamble, because all that is bad." There is no mention of Narcizo performing other cures that many other healers like Rio de Janeiro's Juca Rosa were known for, such as healing emotional and physical illnesses and securing someone's love and devotion.[97]

Pemba was also connected to the wider spiritual community of Black Atlantic Catholicism. Narcizo led the prayers to Saint Anthony, an extremely popular saint in the Kongo and among Black communities in Brazil. The saint was widely worshipped for his power to heal illnesses, find lost objects, and bestow fertility, and

---

89 Thompson, *Flash of the Spirit*, 108–16; Martínez-Ruiz, *Kongo Graphic Writing*, 68–71.

90 K. K. Bunseki Fu-Kiau, "Ntangu-Tandu-Kolo: The Bantu-Kongo Concept of Time," in *Time in the Black Experience*, ed. Joseph K. Adjaye (London, U.K.: Greenwood Publishing Group, 1994), 27.

91 Jacobson-Widding, *Red-White-Black*, 196–97.

92 Ras Michael Brown, personal communication, Thompson, *Flash of the Spirit*, 108.

93 Jacobson-Widding, *Red-White-Black*, 226–85, esp. 229 and 233.

94 Slenes states that this ritual is very similar to that described the by

missionary-ethnographer J. Van Wing in a Kongo Kimpasi cult in the early 20th century. My Slenes, "A árvore de Nsanda transplantada," 297. The movement is also strikingly similar to the *tesoura* (scissor) movement in capoeira Angola.

95 Fu-Kiau, *Le Mukongo*, 136. Famed spiritual healer Juca Rosa and his followers also ingested a mixture of white powders they called "pemba" and *aguardente*, which was followed by spirit possession. Sampaio, *Juca Rosa*, 186.

96 On snakes and ndoki (witches and wizards), see Jacobson-Widding, *Red-White-Black*, 59.

97 Narcizo Mina, Fl. 145. See Sampaio, *Juca Rosa*.

was usually portrayed holding the infant Jesus.[98] Saint Anthony already had a long history of veneration among West Central Africans who followed Dona Beatriz Kimpa Vita and her "Antonian movement" in the Kingdom of Kongo (1704-1706), whose monarch had officially converted to Catholicism in 1491. Dona Beatriz, who died due to a supernatural sickness and was resurrected as Saint Anthony (known as Toni Malau or "Anthony of Good Fortune" among Kongo), began a movement to restore the war-torn Kingdom. In her sermons she preached that, as the patron saint of Portugal and of the Kongo, Saint Anthony was the most important of saints, with the power to heal illnesses and infertility.[99]

Veneration of Saint Anthony continued among West Central Africans in Brazil, including Pemba initiates. Low birth rates and relatively small number of children among the enslaved owned by Lima suggests that the community suffered from low fertility, high mortality rates, and/or sales of their children, which threatened their community and caused tremendous anguish.[100] Pemba initiates thus existed in a complex religious field in Brazil, wherein a large number of African-based religions flourished, often in symbiotic relationships with Catholic Christianity and Indigenous religions.

ON OPACITY, SECRECY, AND OTHER FINAL THOUGHTS

It's not my intention to define Pemba. The initiates possess what Édouard Glissant called the "right to opacity," and I have to resist rendering Pemba intelligible on my terms. "Give up this old obsession with discovering what lies at the bottom of natures," he admonished.[101] I had initially spent many hours

trying to decipher Pemba's purpose along categories defined by other scholars. Was it a cult of affliction?[102] A crisis society? A healing society? A mutual aid society? A political or spiritual organization? What elements are Kongo or Mina? Which are Catholic? What parts are syncretic or creolized? Such distinctions, I eventually understood, could satisfy my own desire to categorize and define but held no meaning for the initiates themselves, because Pemba could encompass all these things. Would we compartmentalize Christianity or Buddhism into such narrow categories?[103] The same could be said for categories we historians of slavery regularly employ in our work, such as African versus Brazilian-born, Black versus *pardo* (mulato), freed or free versus enslaved, and so forth. They are certainly important in enriching our understanding of demographics and social relations across race, status, generation, and birthplace, and so forth. But when they become explanatory, they could lead to narrow readings of spirituality by suggesting, for instance, that freedpeople participated with the enslaved in Pemba because they also opposed slavery. While that may be true, that could hardly be the full picture.

The idea of a "secret society" also warrants caution. As art historian Mary Nooter notes, secrecy is as an "important dimension of African knowledge, power, and aesthetic experience."[104] The justice system, however, was not evoking it in a nod to African thought. Judge Castro mentioned that the "society's goals were secret, and it was prohibited to reveal them under oath and penalty of death." But this isn't what the initiates said

---

98 Mary Karasch, *Slave Life in Rio de Janeiro, 1808-1850* (Princeton: Princeton University Press, 1987), 266–72, 280–84; Robert W. Slenes, "'Malungu, ngoma vem!': África coberta e descoberta do Brasil," *Revista USP*, no. 12 (February 28, 1992): 64–65, https://doi.org/10.11606/issn.2316-9036.v0i12p48-67.

99 John K Thornton, *The Kongolese Saint Anthony: Dona Beatriz Kimpa Vita and the Antonian Movement, 1684-1706* (Cambridge, U.K.; New York: Cambridge University Press, 1998), 110–12, 132–33. Dona Beatriz was burned at the stake in 1706. See also Cécile Fromont, *The Art of Conversion: Christian Visual Culture in the Kingdom of Kongo* (Chapel Hill: University of North Carolina Press, 2014).

100 Thanks to Ras Michael Brown for this analysis based on Lima and his wife's inventories.

101 Édouard Glissant, *Poetics of Relation*, trans. Betsy Wing (Ann Arbor: University of Michigan Press, 1997), 189–90.

102 Robert Slenes describes such groups in the lower Congo whose purpose was to address individual and communal ills or afflictions, and contends that the enslaved in Brazil also relied on such groups to address the "witchcraft" of slavery. Slenes, "A árvore de Nsanda transplantada," 287–91.

103 The scholarship on Vodun offers a helpful perspective. In her work on contemporary Vodun in the Republic of Benin and the diaspora, for example, Dana Rush describes Vodun's "open-ended structure" which is "constantly reinvigorating old ideas and components while welcoming newly arriving ideas or components—local and international." Dana Rush, *Vodun in Coastal Bénin: Unfinished, Open-Ended, Global* (Nashville: Vanderbilt University Press, 2013), 5. Consentino also recognizes the capaciousness of the enslaved and free people of Haiti "who imagined a myth broad enough and fabricated a ritual complex enough to encompass all this disparate stuff" e.g. St. Anthony, the Buddha, rosaries, Masonic insignia, goat skulls, Arawak celts. Donald Cosentino, *Sacred Arts of Haitian Vodou* (Los Angeles: UCLA Fowler Museum of Cultural History, 1998), 27.

104 Mary H. Nooter, "Secrecy: African Art That Conceals and Reveals," *African Arts* 26, no. 1 (January 1993): 58.

---

at all. If they refused to speak, it was because they knew their enslavers and law enforcement could not understand, and moreover would respond with violence. Fu-Kiau dismisses the "secret society" concept as a fabrication by colonial states (in his case France and Belgium, whose king Leopold II seized the Lower Congo in 1885) for whom the penetration of Indigenous institutions such as Lemba became an important component of the colonial project. Lemba initiation was open to anyone who underwent the proper rites of initiation and possessed the necessary wealth. Colonial agents who were denied access because they eschewed proper initiation retaliated by denouncing Lemba's "secrecy."[105] By the 1920s, Belgians banned Lemba in the lower Congo for its perceived resistance to colonial progress and civilization. Missionaries condemned it. Ethnologist Edward DeJonghe deemed it "one of the largest and most serious infections on Africa," misappropriating Lemba's language of sickness and healing.[106] Whether Brazil in the 1860s or the Belgian Congo in the 1920s, calling Pemba or Lemba a "secret society" shrouded them in an aura of mystery that was more a projection of slaveholder and colonial fantasies.

As a historian, I do think we need to approach our archival work with caution, so that we don't get seduced by its stories, no matter how exciting—like an insurrection by enslaved Africans. We need to read along the archival grain first in order to understand how they project the epistemology of enslavers. Only then can we recognize when it is shaping our own thinking, whether we are focusing on the veracity of an insurrection, or confining African spiritualities to the realm of resistance to slavery.

Scholars of slavery and Black life have been increasingly vocal about the gaps, silences, and distortions of documentary archives, which were overwhelmingly created by people and institutions who trafficked, owned, and criminalized people of African descent.

But they've also introduced and embraced different archives and ways of writing about Black life. They travel between the written and spoken, fiction and non-fiction, sound and memory. They are unafraid to speculate, because they recognize that "archivally verifiable" history and its positivist presumptions too often replicate existing hierarchies and impoverish our possibility to imagine.[107]

Writing this piece about Pemba has allowed me to discern a different archive that pushes beyond the boundaries of the sayable, an embodied archive of spirituality crossing not only Atlantic space but past and present, living and ancestral, that bleeds into the archives of slavery. The Africans' bodies themselves are palimpsests. Just before the Middle Passage, the Africans were probably marked by one of the most violent signs of slavery: the iron brand. Seared into their arms, chests, legs, and torsos, they signaled their transformation into merchandise and property. But when a dikenga was drawn onto those very same bodies with mpemba, their souls began another journey that could not be contained by the violent denial of their personhood.[108] Their bodies are what José Esteban Muñoz called "ephemeral evidence," which "describe and imagine contemporary identities that do not fit into a single preestablished archive of evidence." Our world is so much richer for it.[109]

Let's close with one final question: why was Pemba important to the initiates? Many had been kidnapped, sold, or condemned to slavery on the other side of the Atlantic. In the Middle Passage they witnessed disease

---

105 K. K. Bunseki Fu-Kiau, "Makuku Matatu: les fondements culturels Bantu chez les Kongo" (1980), 423–24; Fu-Kiau, *Le Mukongo*, 148.

106 Janzen, *Lemba, 1650-1930*, 9–12. Nooter similarly critiques the Eurocentric biases present in many descriptions of "secret societies" and the "authors' ignorance of the nature and necessity of secrecy, and of its sophisticated role in African life." Nooter, "Secrecy," 55.

107 Herman L. Bennett, "Writing into a Void: Representing Slavery and Freedom in the Narrative of Colonial Spanish America," *Social Text* 25, no. 4 (93) (December 1, 2007): 67–90; Hartman, "Venus in Two Acts"; Saidiya Hartman, *Wayward Lives, Beautiful Experiments: Intimate Histories of Social Upheaval* (New York: W. W. Norton & Company, 2019); Tiya Miles, *All That She Carried: The Journey of Ashley's Sack, a Black Family Keepsake* (New York: Random House, 2021); Brent Hayes Edwards, "The Taste of the Archive," *Callaloo* 35, no. 4 (2012): 944–72, https://doi.org/10.1353/cal.2013.0002; Smallwood, "The Politics of the Archive."

108 Elsewhere I discuss how Brazilian sources listing the physical description of African people's teeth, head shape, height, and slave brandings constitute an "archive of signs." See Miki, "In the Trail of the Ship," 93–94.

109 José Esteban Muñoz, "Ephemera as Evidence: Introductory Notes to Queer Acts," *Women & Performance: A Journal of Feminist Theory* 8, no. 2 (January 1, 1996): 9, https://doi.org/10.1080/07407709608571228. I thank Arnaldo Cruz-Malavé for this reference and Matthew Chin for his insights on embodied archives.

and despair extinguish the lives of countless shipmates. They barely survived themselves. Their sorrow continued once their lives converged in Itapemirim, Brazil, where they toiled in the coffee fields from dawn to dusk. The men who came to own them beat and whipped them for the most trifling matters. Still, they found solace in each other. They married and had children, but not many, and lost many. Family and loss were always bound together. After Lima's death in 1867, Narcizo Mina and Umbelina's two children were split up among Lima's heirs and creditors, his small family destroyed. In 1872 two of Caspar Moange and Maria's sons, Zacharias and Leopoldo, would run away after they were sold to another buyer.[110] Africans worried for their children born into slavery and grieved for those who were missing because they had been sold away, died young, or were never born. They lit candles to Saint Anthony to protect them and their children. Slavery was affliction and malevolence, and masters had to be tamed.

But terror and violence were not the entirety of their lives. When Narcizo traced the cosmogram on their bodies with mpemba, a path opened to another world. In their initiation they came face to face with the dead but knew that death was not the end of existence. When they died in this world, they would cross the ocean to be reborn in mpemba, the land of the ancestors, and return to the land of the living, just as the sun rises and sets each day. They could heal the illness that had afflicted them. They were endowed with justice, which guided their commitment to their community, to one another. Lemba meant rebirth, but also to calm, to make gentle, to tame: *Abranda Mundo*. Calm the world. For a fleeting moment, Pemba appears in the Brazilian archives, allowing us to glimpse African people's spirituality whose complexity and richness transport us far deeper and beyond the world of slavery.

— **Yuko Miki**

---

110 "Inventory of José Barboza de Lima"; *O Estandarte*, April 28, 1872.

BIBLIOGRAPHY

Almada, Vilma Paraíso Ferreira de. *Escravismo e transição: o Espírito Santo (1850-1888)*. Rio de Janeiro-RJ-Brasil: Graal, 1984.

Bennett, Herman L. "Writing into a Void: Representing Slavery and Freedom in the Narrative of Colonial Spanish America." *Social Text* 25, no. 4 (93) (December 1, 2007): 67–90.

Bentley, W. Holman. *Dictionary and Grammar of the Kongo Language: English-Kongo Dictionary. Kongo-English Dictionary.* Baptist Missionary Society and Trübner, 1887.

Carlos Sandroni. *A Respectable Spell: Transformations of Samba in Rio de Janeiro*. Champaign: University of Illinois Press, 2021.

Cosentino, Donald. *Sacred Arts of Haitian Vodou*. Los Angeles: UCLA Fowler Museum of Cultural History, 1998.

Domingues da Silva, Daniel B. *The Atlantic Slave Trade from West Central Africa, 1780-1867*. Cambridge [England]; New York: Cambridge University Press, 2017.

Edwards, Brent Hayes. "The Taste of the Archive." *Callaloo* 35, no. 4 (2012): 944–72. https://doi.org/10.1353/cal.2013.0002.

Farias, Juliana Barreto, Flávio dos Santos Gomes, Carlos Eugenio Libano Soares, and Arquivo Nacional (Rio de Janeiro). *No labirinto das nações: africanos e identidades no Rio de Janeiro, século XIX*. Rio de Janeiro: Arquivo Nacional, 2005.

Ferreira, Roquinaldo. "The Suppression of the Slave Trade and Slave Departures from Angola, 1830s-1860s." In *Extending the Frontiers: Essays on the New Transatlantic Slave Trade Database*, edited by David Eltis and David Richardson, 313–34. New Haven, CT: Yale University Press, 2008.

Finch, Aisha K. *Rethinking Slave Rebellion in Cuba: La Escalera and the Insurgencies of 1841-1844*. Chapel Hill: University of North Carolina Press, 2015.

Fromont, Cécile. *The Art of Conversion: Christian Visual Culture in the Kingdom of Kongo*. Chapel Hill: University of North Carolina Press, 2014.

Fu-Kiau, K. K. Bunseki. *Le Mukongo et le monde qui l'entourait: Cosmogonie Kôngo*. Translated by C. Zamenga-Batukezanga. Kinshasa: Office National de la Recherche et Développement, 1969.

———. "Makuku Matatu: les fondements culturels Bantu chez les Kongo," 1980.

———. "Ntangu-Tandu-Kolo: The Bantu-Kongo Concept of Time." In *Time in the Black Experience*, edited by Joseph K. Adjaye, 17–34. London, U.K.: Greenwood Publishing Group, 1994.

Glissant, Édouard. *Poetics of Relation*. Translated by Betsy Wing. Ann Arbor: University of Michigan Press, 1997.

Gomes, Flávio dos Santos. *Histórias de quilombolas: mocambos e comunidades de senzalas no Rio de Janeiro, século XIX*. São Paulo: Companhia das Letras, 2006.

Gomez, Michael A. *Exchanging Our Country Marks: The Transformation of African Identities in the Colonial and Antebellum South*. Chapel Hill: University of North Carolina Press, 1998.

Grinberg, Keila. *Liberata, a lei da ambiguidade: as ações de liberdade da Corte de Apelação do Rio de Janeiro no século XIX*. Relume Dumara, 1994.

Hall, Gwendolyn Midlo. *Slavery and African Ethnicities in the Americas: Restoring the Links*. Chapel Hill: University of North Carolina Press, 2005.

Hartman, Saidiya. "Venus in Two Acts." *Small Axe* 12, no. 2 (July 17, 2008): 1–14. https://doi.org/doi.org/10.1215/-12-2-1.

———. *Wayward Lives, Beautiful Experiments: Intimate Histories of Social Upheaval*. New York: W. W. Norton & Company, 2019.

Jacobson-Widding, Anita. *Red-White-Black as a Mode of Thought: A Study of Triadic Classification by Colours in the Ritual Symbolism and Cognitive Thought of the Peoples of the Lower Congo*. Uppsala, Sweden: Almqvist & Wiksell, 1979.

Janzen, John M. *Lemba, 1650-1930: A Drum of Affliction in Africa and the New World*. New York: Garland, 1982.

Johnson, Michael P. "Denmark Vesey and His Co-Conspirators." *The William and Mary Quarterly* 58, no. 4 (2001): 915–76. https://doi.org/10.2307/2674506.

Jordan, Winthrop D. *Tumult and Silence at Second Creek: An Inquiry Into a Civil War Slave Conspiracy*, 1996.

Karasch, Mary. *Slave Life in Rio de Janeiro, 1808-1850*. Princeton: Princeton University Press, 1987.

Keefer, Katrina H. B. "Scarification and Identity in the Liberated Africans Department Register, 1814-1815." *Canadian Journal of African Studies* 47, no. 3 (2013): 537–53.

Lago, Rafaela Domingos. "Sob os olhos de Deus e dos homens: escravos e parentesco ritual na província do Espírito Santo (1831-1888)." M.A. Thesis, UFES, 2013.

Langfur, Hal. *The Forbidden Lands: Colonial Identity, Frontier Violence, and the Persistence of Brazil's Eastern Indians, 1750-1830*. Stanford: Stanford University Press, 2006.

Lara, Silvia Hunold. *Palmares e Cucaú: o aprendizado da dominação*. São Paulo, Brazil: EdUSP, 2021.

Lovejoy, Paul E. "Ethnic Designations of the Slave Trade and the Reconstruction of the History of Trans-Atlantic Slavery." In *Trans-Atlantic Dimensions of Ethnicity in the African Diaspora*, edited by Paul E. Lovejoy and David V. Trotman, 9–42. London and New York: Continuum, 2003.

MacGaffey, Wyatt, ed. *Art and Healing of the Bakongo Commented by Themselves: Minkisi from the Laman Collection*. Stockholm: Folkens Museum-etnografiska and Indiana University Press, 1991.

———. *Kongo Political Culture: The Conceptual Challenge of the Particular*. Bloomington, IN: Indiana University Press, 2000.

Machado, Laryssa da Silva. "Retratos da escravidão em Itapemirim, ES: uma análise das famílias escravas enre 1831-1888." M.A. Thesis, UFES, 2019.

Mahony, Mary Ann. "Creativity under Constraint: Enslaved Afro-Brazilian Families in Brazil's Cacao Area, 1870–1890." *Journal of Social History* 41, no. 3 (2008): 633–66.

Mamigonian, Beatriz Gallotti. *Africanos livres: a abolição do tráfico de escravos para o Brasil*. São Paulo: Companhia das Letras, 2017.

Martínez, María Elena. "Archives, Bodies, and Imagination: The Case of Juana Aguilar and Queer Approaches to History, Sexuality, and Politics." *Radical History Review* 2014, no. 120 (October 1, 2014): 159–82. https://doi.org/10.1215/01636545-2703787.

Martínez-Ruiz, Barbaro. *Kongo Graphic Writing and Other Narratives of the Sign*. Philadelphia: Temple University Press, 2013.

Mattos, Hebe Maria Mattos de, and Martha Abreu. "Jongo, registros de uma história." In *Memória do jongo: as gravaçõcoes históricas de Stanley J. Stein, Vassouras, 1949*, edited by Silvia Hunold Lara and Gustavo Pacheco, 69–106. Rio de Janeiro: Folha Seca, 2007.

Maxwell, David. "Freed Slaves, Missionaries, and Respectability: The Expansion of the Christian Frontier from Angola to Belgian Congo." *The Journal of African History* 54, no. 1 (March 2013): 79–102. https://doi.org/10.1017/S0021853713000030.

Miki, Yuko. *Frontiers of Citizenship: A Black and Indigenous History of Postcolonial Brazil*. Afro-Latin America. New York and Cambridge: Cambridge University Press, 2018.

———. "In the Trail of the Ship: Narrating the Archives of Illegal Slavery." *Social Text* 37, no. 1 (138) (March 1, 2019): 87–105. https://doi.org/10.1215/01642472-7286276.

Miles, Tiya. *All That She Carried: The Journey of Ashley's Sack, a Black Family Keepsake*. New York: Random House, 2021.

Mintz, Sidney W., and Richard Price. *The Birth of African-American Culture: An Anthropolgial Perspective*. Boston: Beacon Press, 1992.

Muñoz, José   Esteban. "Ephemera as Evidence: Introductory Notes to Queer Acts." *Women & Performance: A Journal of Feminist Theory* 8, no. 2 (January 1, 1996): 5–16. https://doi.org/10.1080/07407709608571228.

Nooter, Mary H. "Secrecy: African Art That Conceals and Reveals." *African Arts* 26, no. 1 (January 1993): 54-69+102.

Reis, João José. *Domingos Sodré, um sacerdote africano : escravidão, liberdade e candomblé na Bahia do século XIX*. São Paulo: Companhia das Letras, 2008.

———. *Rebelião escrava no Brasil: a história do levante dos malês em 1835*. [São Paulo, Brazil]: Companhia das Letras, 2003.

———. "'The Revolution of the Ganhadores': Urban Labour, Ethnicity and the African Strike of 1857 in Bahia, Brazil." *Journal of Latin American Studies* 29, no. 2 (1997): 355–93.

Reis, João José, and Flávio dos Santos Gomes, eds. *Revoltas escravas no Brasil*. São Paulo, Brazil: Companhia das Letras, 2021.

Ribeiro, Geisa Lourenço. "Enlaces e desenlaces: família escrava e reprodução endógena no Espírito Santo (1790-1871)." M.A. Thesis, UFES, 2012.

Rodrigues, Aldair. "African Body Marks, Stereotypes and Racialization in Eighteenth-Century Brazil." *Slavery & Abolition* 42, no. 2 (April 3, 2021): 315–44. https://doi.org/10.1080/0144039X.2020.1814055.

Rush, Dana. *Vodun in Coastal Bénin: Unfinished, Open-Ended, Global*. Nashville: Vanderbilt University Press, 2013.

Sampaio, Gabriela dos Reis. *Juca Rosa: um pai-de-santo na corte imperial*. Rio de Janeiro: Arquivo Nacional, 2009.

Slenes, Robert W. "A árvore de Nsanda transplantada: cultos Kongo de afilição e identidade escrava no sudeste brasllelro (século XIX)." In *Trabalho livre, trabalho escravo: Brasil e Europa, séculos XVIII e XIX*, edited by Douglas C. Libby and Júnia Ferreira Furtado, 273–314. São Paulo, Brazil: Annablume, 2006.

———. "'Eu venho de muito longe, eu venho cavando': jongueiros cumba na senzala centro-africana." In *Memória do jongo: as gravaçõcoes históricas de Stanley J. Stein, Vassouras, 1949*, edited by Silvia Hunold Lara and Gustavo Pacheco, 109–56. Rio de Janeiro: Folha Seca, 2007.

———. "'Malungu, ngoma vem!': África coberta e descoberta do Brasil." *Revista USP*, no. 12 (February 28, 1992): 48–67. https://doi.org/10.11606/issn.2316-9036.v0i12p48-67.

———. *Na senzala, uma flor: esperanças e recordações na formação da família escrava : Brasil Sudeste, século XIX*. Rio de Janeiro, RJ, Brasil: Editora Nova Fronteira, 1999.

Smallwood, Stephanie E. "The Politics of the Archive and History's Accountability to the Enslaved." *History of the Present* 6, no. 2 (2016): 117–32. https://doi.org/DOI: 10.5406/historypresent.6.2.0117.

Souza, Laura de Mello e. *O Diabo e a Terra de Santa Cruz*. São Paulo, Brazil: Companhia das Letras, 1986.

Stoler, Ann Laura. *Along the Archival Grain: Epistemic Anxieties and Colonial Common Sense*. Princeton, N.J.: Princeton University Press, 2009.

Sweet, James H. *Domingos Álvares, African Healing, and the Intellectual History of the Atlantic World*. Chapel Hill: University of North Carolina Press, 2011.

Symanski, Luís Cláudio P., and Flávio dos Santos Gomes. "Iron Cosmology, Slavery, and Social Control: The Materiality of Rebellion in the Coffee Plantations of the Paraíba Valley, Southeastern Brazil." *Journal of African Diaspora Archaeology and Heritage* 5, no. 2 (May 3, 2016): 174–97. https://doi.org/10.1080/21619441.2016.1204794.

Thompson, Robert Farris. *Flash of the Spirit: African and Afro-American Art and Philosophy*. 1st Vintage Books ed. New York: Vintage Books, 1984.

Thornton, John K. *The Kongolese Saint Anthony: Dona Beatriz Kimpa Vita and the Antonian Movement, 1684-1706*. Cambridge, U.K.; New York: Cambridge University Press, 1998.

Wied-Neuwied, Maximilian. *Travels in Brazil in 1815, 1816, and 1817*. London: Sir Richard Phillips & Co., 1820.

SAND DECAY
AND TIME

As a child growing up in North West London, I accompanied my father on weekly visits to the local barber. I listened to the stories of the Afro-Caribbean elders who were taking their turn in the barber's chair, and quickly understood the space as one of communal comradery where cultural wisdom was shared. Before entering the barber's, my father would remind us, "Children are seen and not heard." My brother and I would read comics, draw, and intermittently listen to the elders' saucy exploits and pearls of wisdom. The enforced stoicism of being seen but not heard sharpened my visual awareness and imagination. We sat in silence, observing, while I invented characters for each elder as they spoke. I eventually realized that this space was my first institute of learning and unlearning. The relationship between the barber and the subject establishes an intimacy where renewal is entrusted in the hands of the barber, leading to human transformation. To cut away the old and reveal the new.

Spending time in the expanse of the Mleiha Desert of Sharjah with little human interaction and many moments of solitude served as the gateway to resurrecting mindfulness and unlocking the doors of introspection and self-reflection. The Mleiha Desert became the place of reckoning where I was divested of technology, comfort, and ego. The same emotional response visited me years later when I saw the intact T-beam pulled from the debris of Ground Zero. My father was a minister, and the cross was always present and the conduit to the afterlife. Silence and deep meditation were required for God to hear and answer requests. Some spaces hold your tongue. Mleiha and Ground Zero are spaces of reflection and return, where the ghosts of our personal and political pasts can finally be laid to rest.

— **Faisal Abdu'Allah**

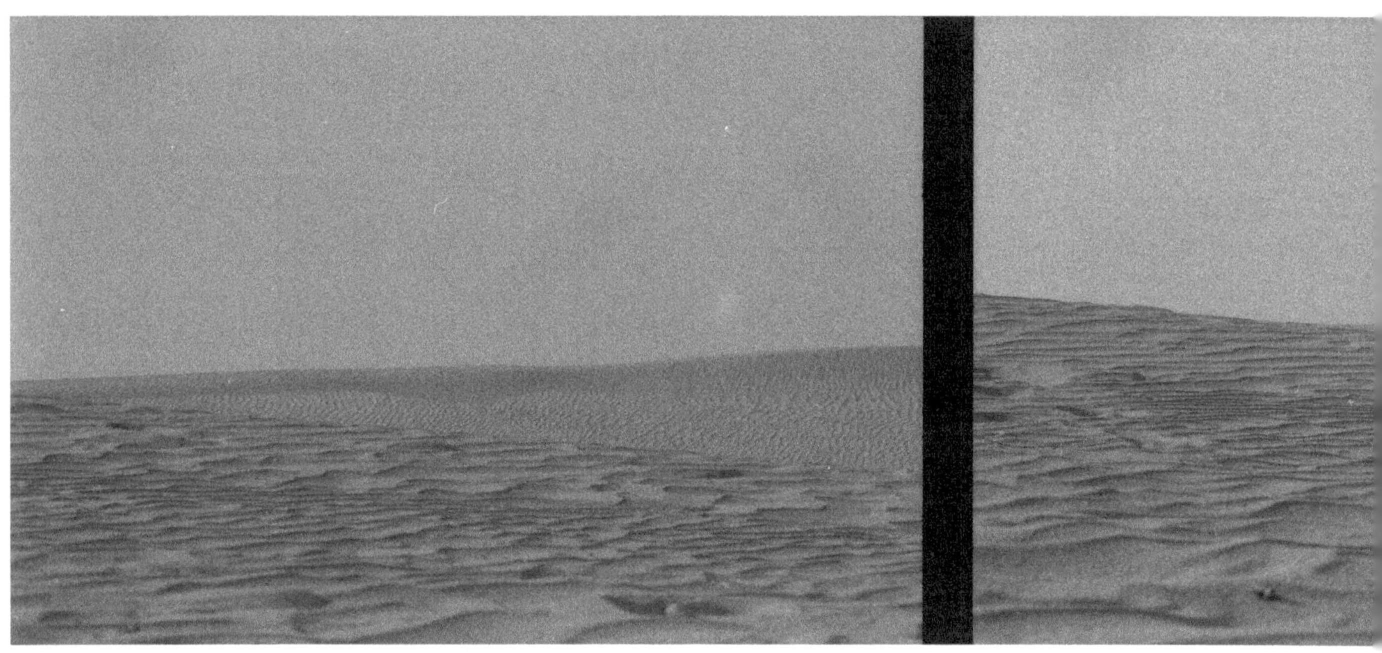

Silent Verses, 2003

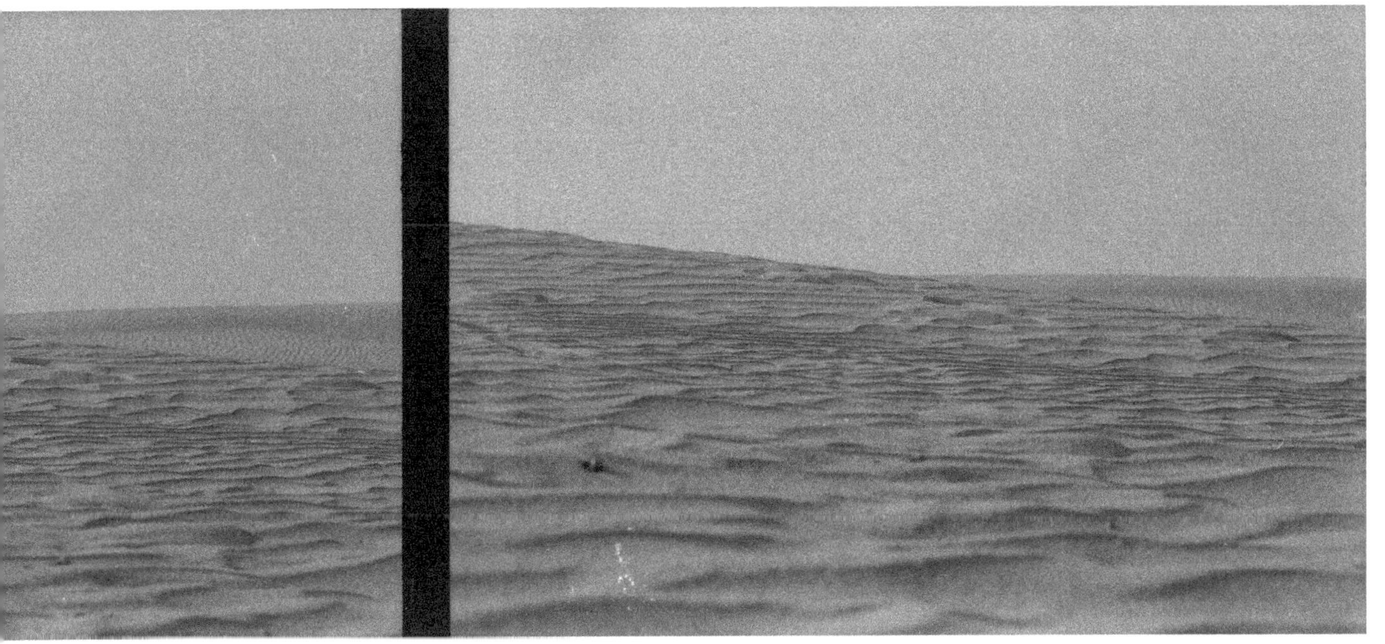

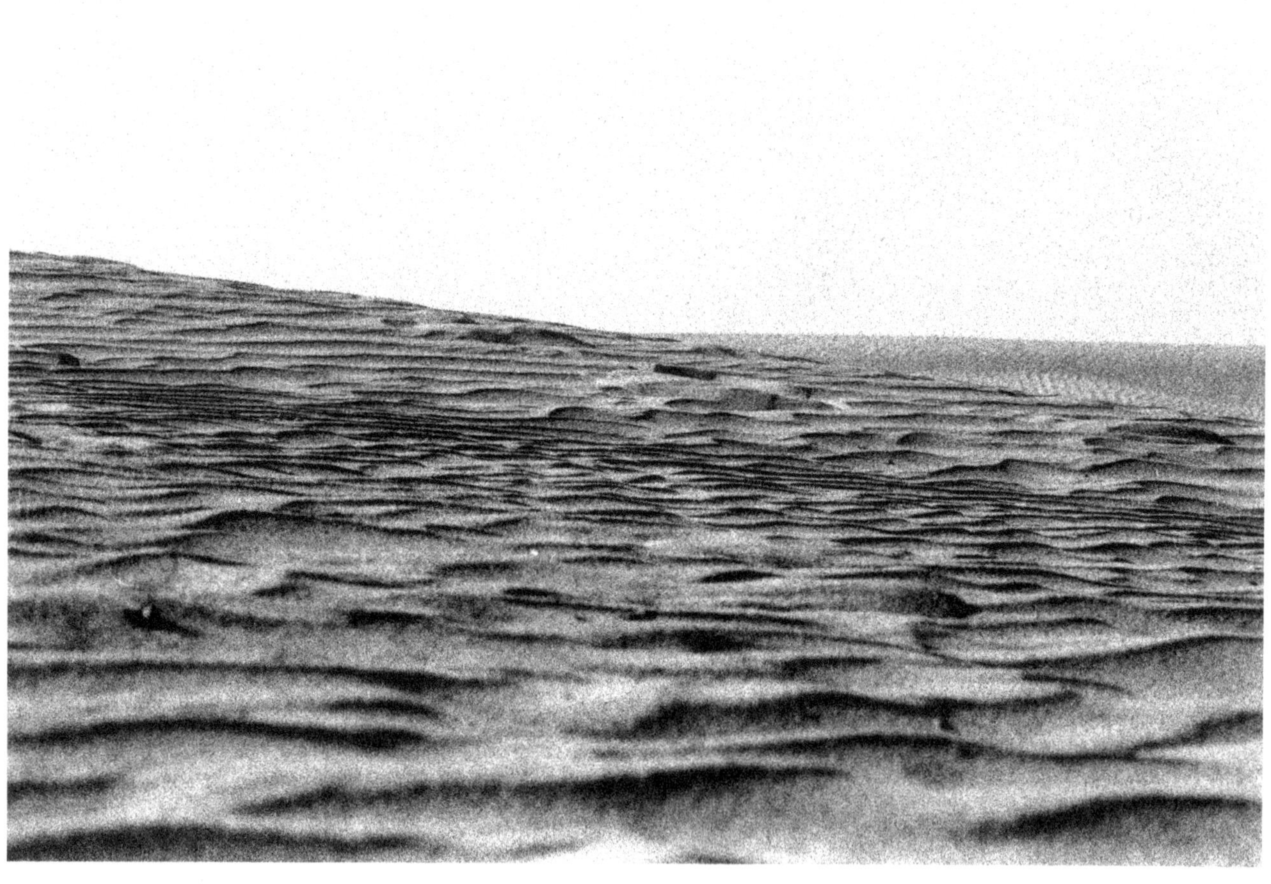

Red Land, 2003

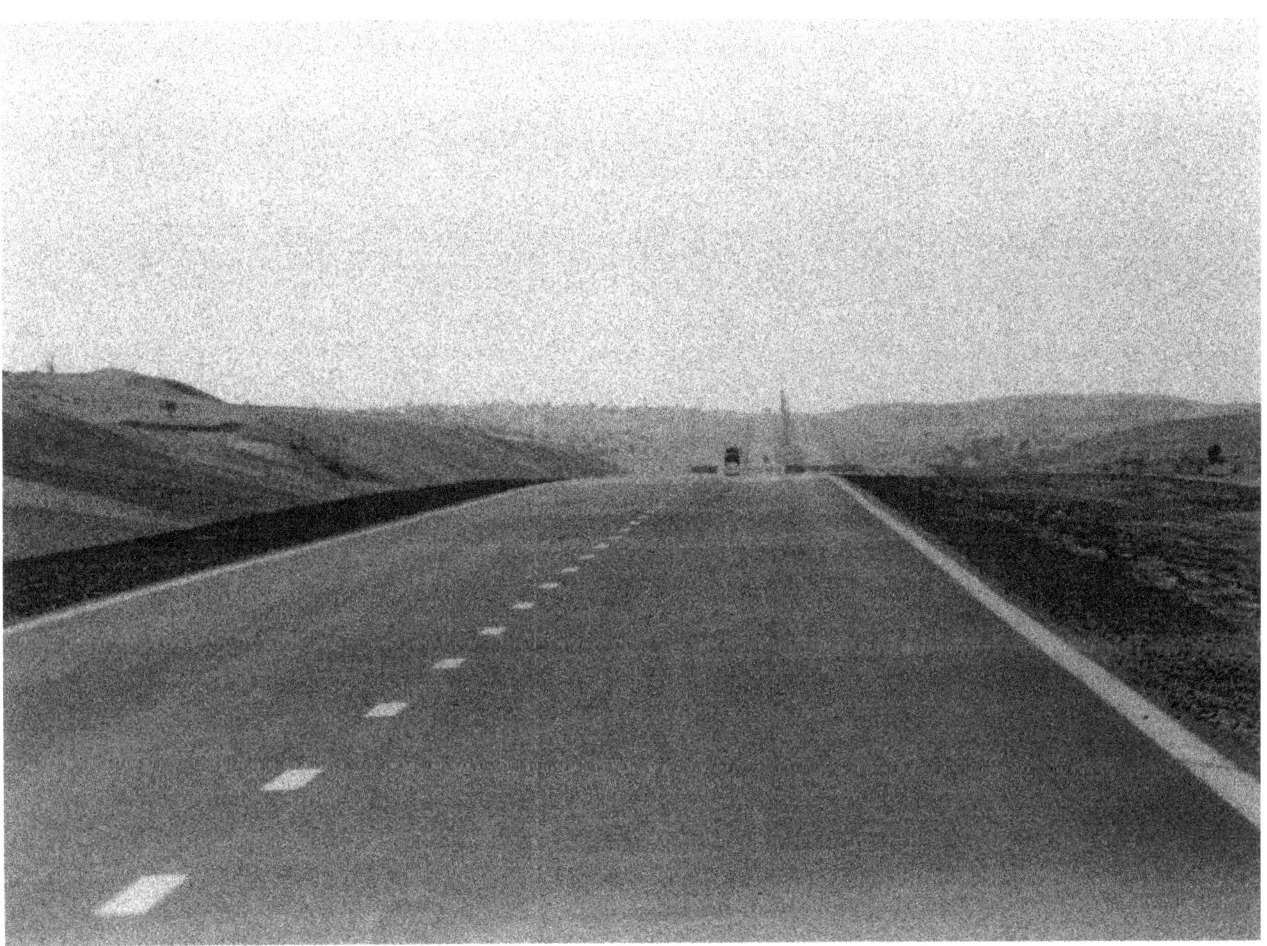

Through Time and Sand, 2003

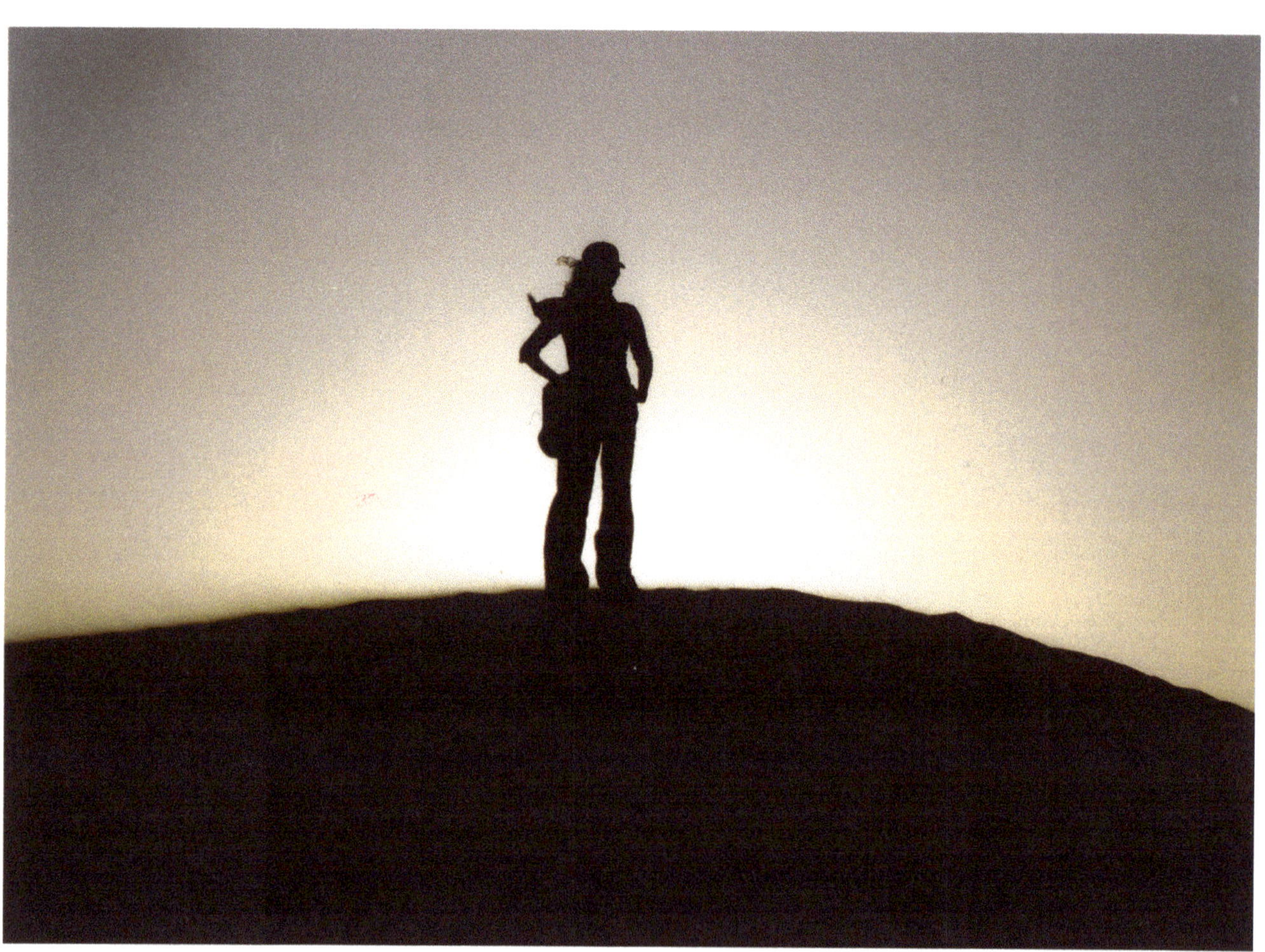

Runa, 2003

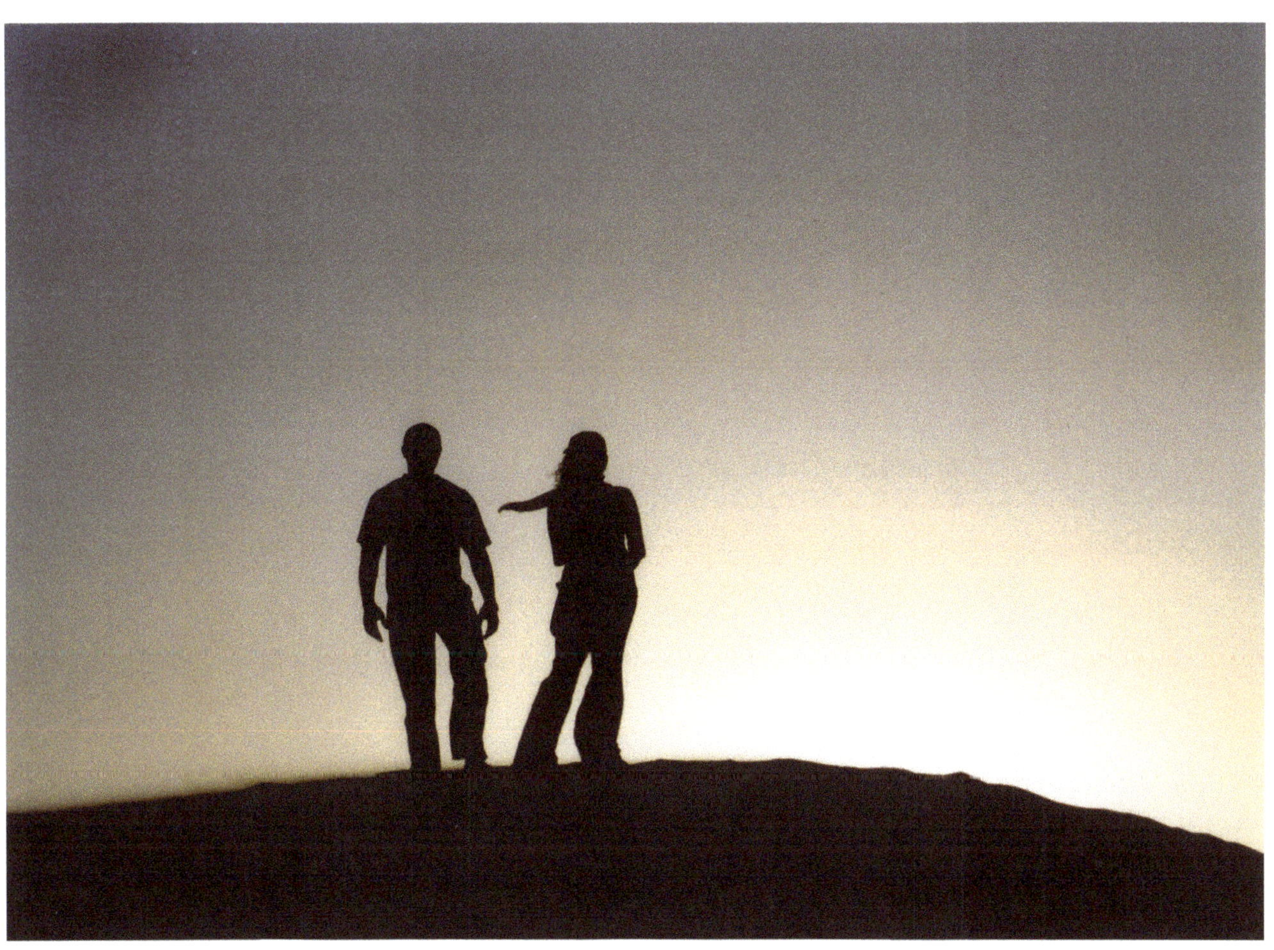

Ruhun, 2003

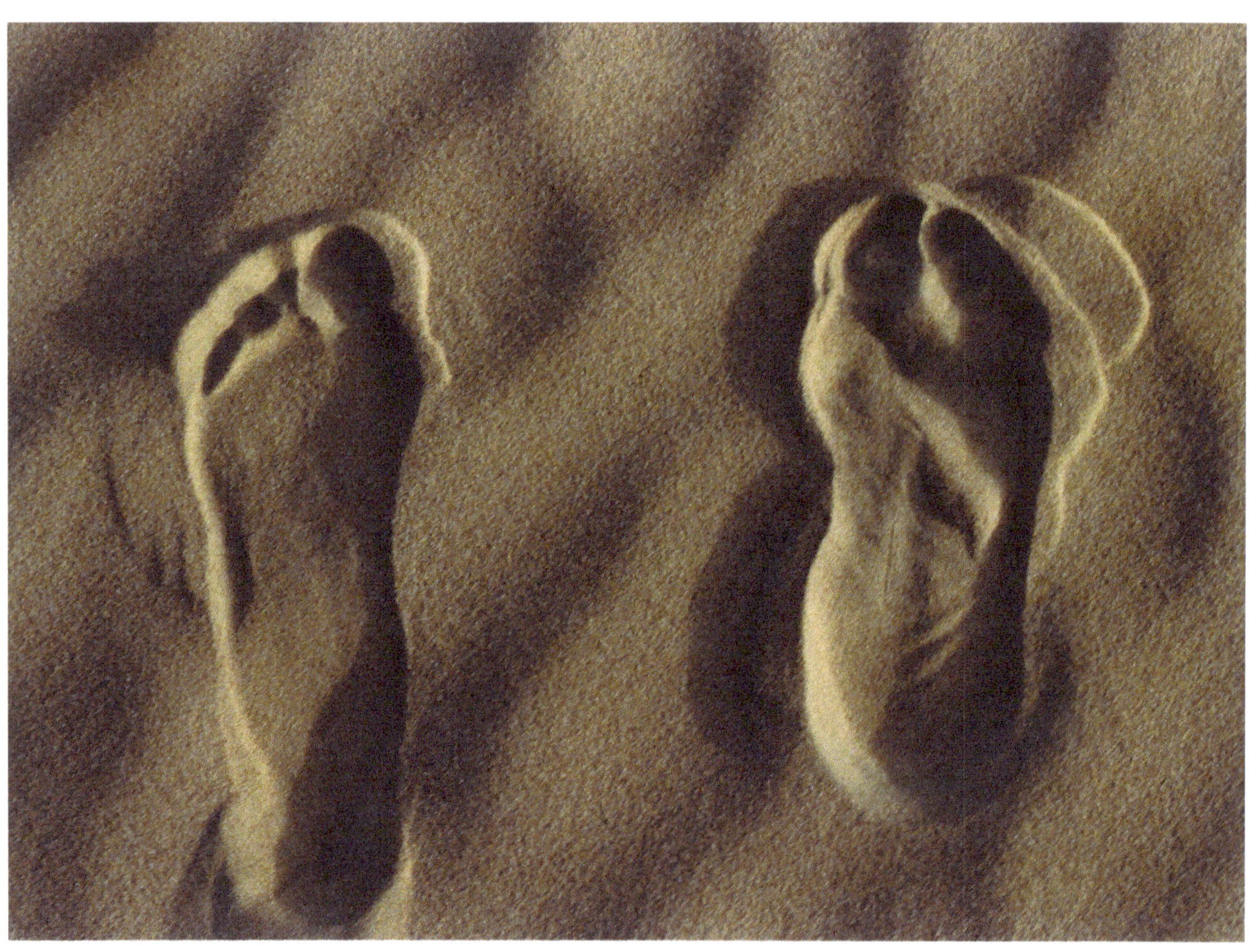

Echoes of the Passing Soul, 2003

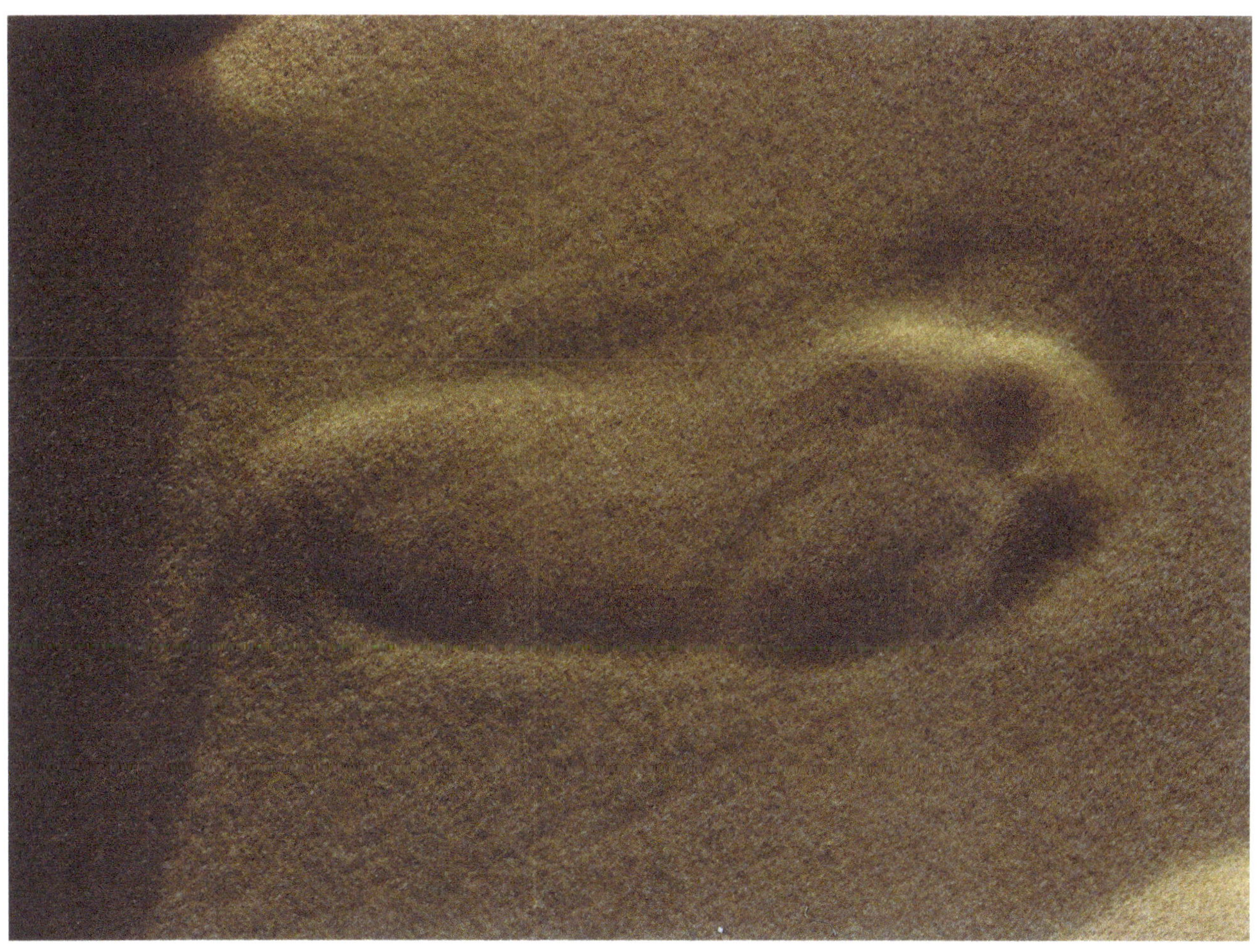

Ephemeral Step, 2003

PHOTO-BOOK 1981-1995

I have been producing both sculptures and photomontages since 1981. The photomontages produced between 1981 and 1995, reproduced in this publication, originally appeared as an artwork in the booklet *Photo-Book*, published in 1995. They are composed of found and captured imagery, mainly referencing Germany and South Africa, linked for me through various common features such as my ancestry and systems of discrimination and displacement. Formally, the images intentionally draw on qualities of some predigital, low light, high film speed, analog photojournalist images: black and white, sometimes characterized by movement and grain in soft focus, reproduced in high contrast halftone for low-cost printed newspapers and journals.

The satirical political photomontages by John Heartfield (1891–1968), published in the *Arbeiter-Illustrierte-Zeitung* (AIZ) in the 1930s, influenced my interest in photomontage as a form of political survey and commentary. In addition to the potential association with reality often assumed of photography, photomontage allows for an unfixed temporality, combined with the improbable and imaginative embedded in any chosen environment; the medium enables the evocation of a particular scenario or condition, unmediated by textual explication. That Heartfield's photomontages were directed at workers through the AIZ—as opposed to exclusive institutional sites of art appreciation— was also significant, hence the pocket-size *Photo-Book* intended to be accessible and dispensable for anyone.

The assembly of the photomontage is genealogically related to sculptural tableaux and site-specific installations I have produced over the last few decades where particular selected found objects and garments have been integrated and combined with created figures, sometimes into selected historical sites. Exhibiting installations site-specifically has often been my ambition for the intertextual resolution of my sculpted works, but has rarely been possible. The photomontage provides the opportunity to construct a contextual specificity and temporal palimpsest with reference to the actual world. From 1985, images of sculpted works were included in the photomontage, which became a medium through which to conceptually expand and elaborate on my three-dimensional figures.

The images in *Photo-Book*, and other sculptural and photomontage artworks before and after, attempt to evoke aspects of authority, its impact and aftermath, and the entitlement that maintains it in various forms of social life. Human and nonhuman animal physiognomy and conduct, techniques of indoctrination and control, acts of complicity and negation, environmental and material traces, and geographic and historical locations have been some of the recurrent considerations in creating these works.

— Jane Alexander

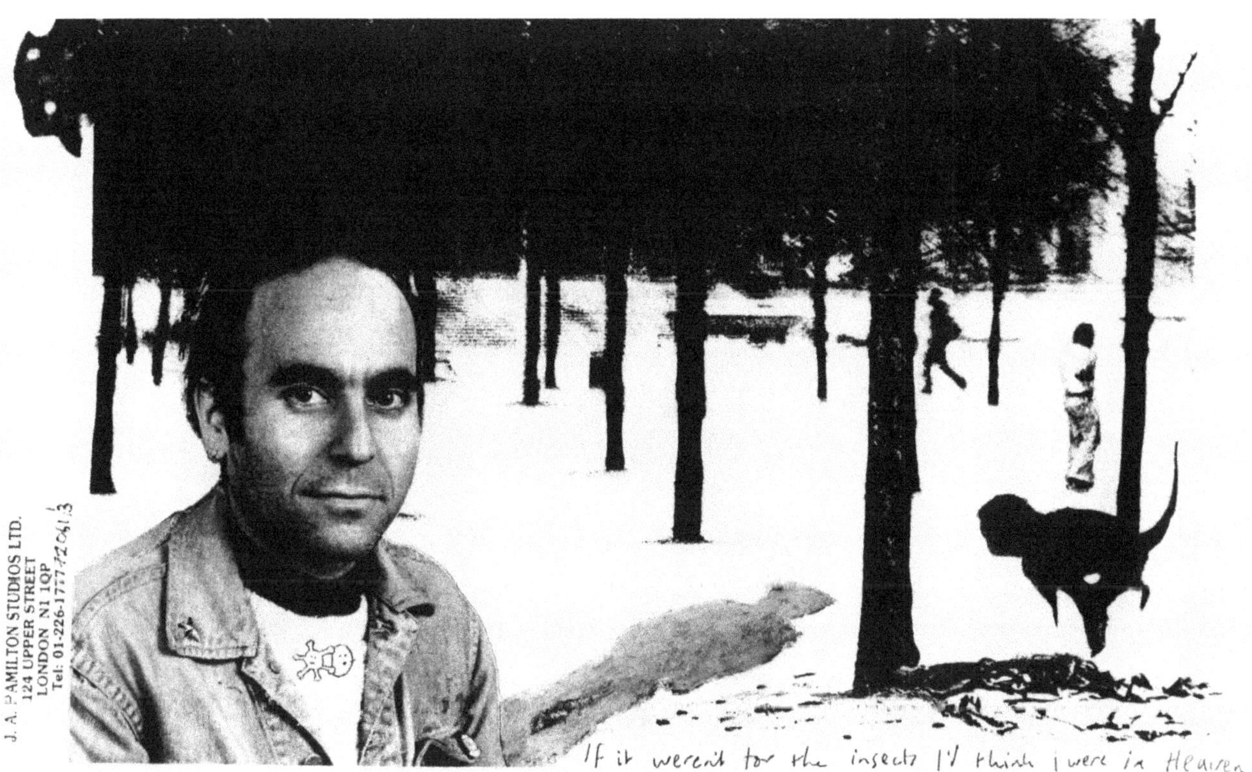

Portrait of a man (adventurer)
by J A Pamilton and J Alexander

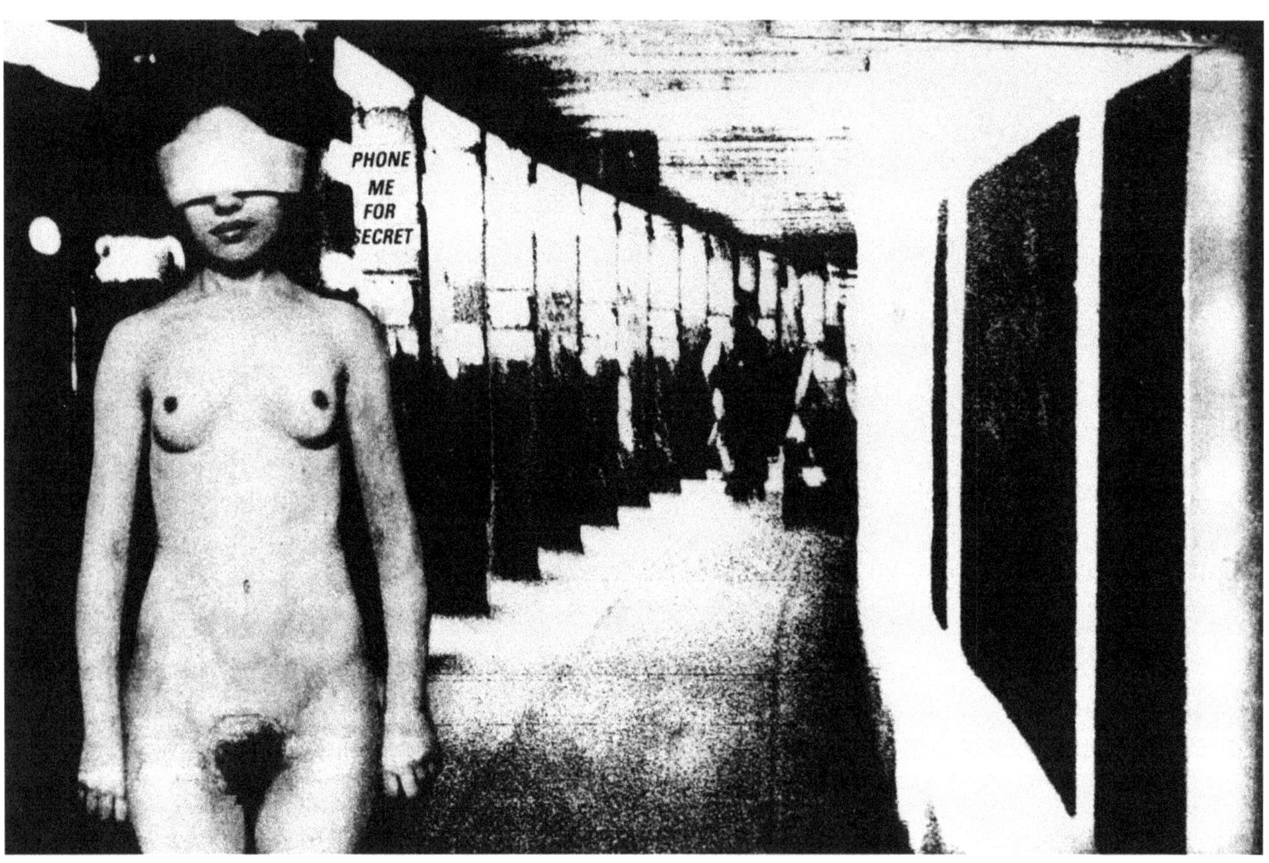

Phone me for secret

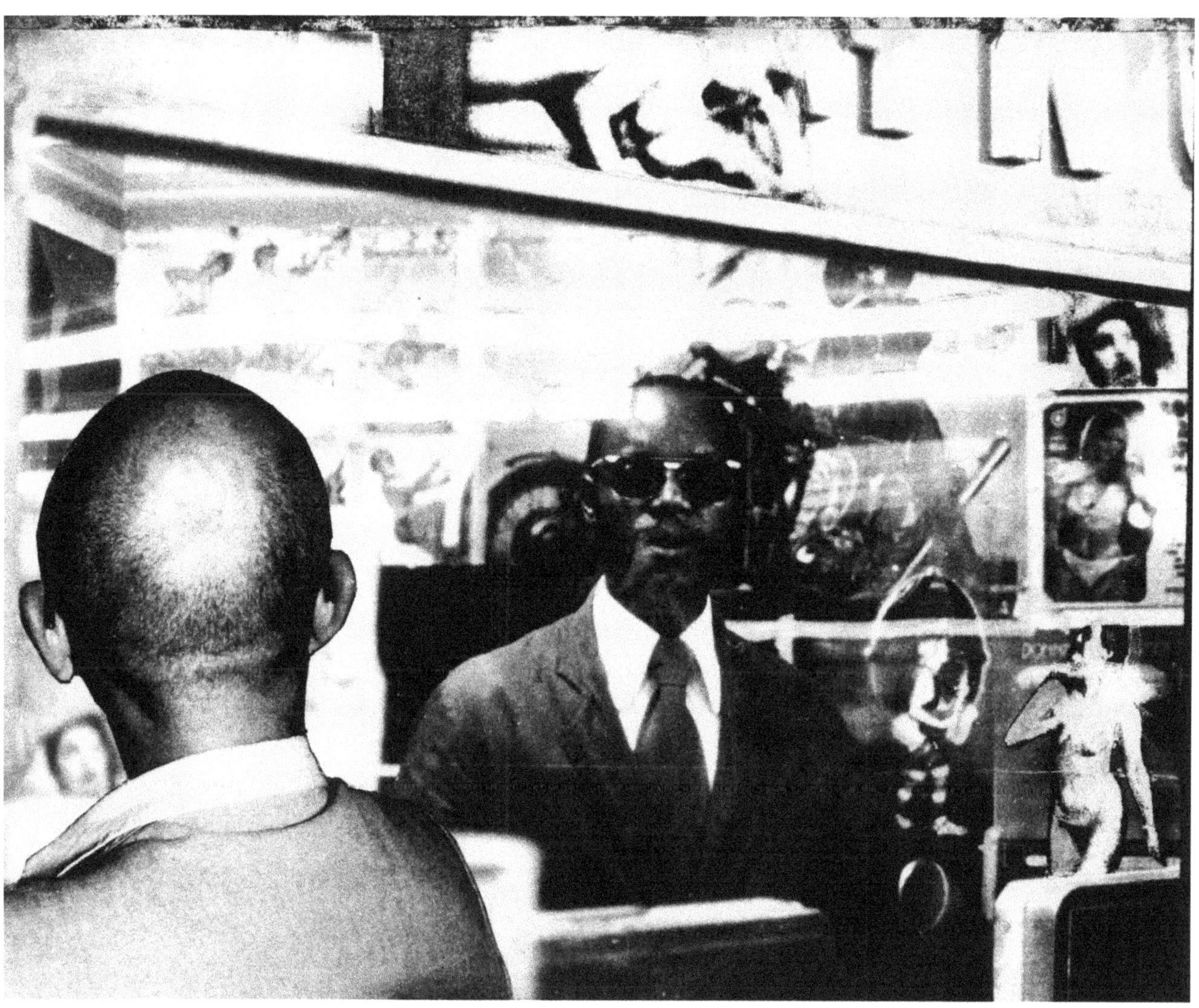

In the arcade

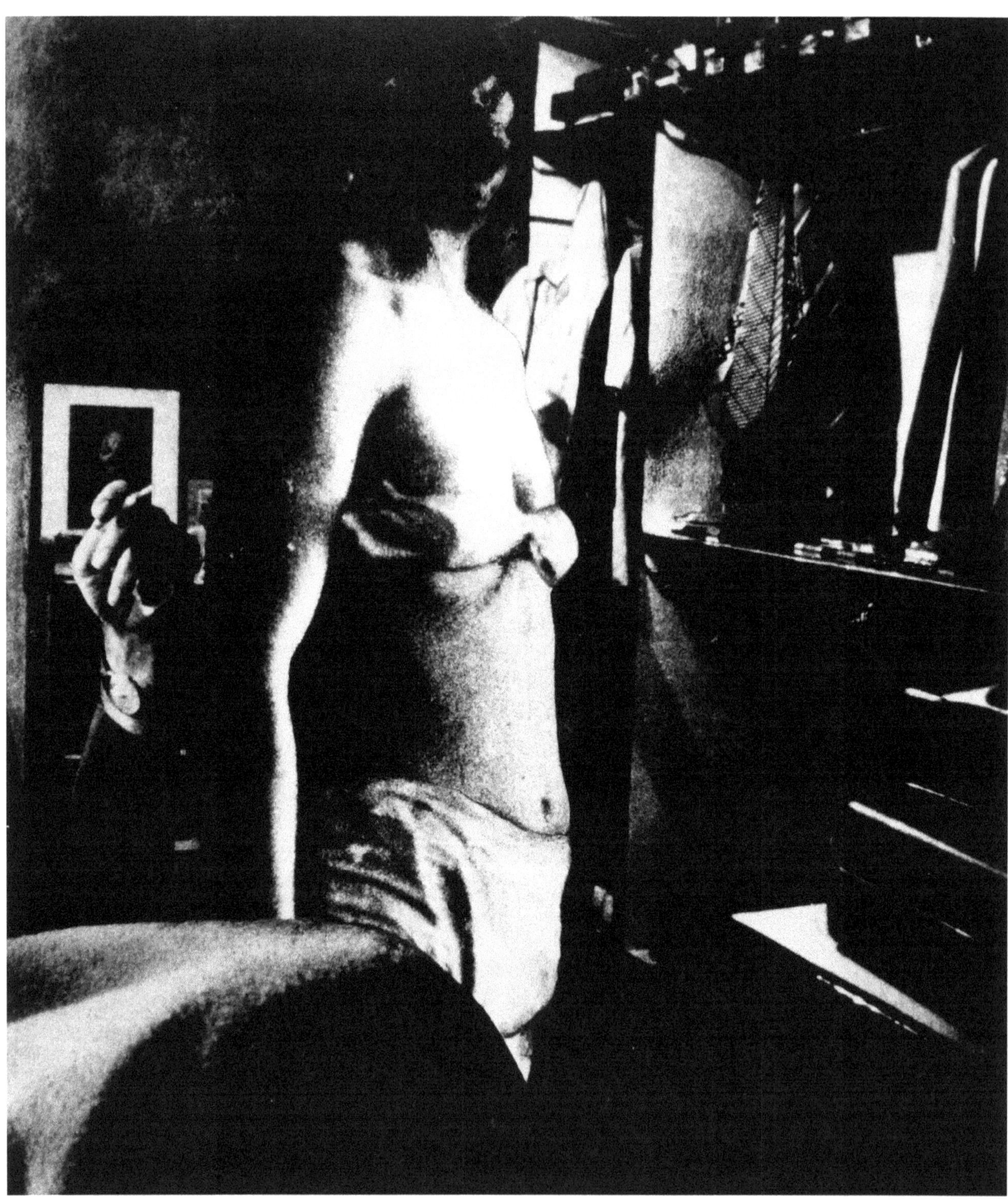

Woman in a two-piece

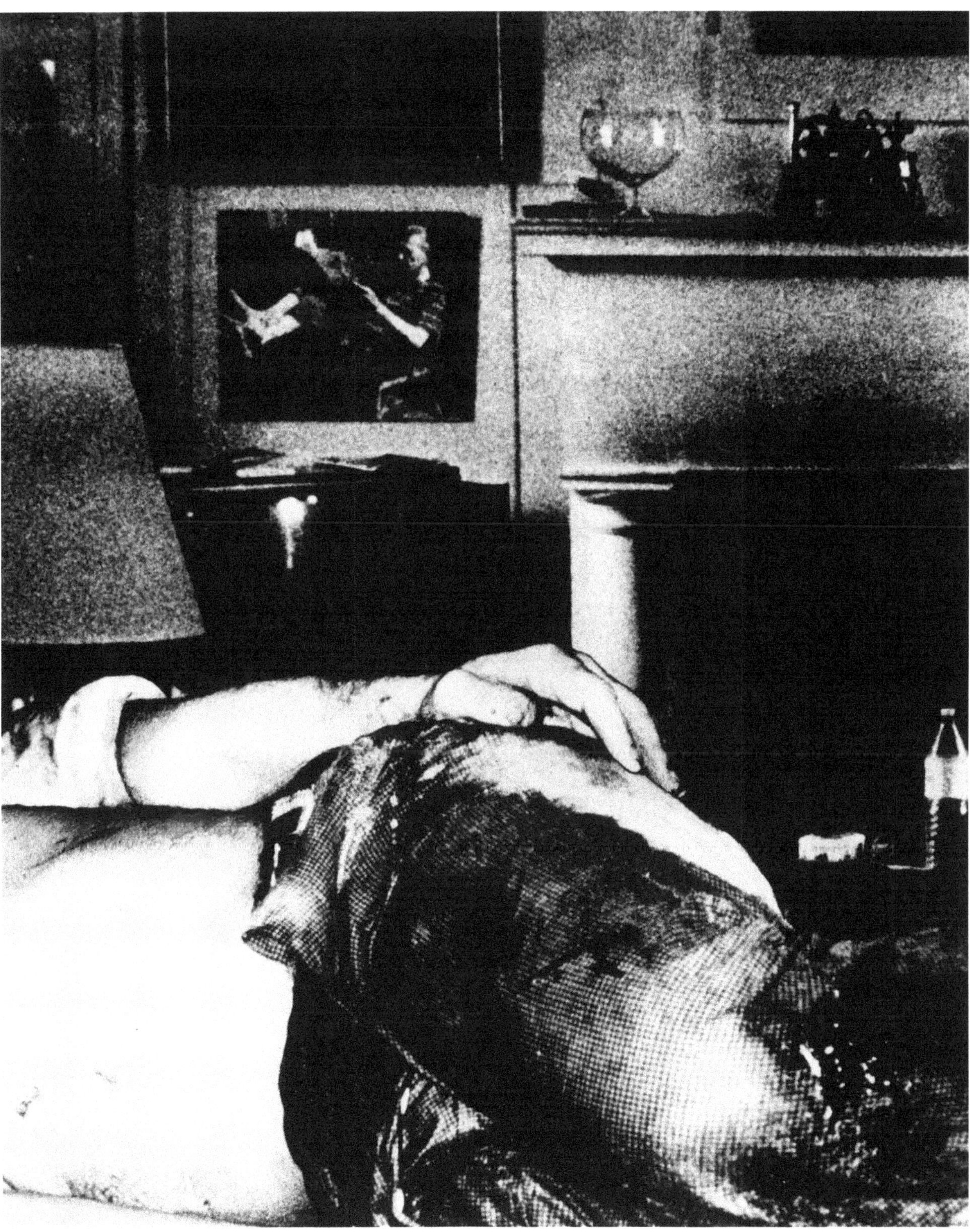

Sleeping man

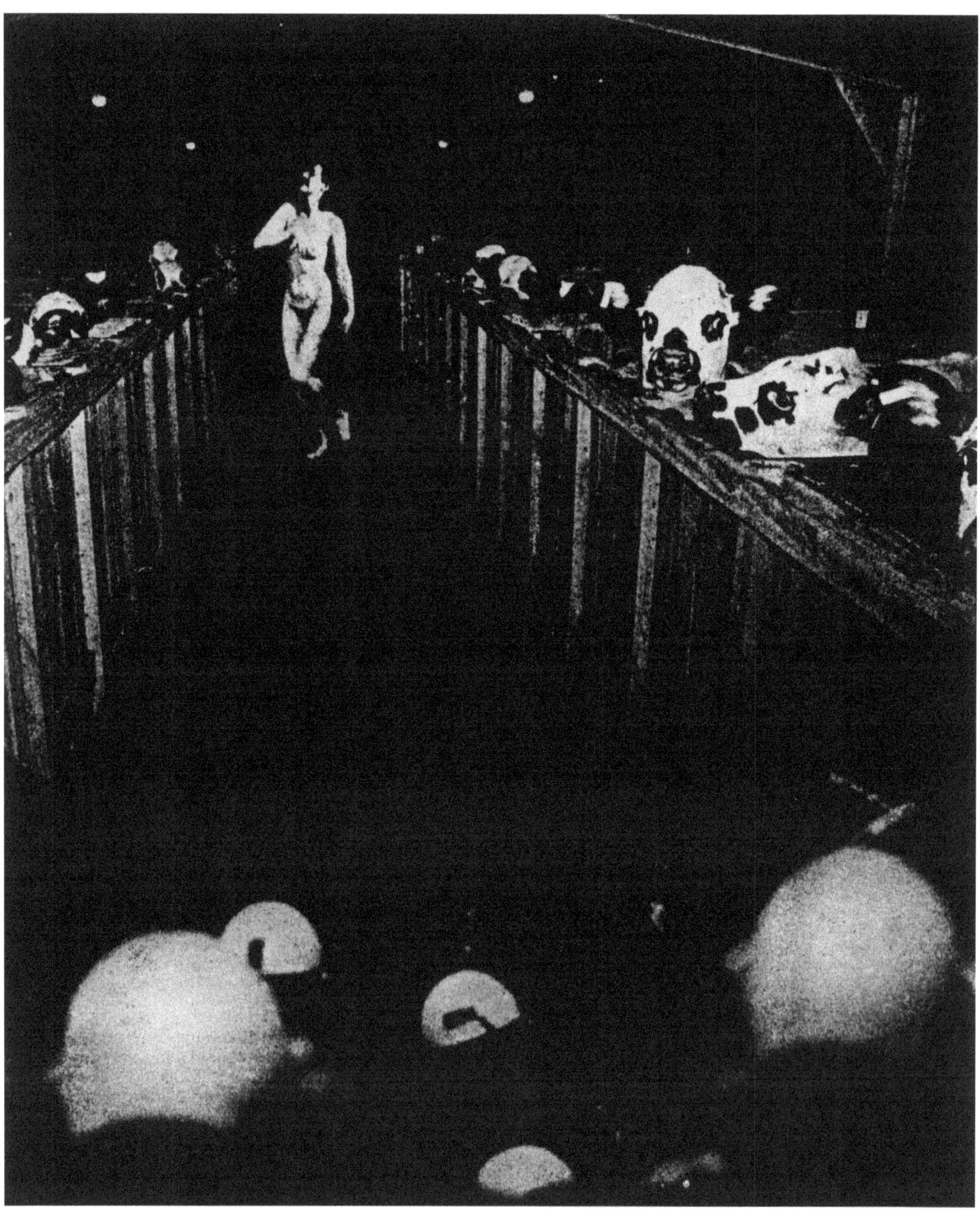

The Cow House

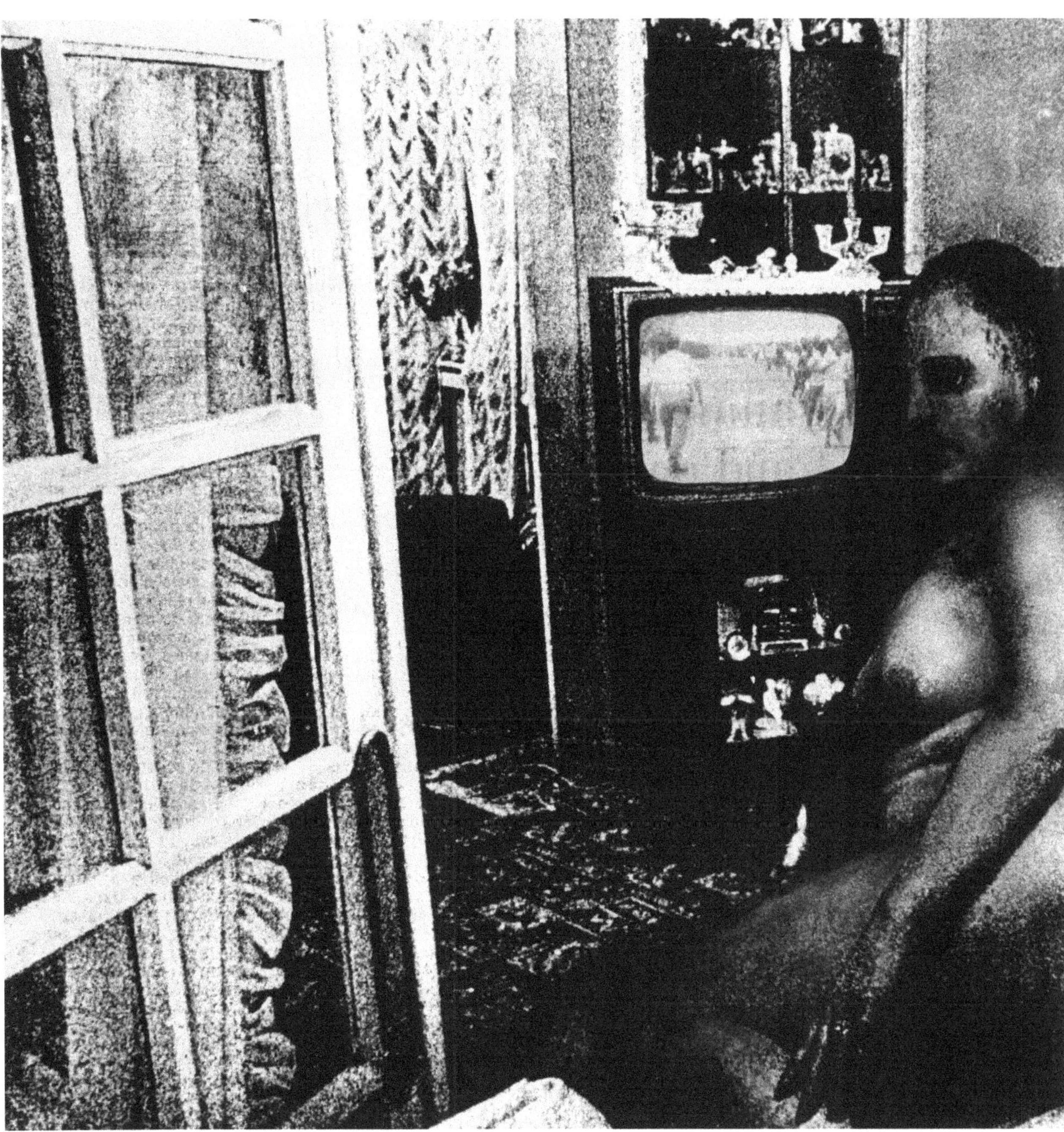

This is Television 1

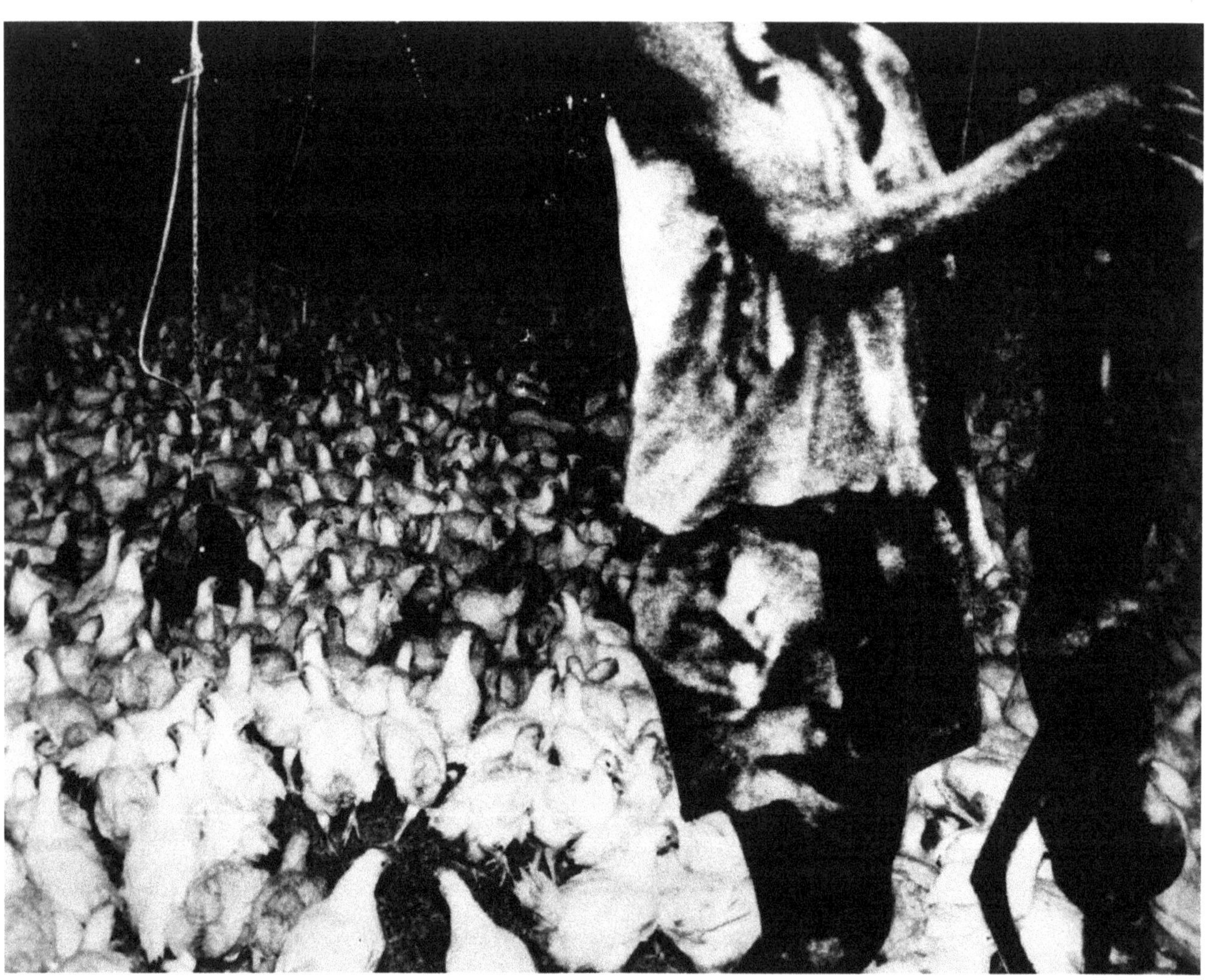

Jane discovers famine

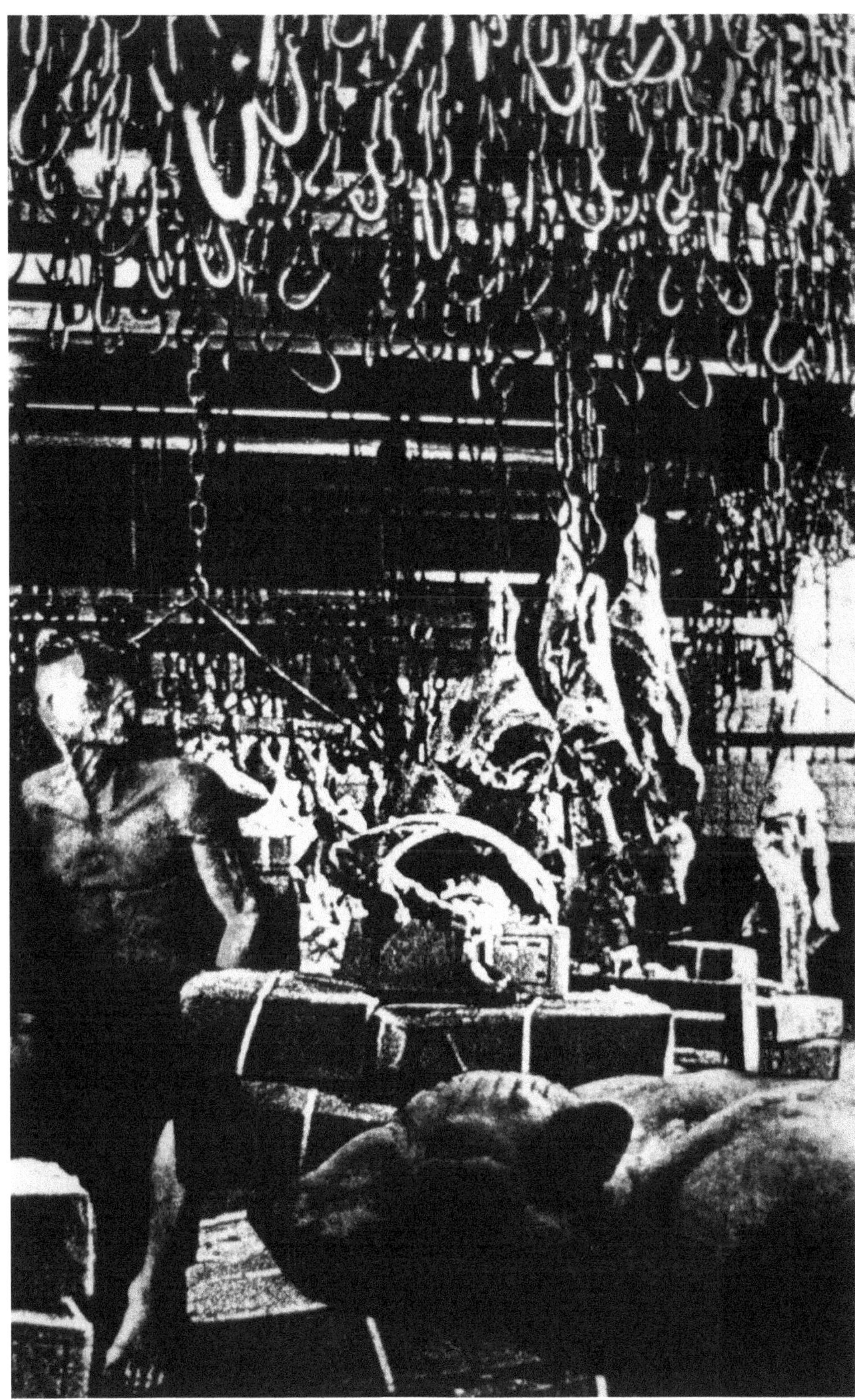

Warehouse

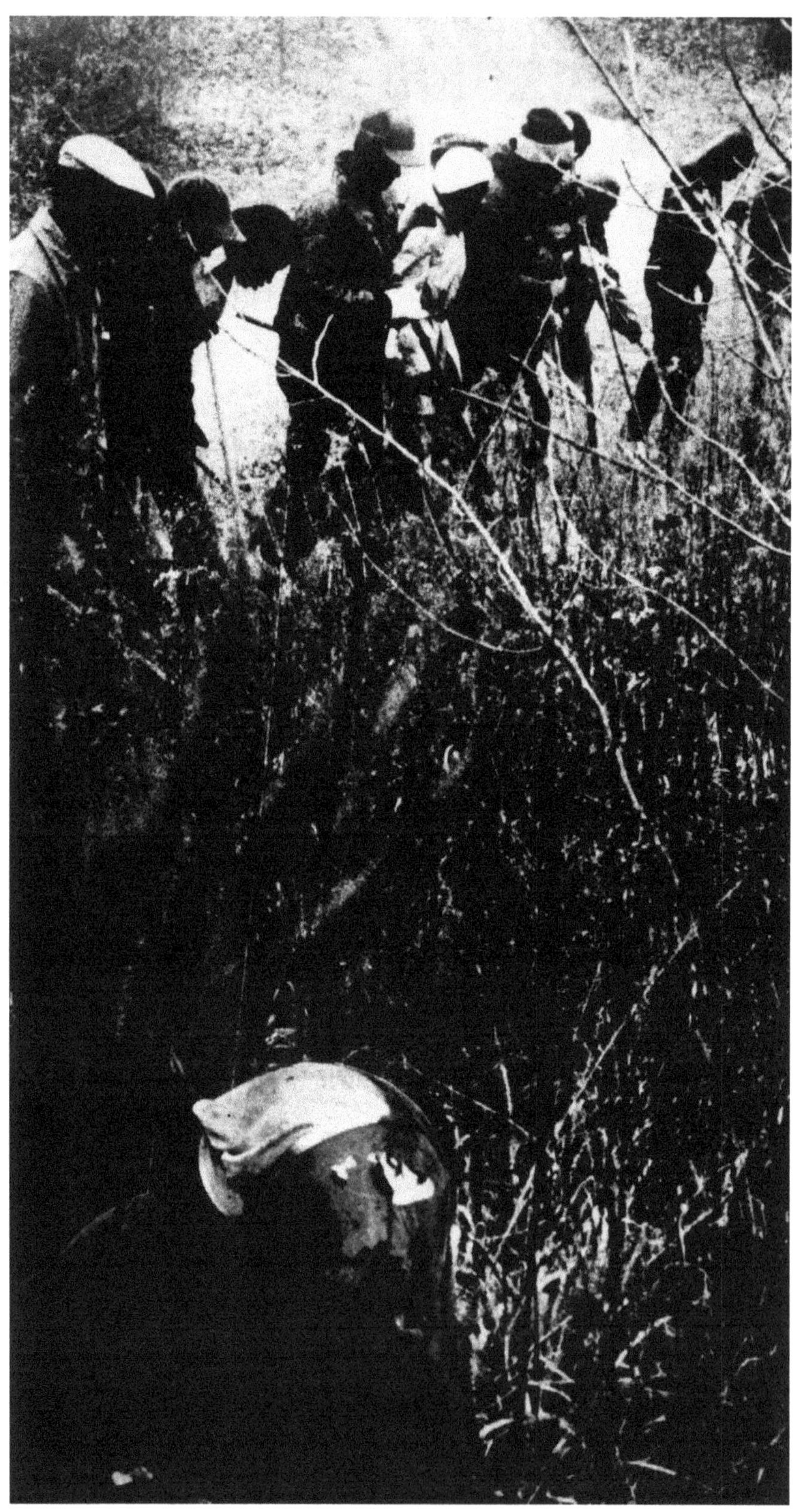

Search

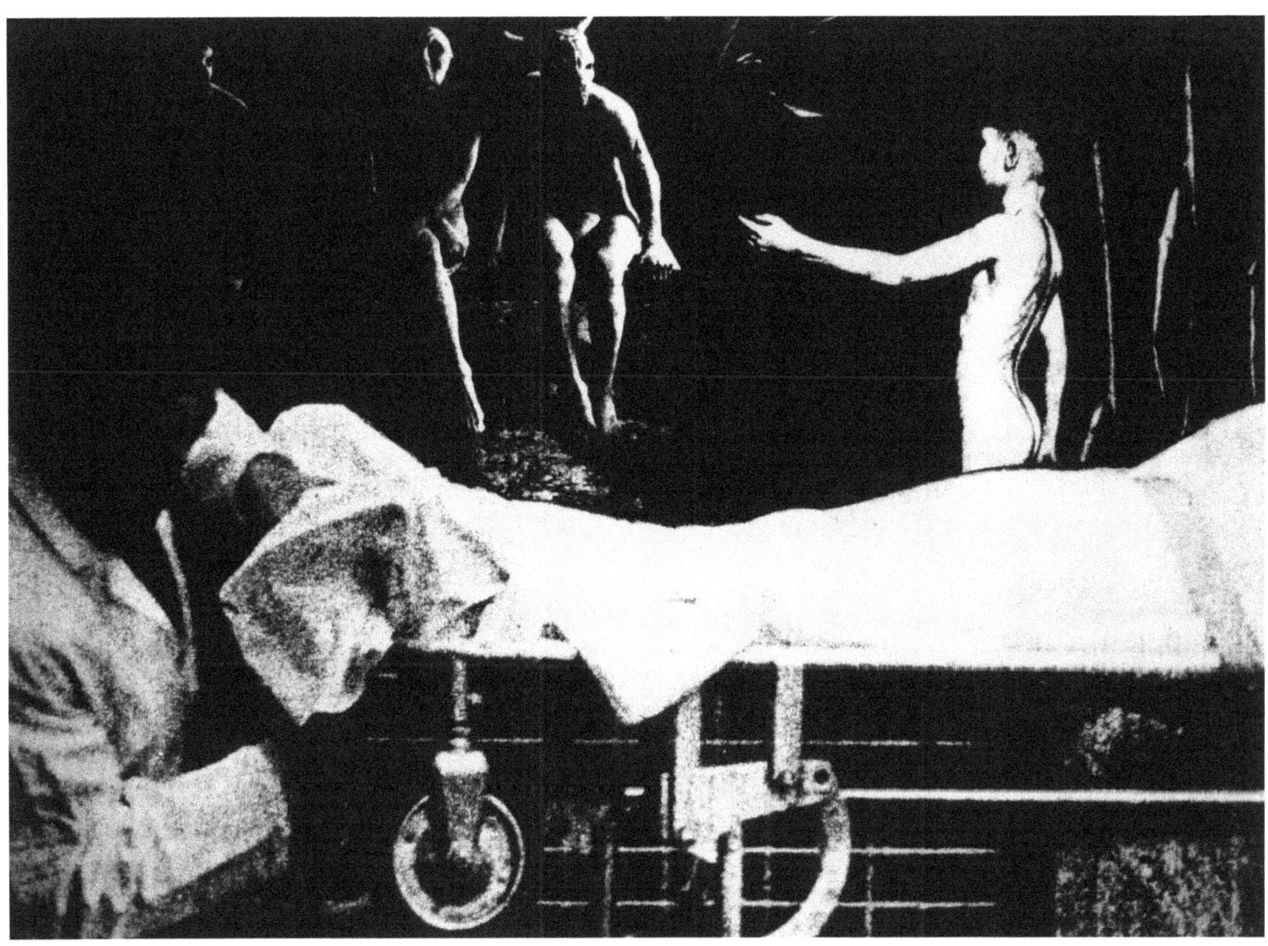

"Purge me with hyssop, and I shall be clean:
Wash me, and I shall be whiter than snow."
Psalm 51, v 7

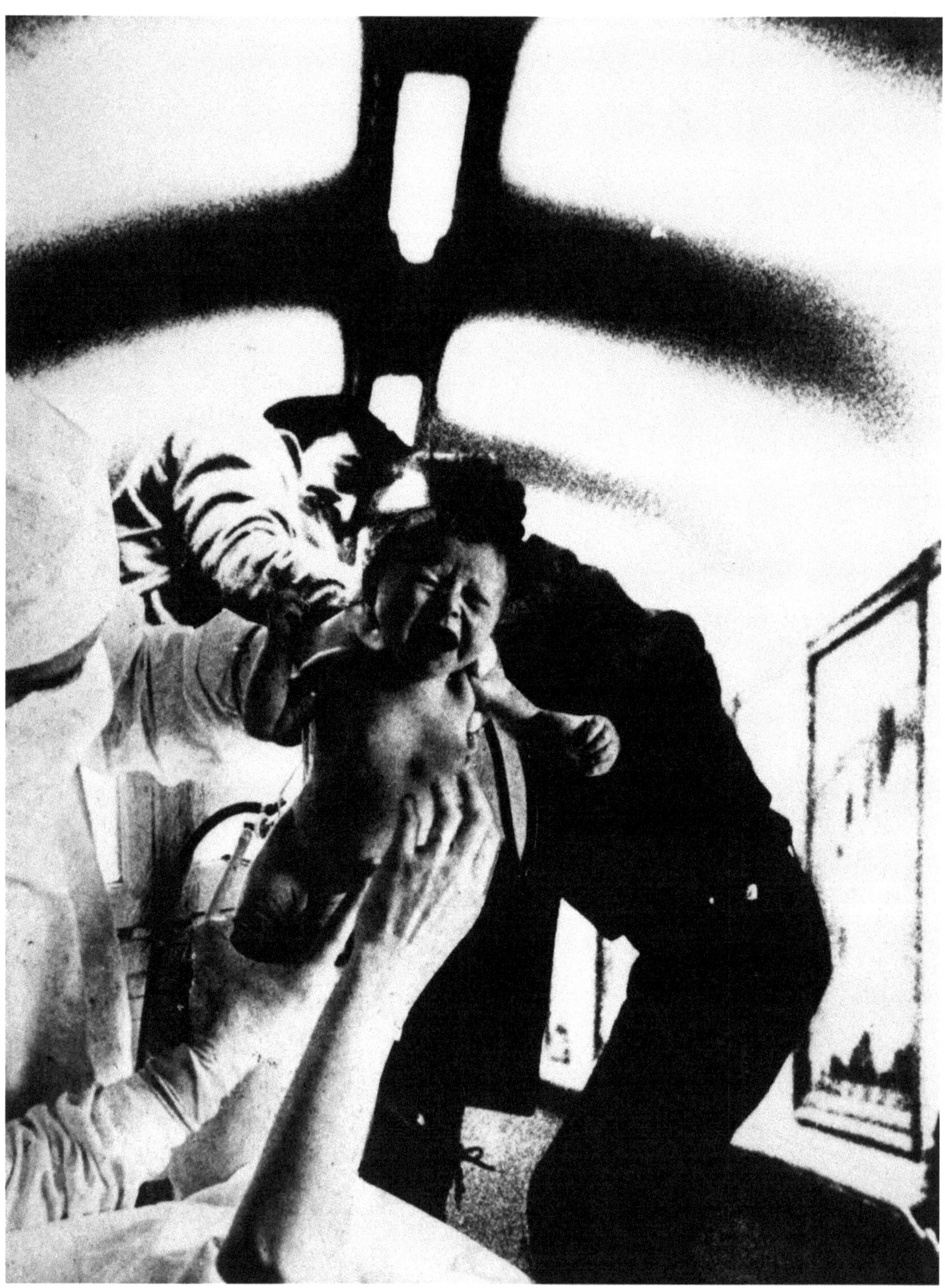

Delivery

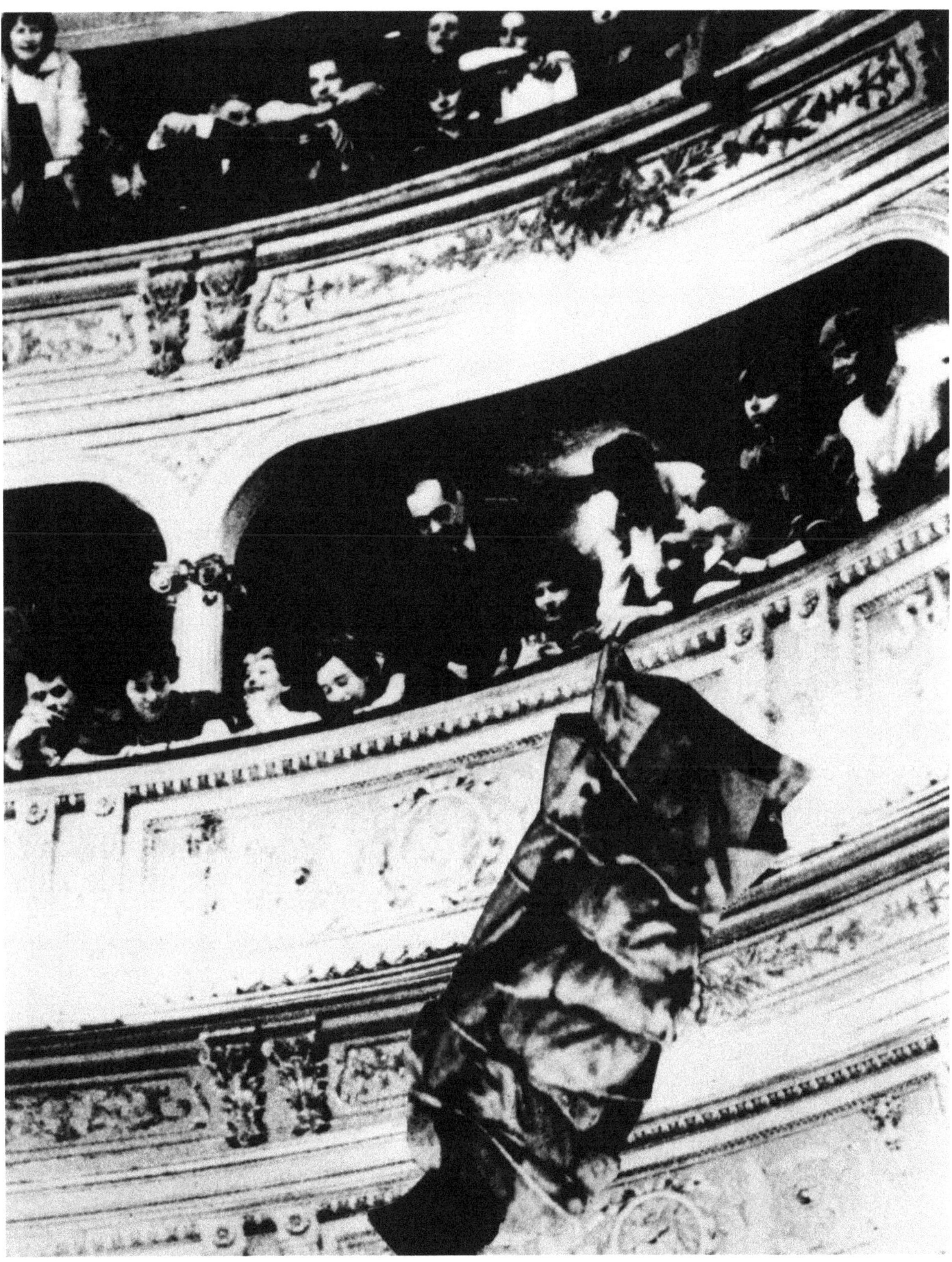

Demonstration with wrapped man

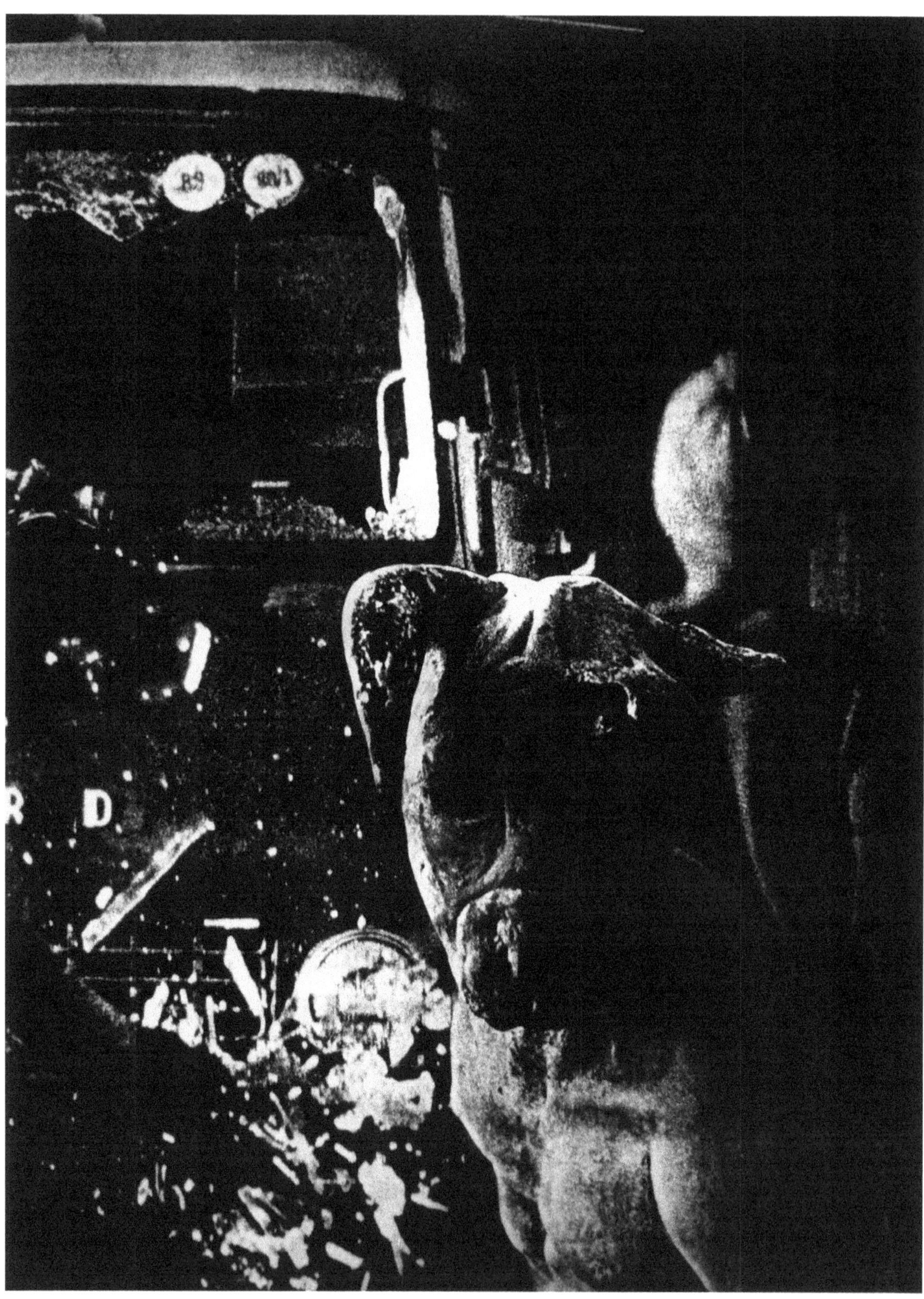

Ford

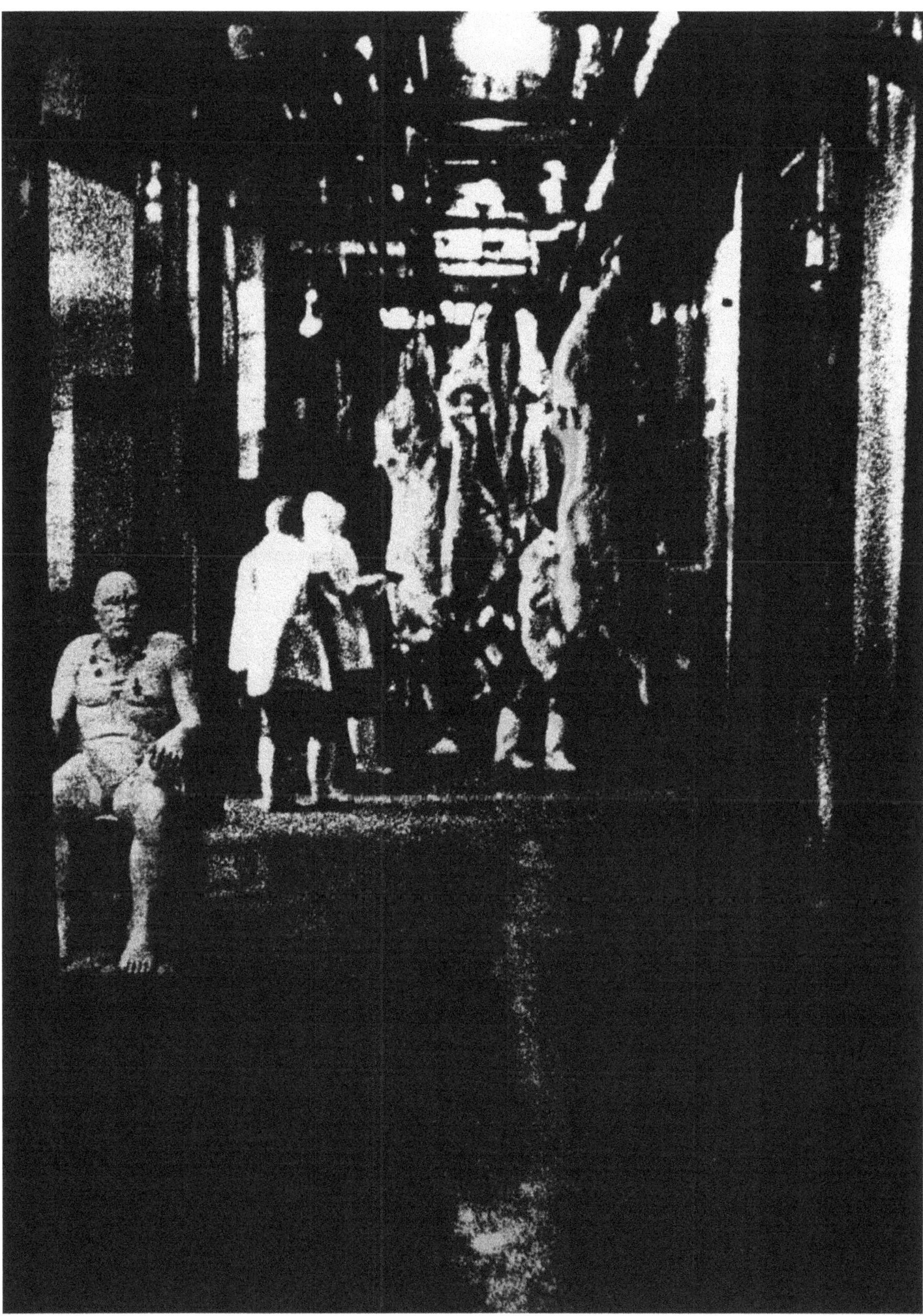

Trading was listless

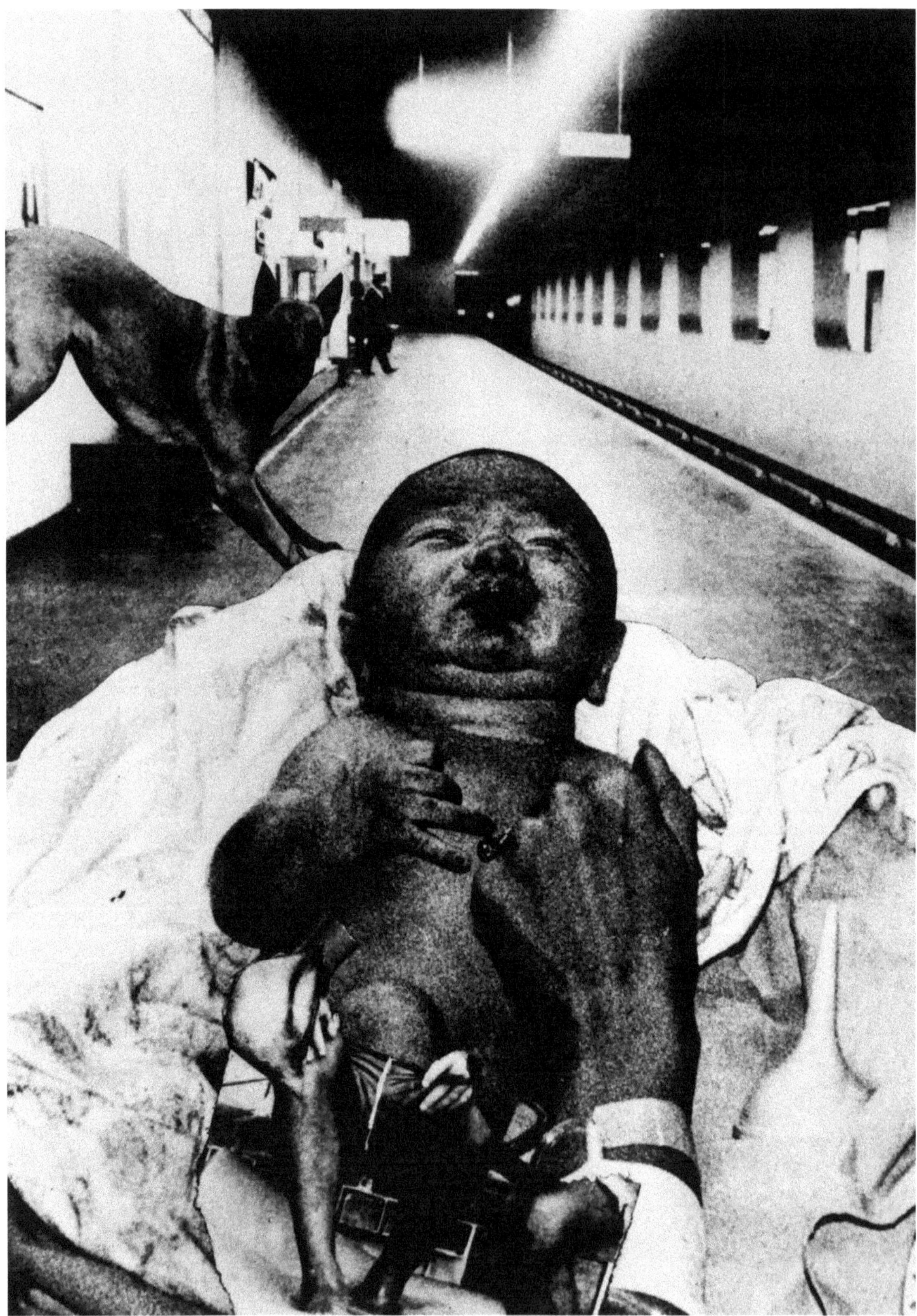

Confinement

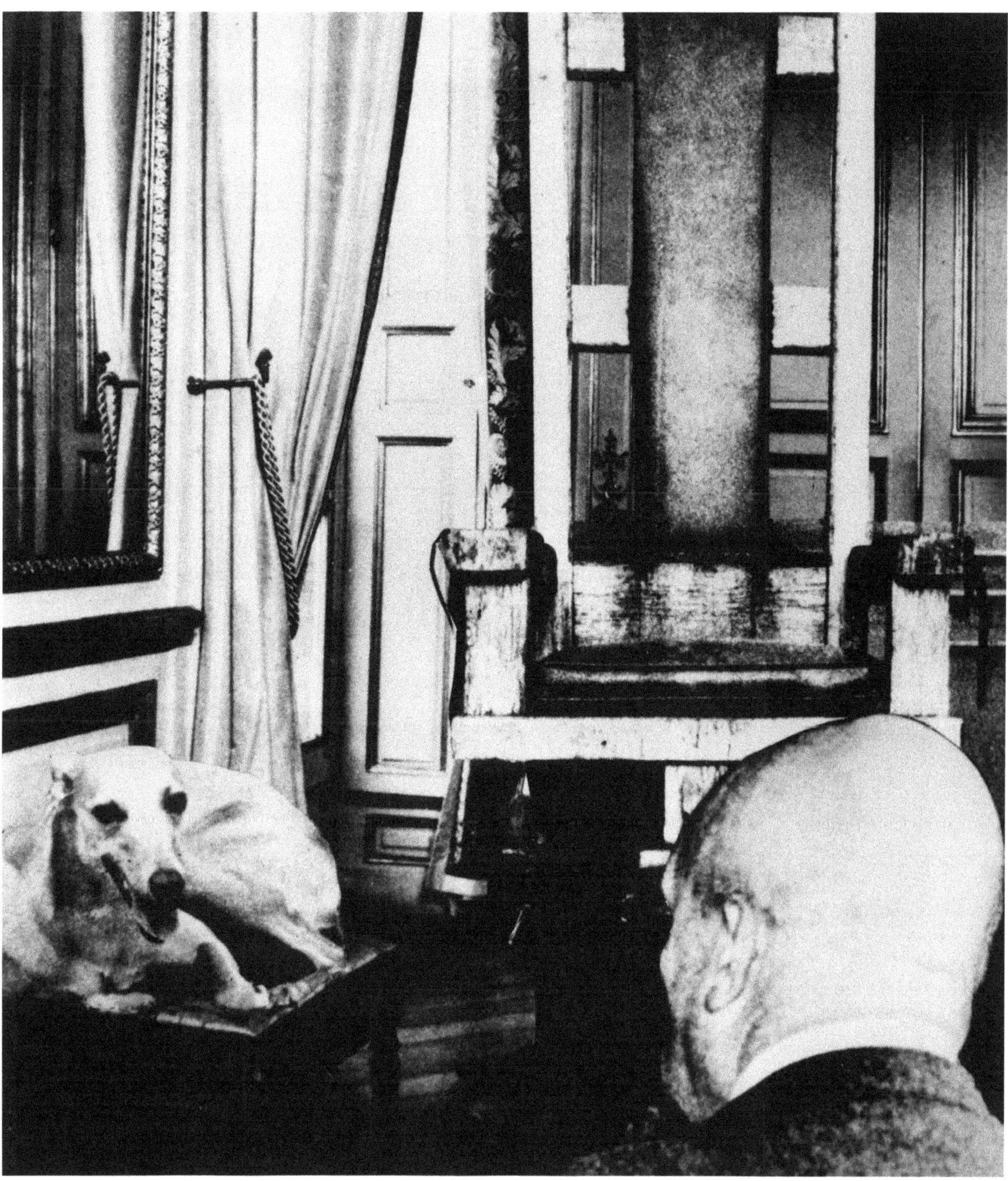

Interior

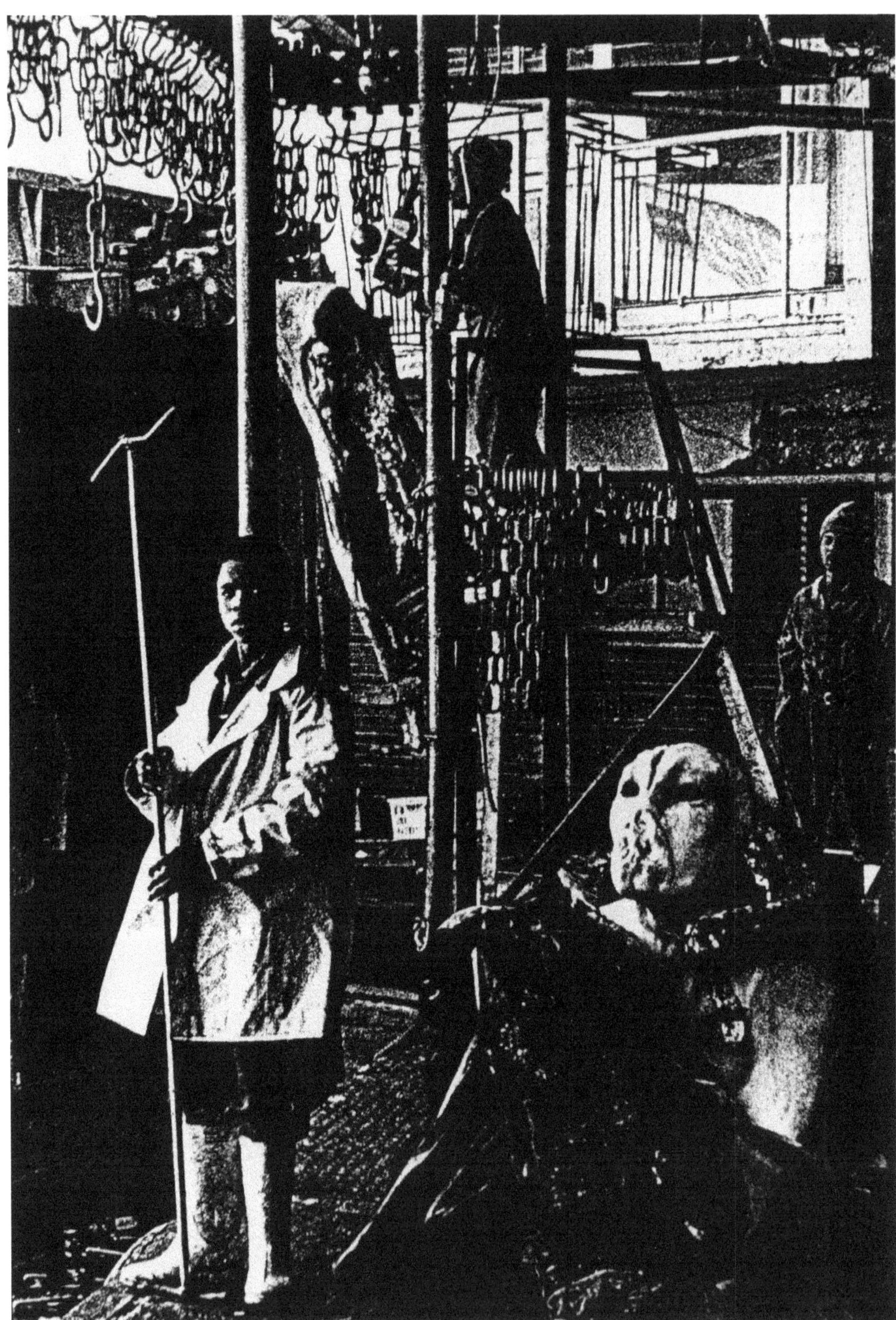

Shepherd

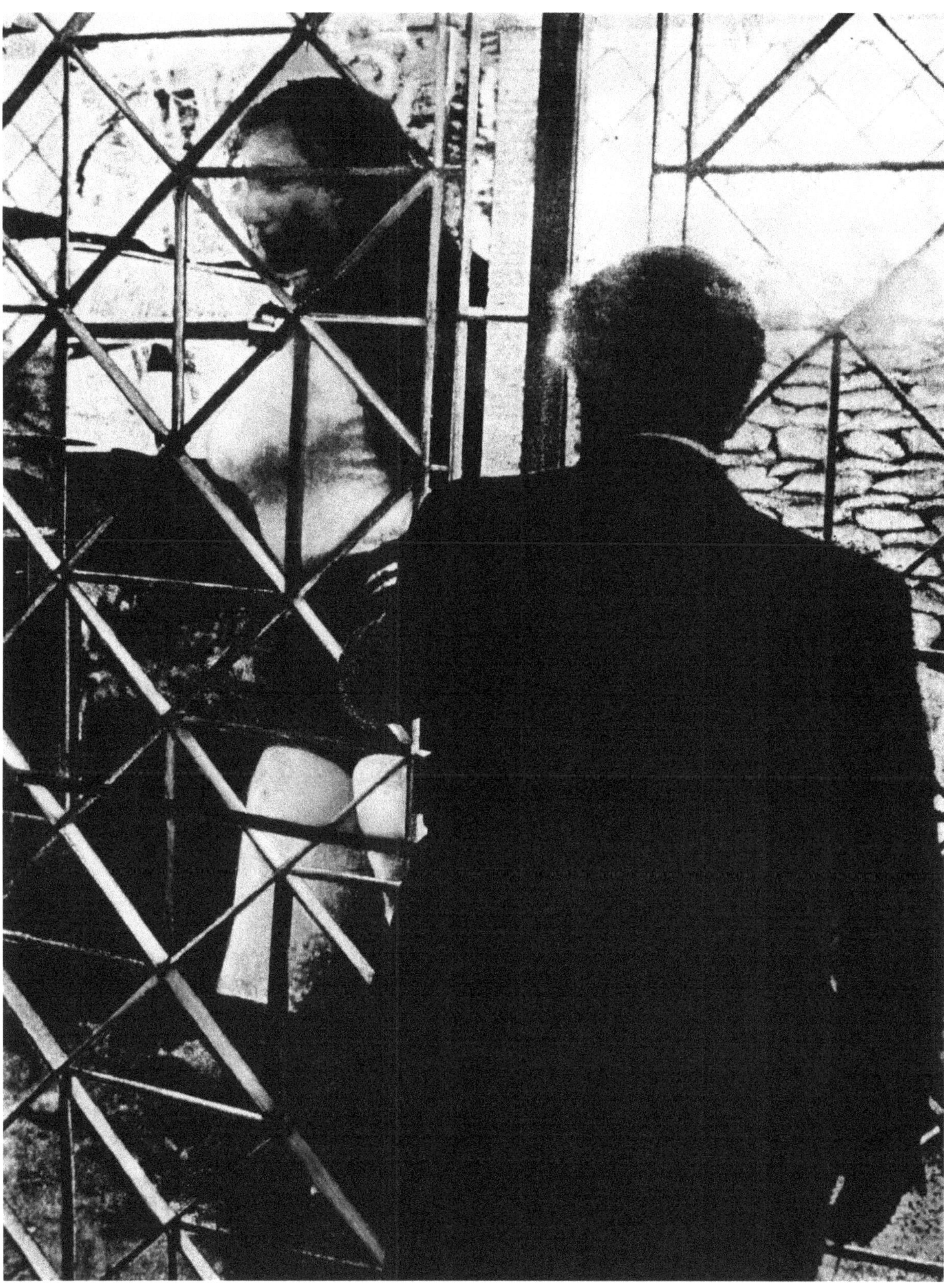

Service

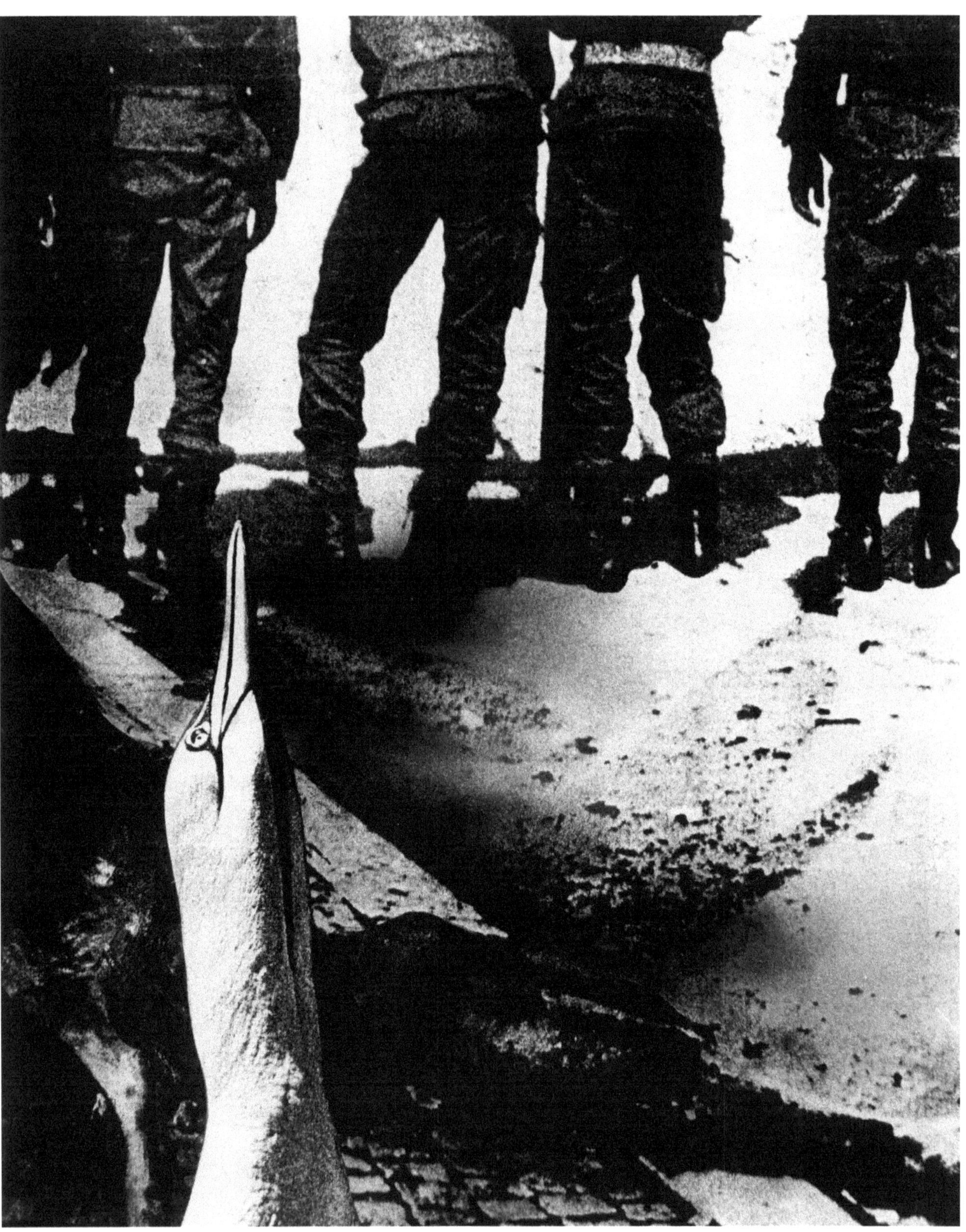

Gannet

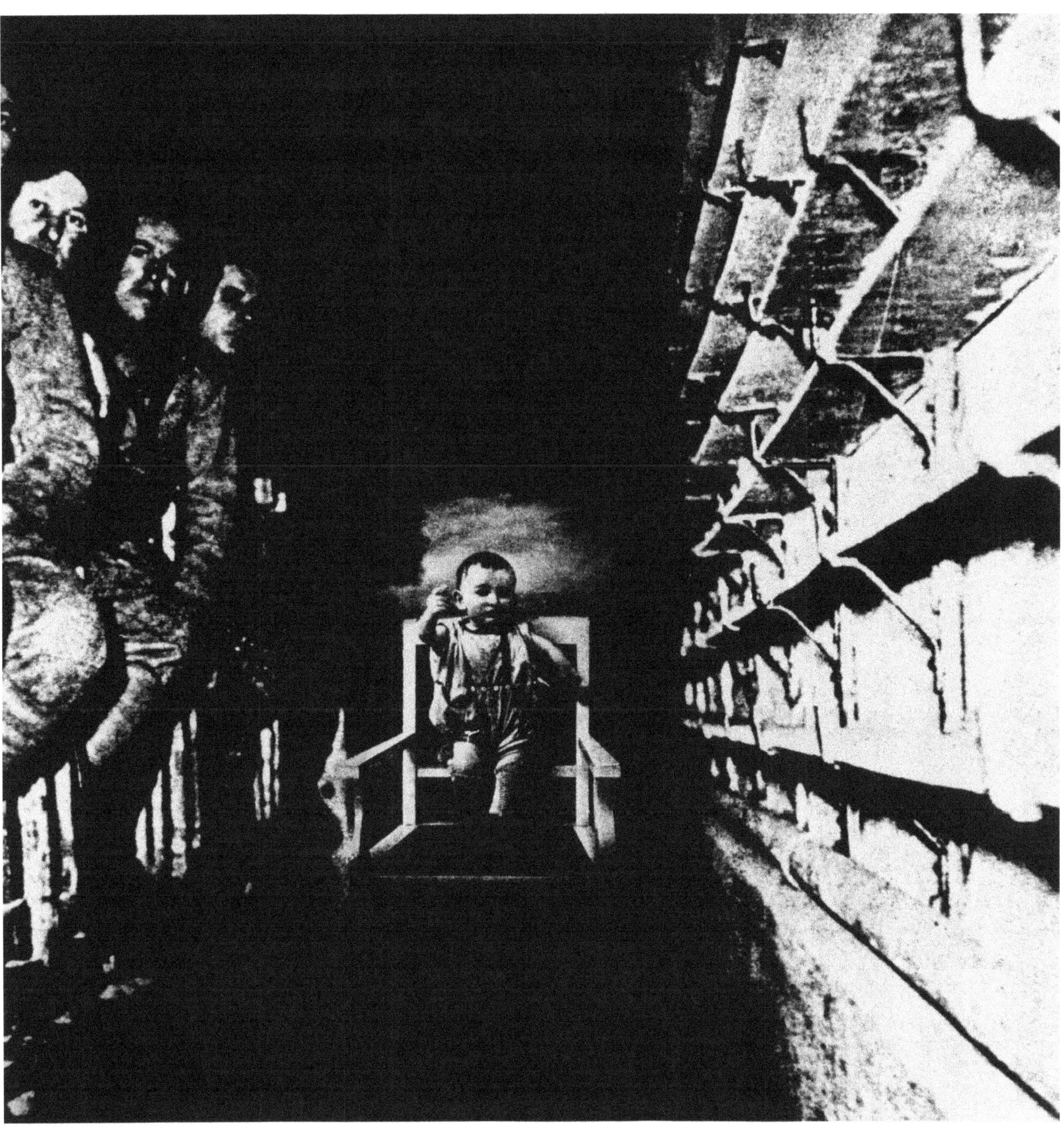

Lost child

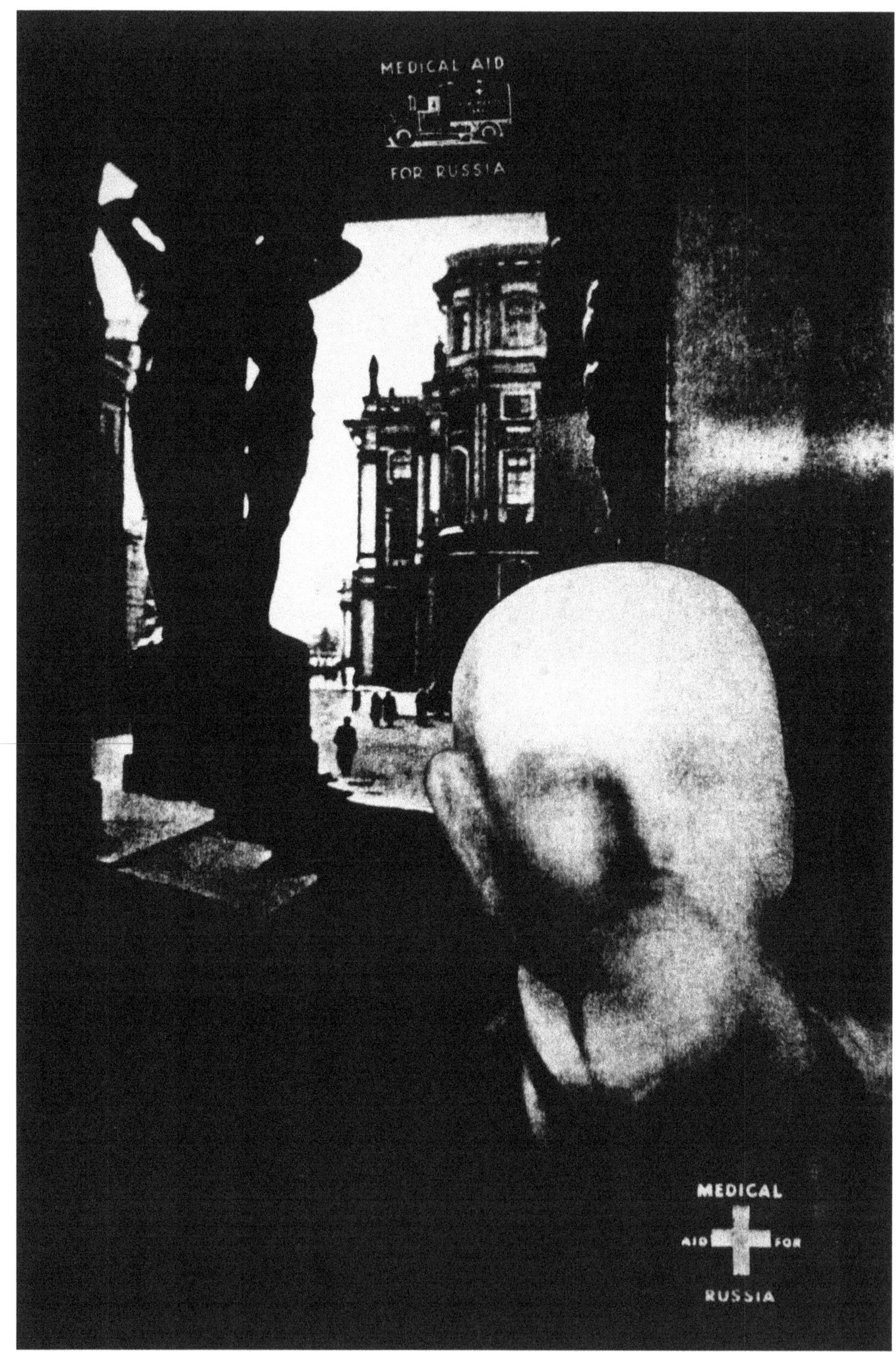

Chernobyl medical aid rally, Leningrad

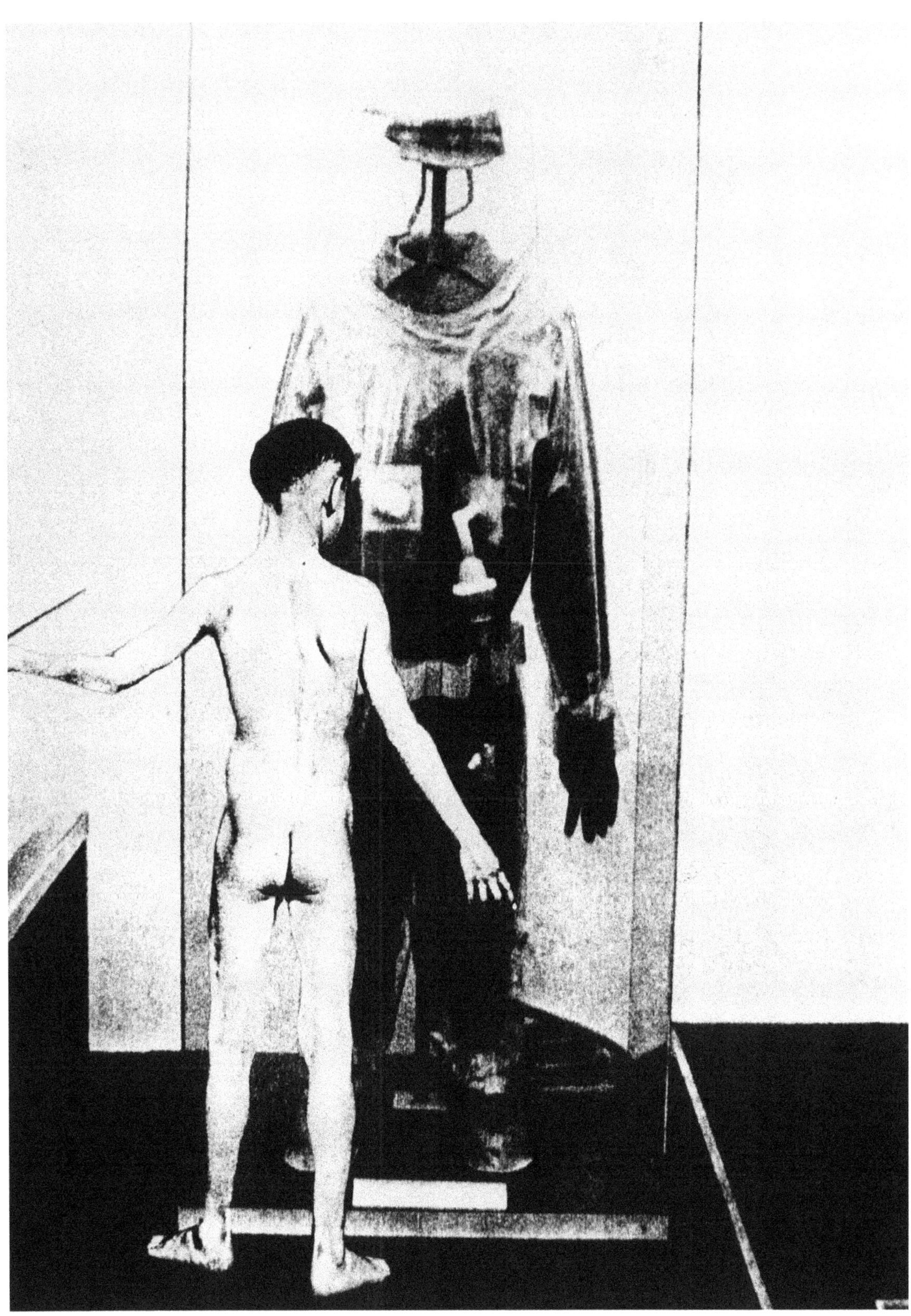

Museum boy

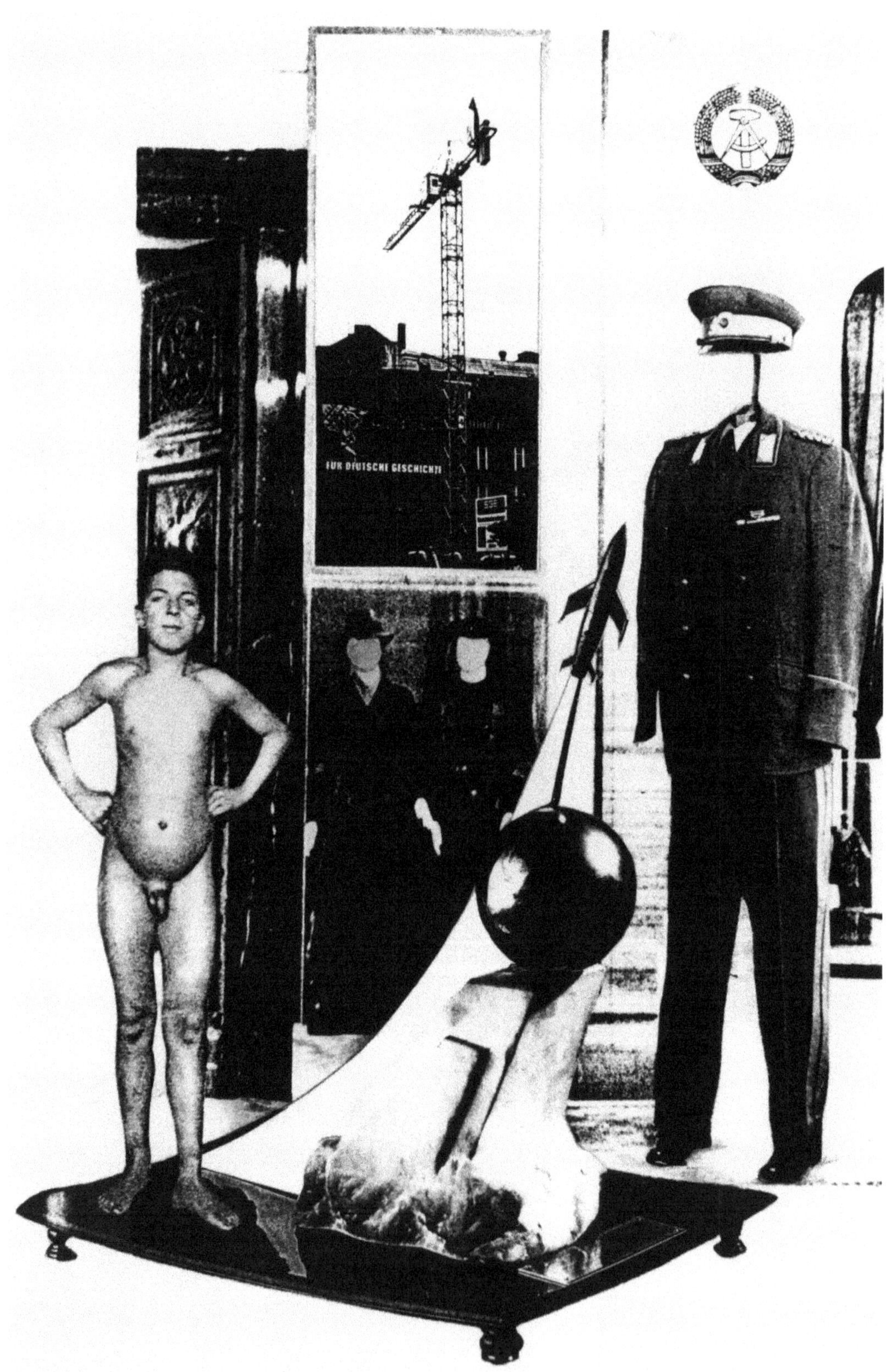

Triumph over capitalism: Für Deutsche Geschichte

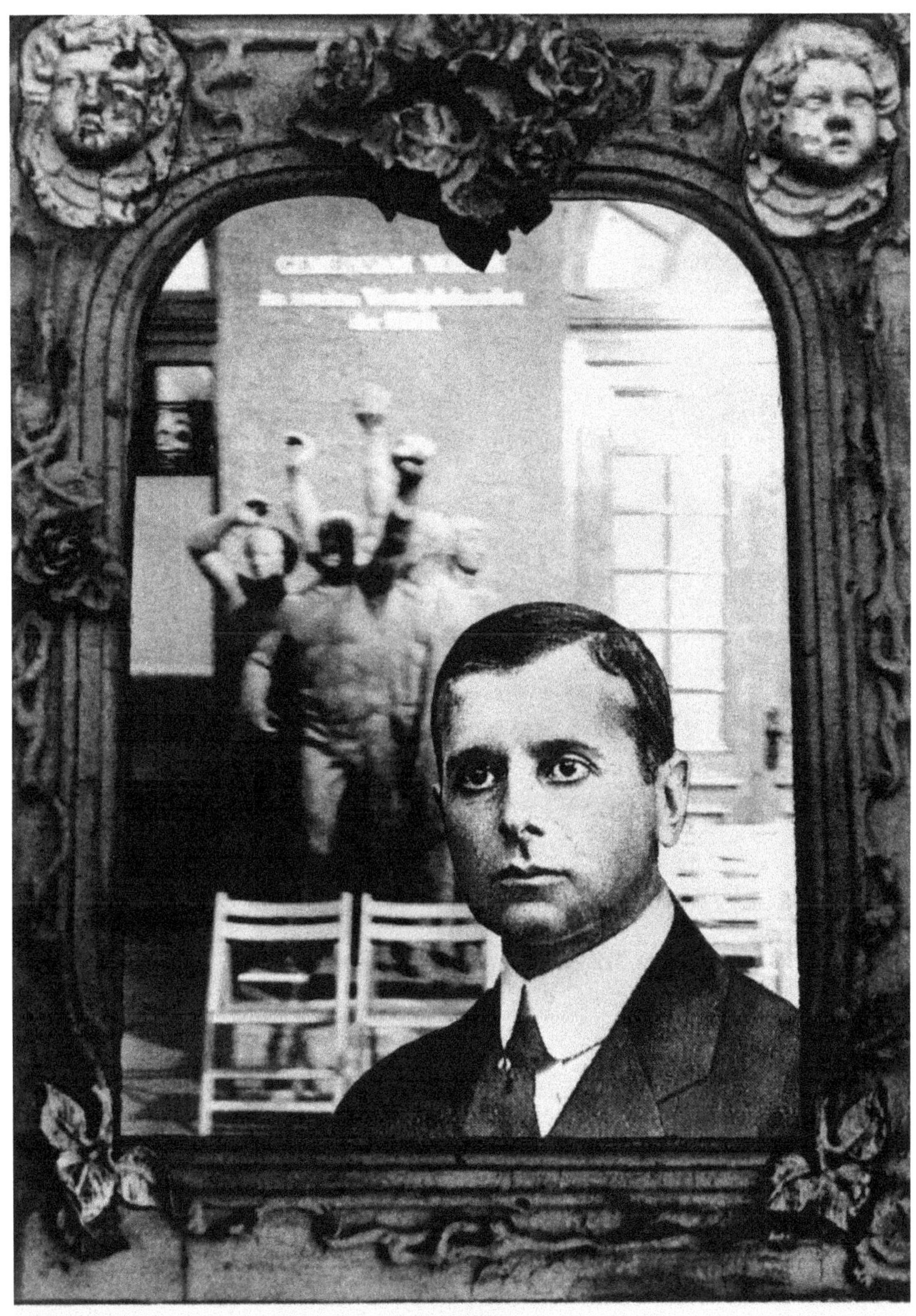

"Sauberkeit ist Gesundheit": ancestor

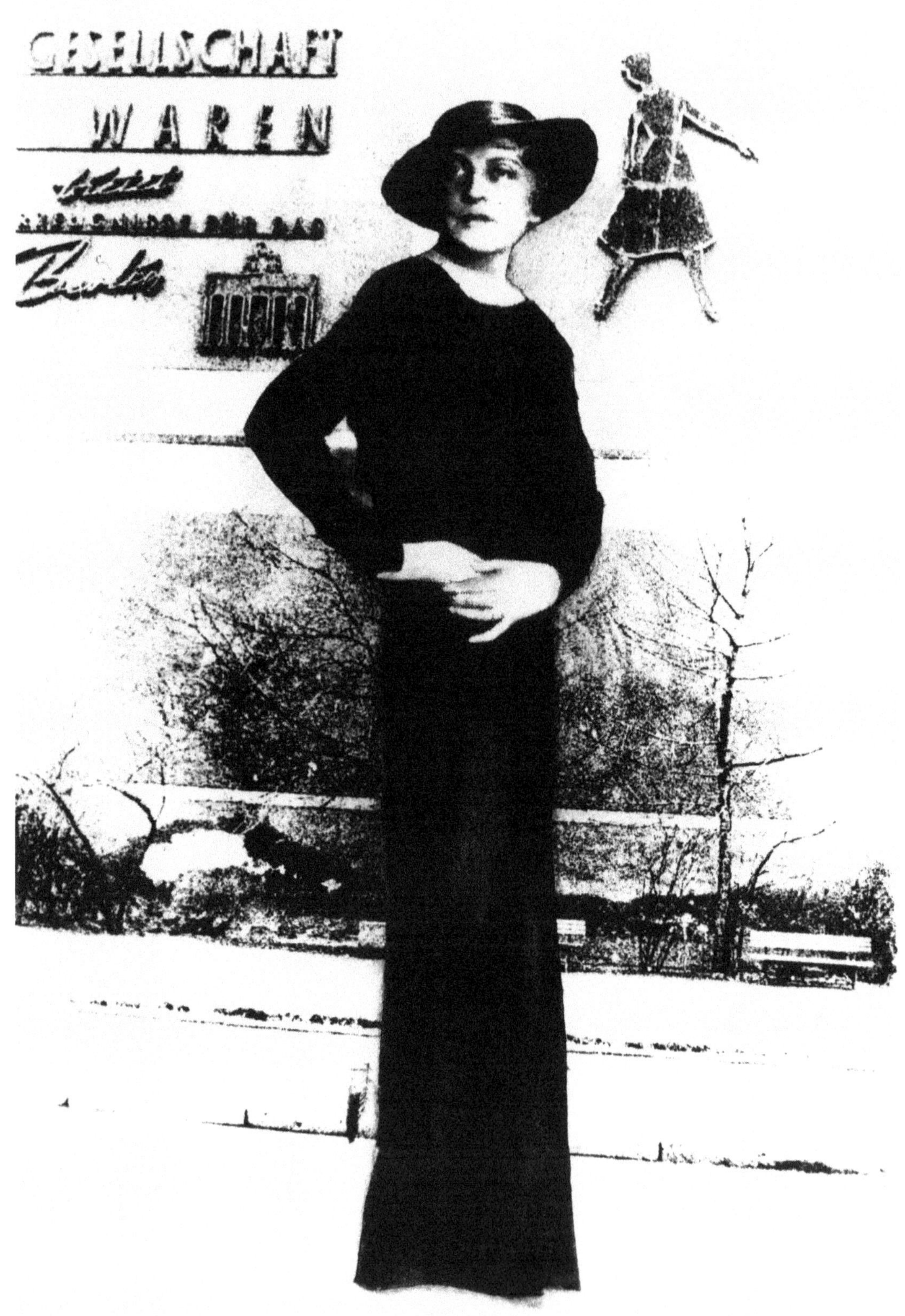

Gesellschaft Waren: Merchandise for society

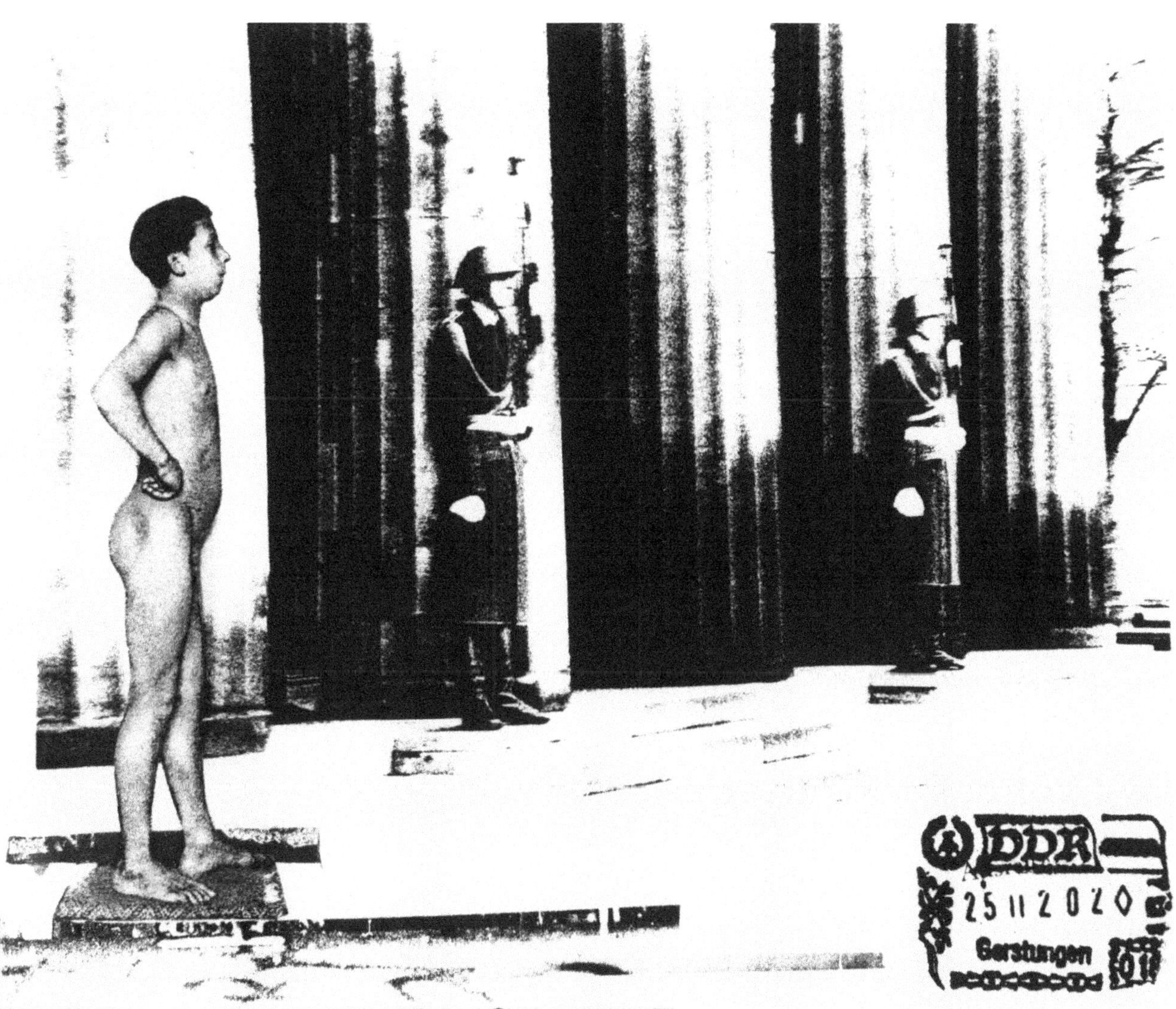

Triumph over capitalism: "Die Ewige Flamme"

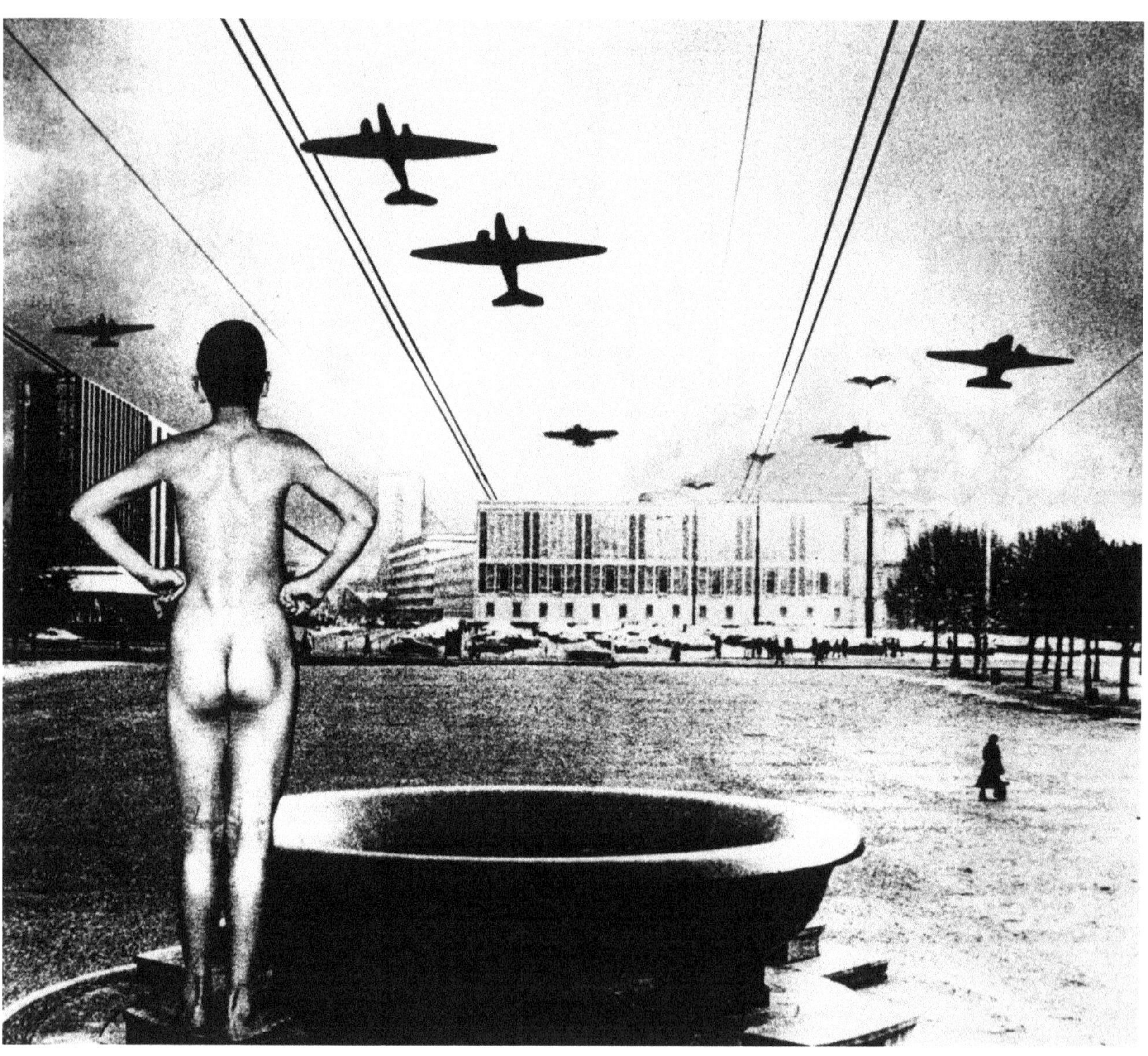

Triumph over capitalism: Lustgarten

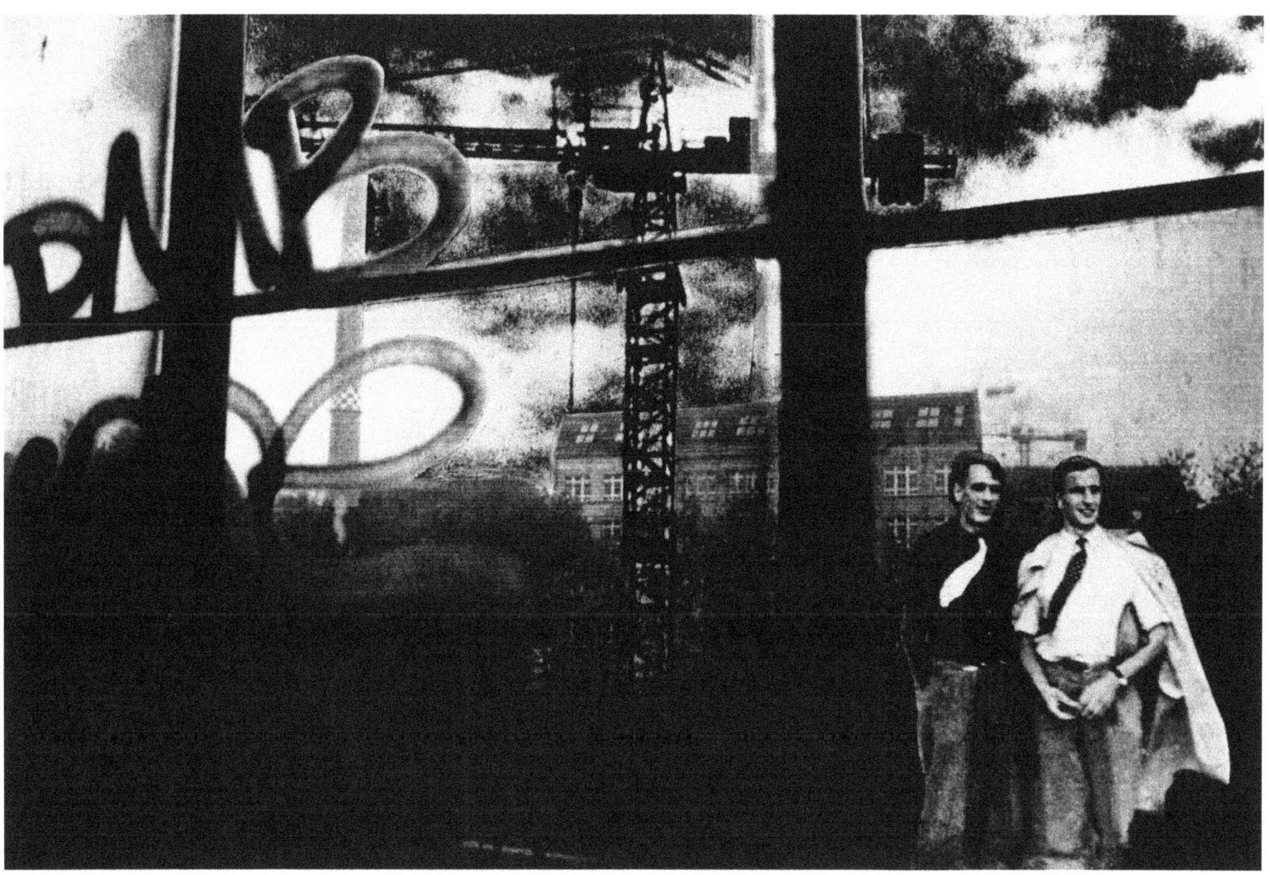

Reconstruction

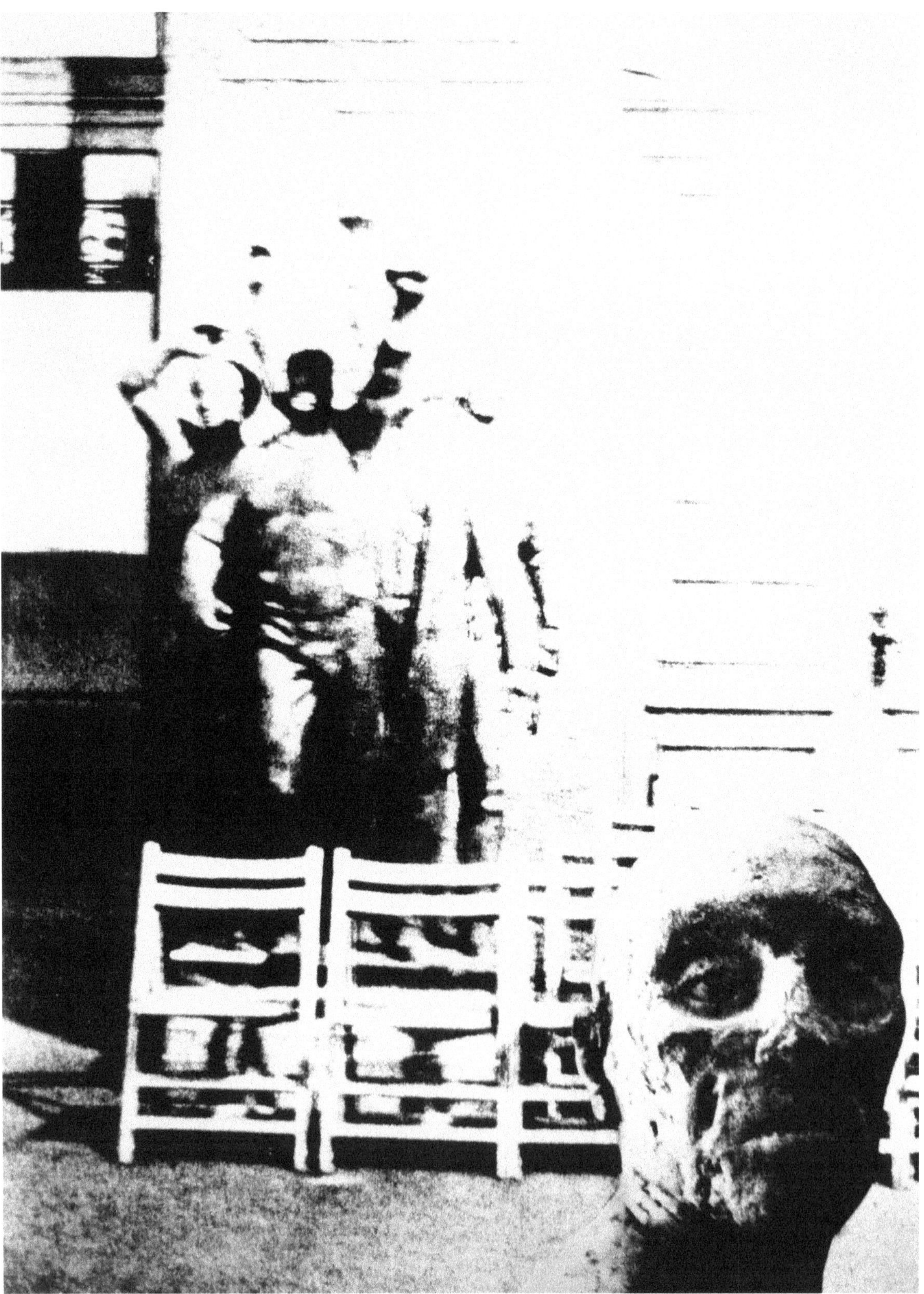

Volk

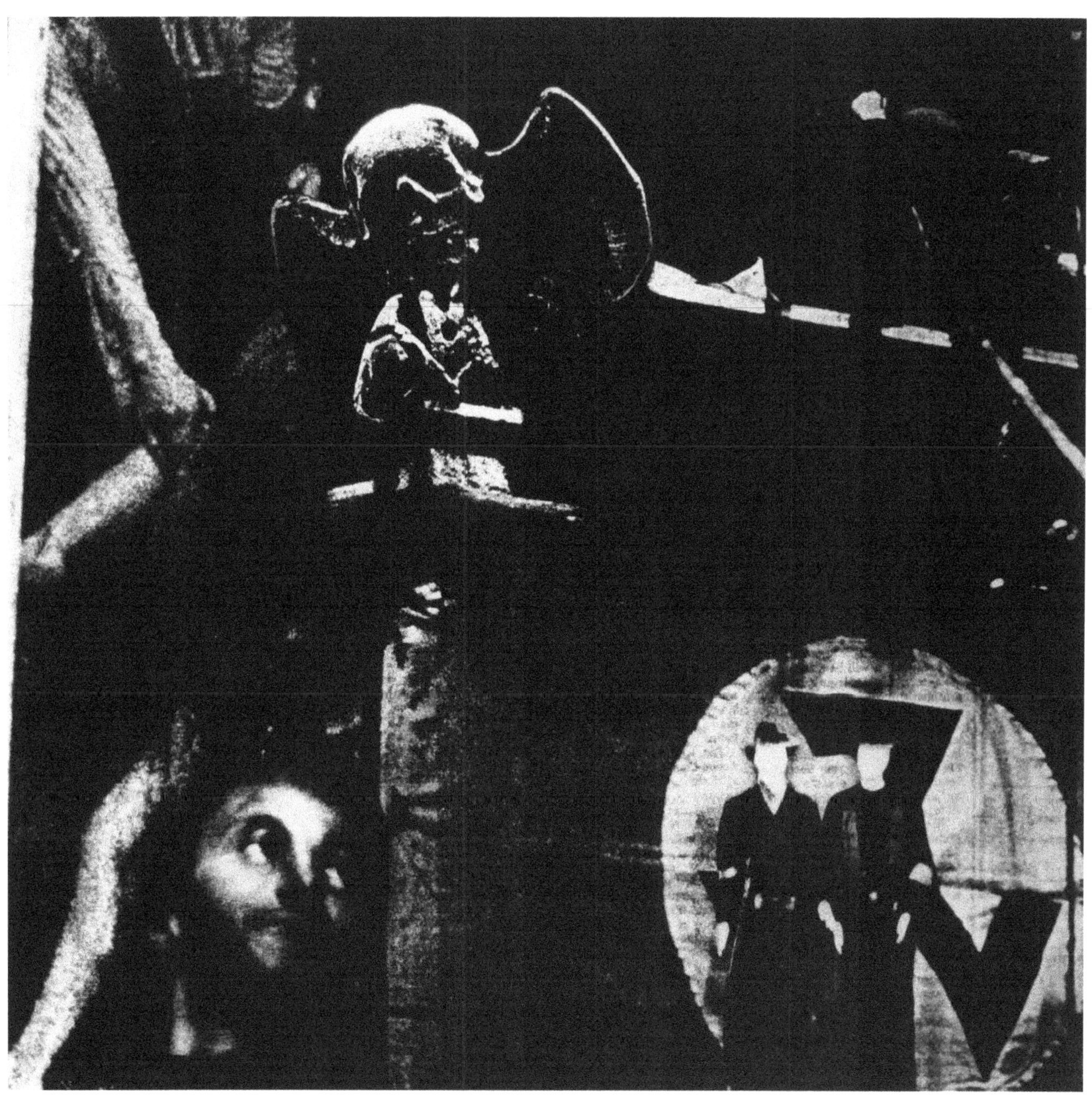

Jamboree

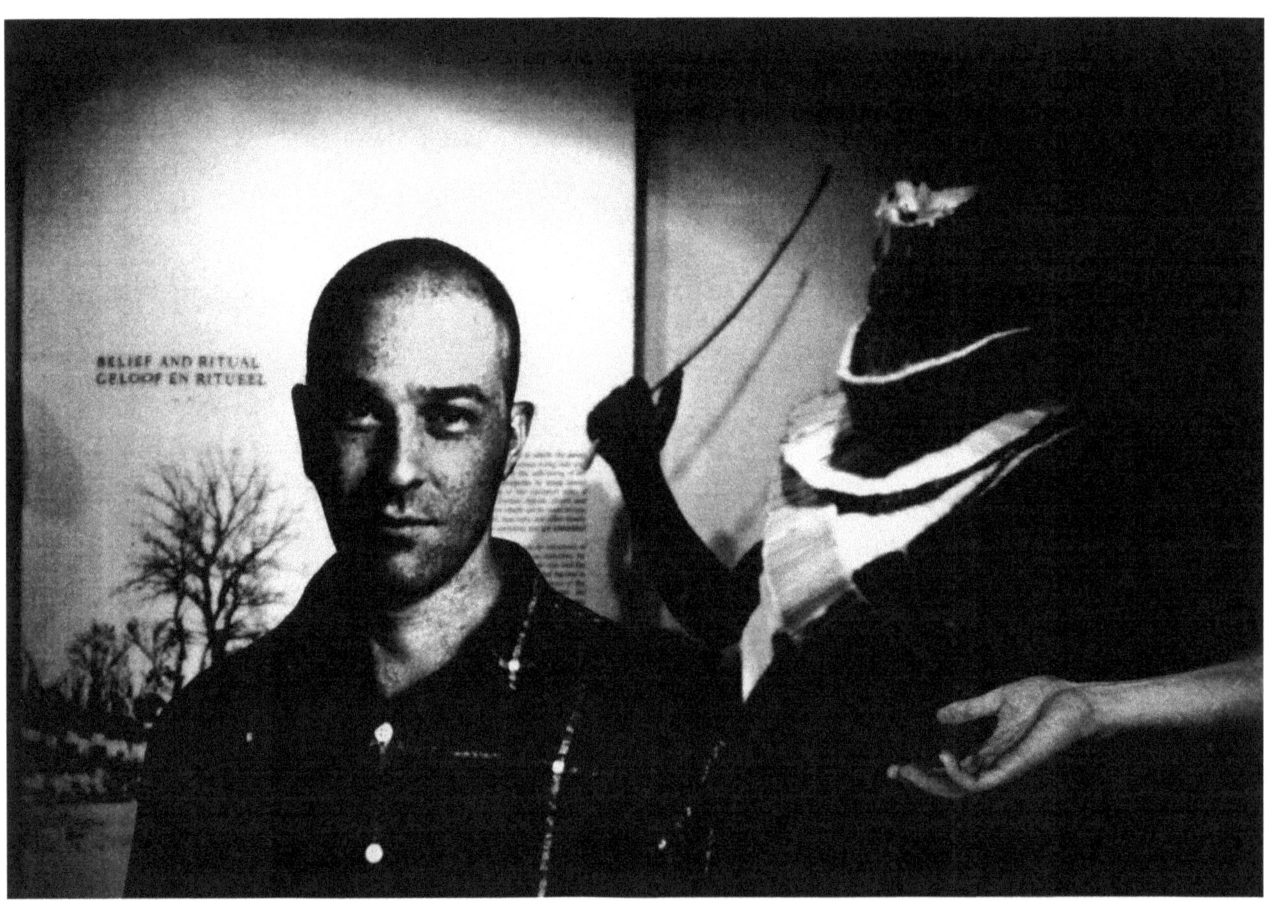

Belief and Ritual / Geloof en Ritueel:
Portrait of a Man

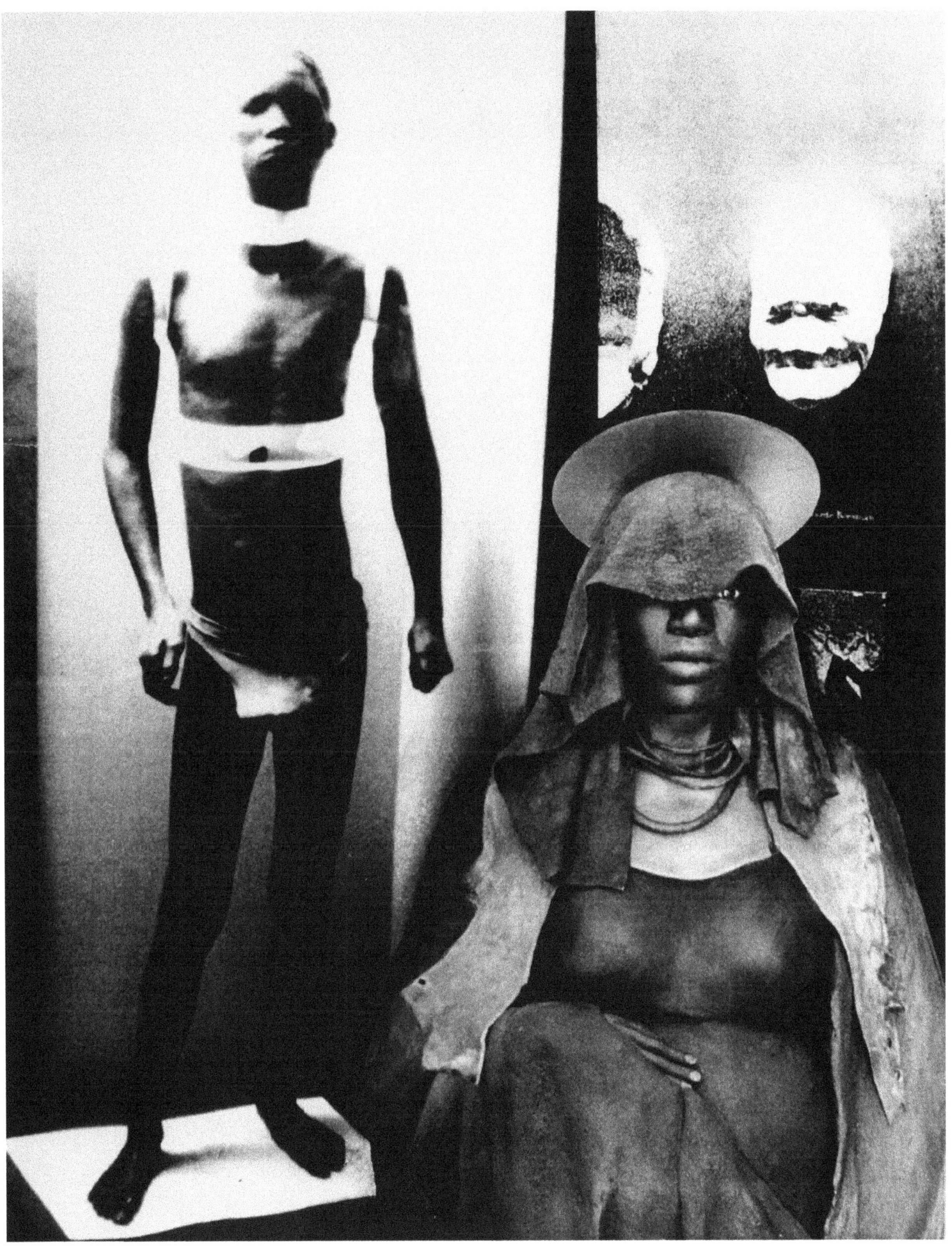

Fragmented Group

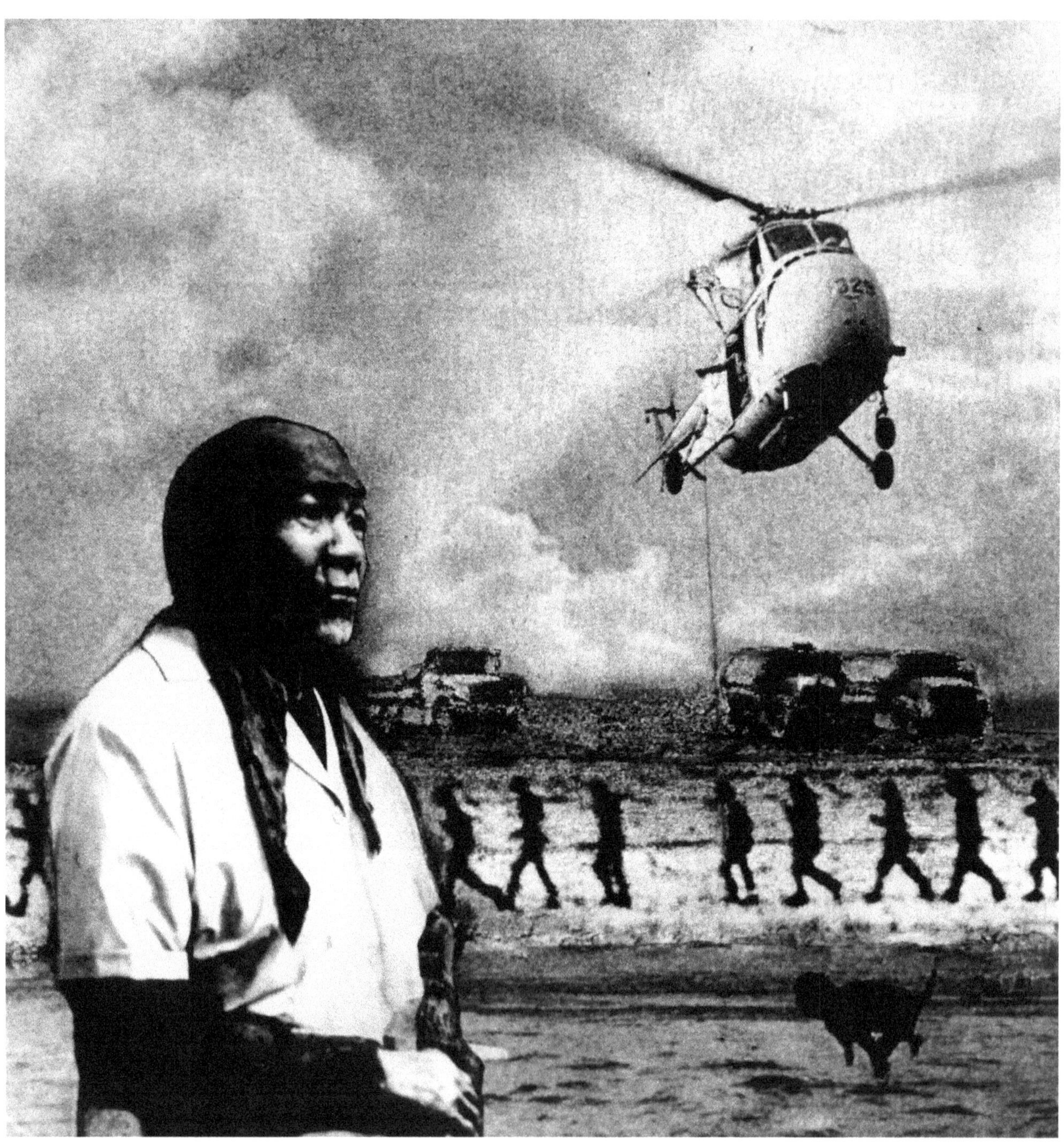

Beauty in a landscape:
born Aliwal North 19-?, died Boksburg 1992

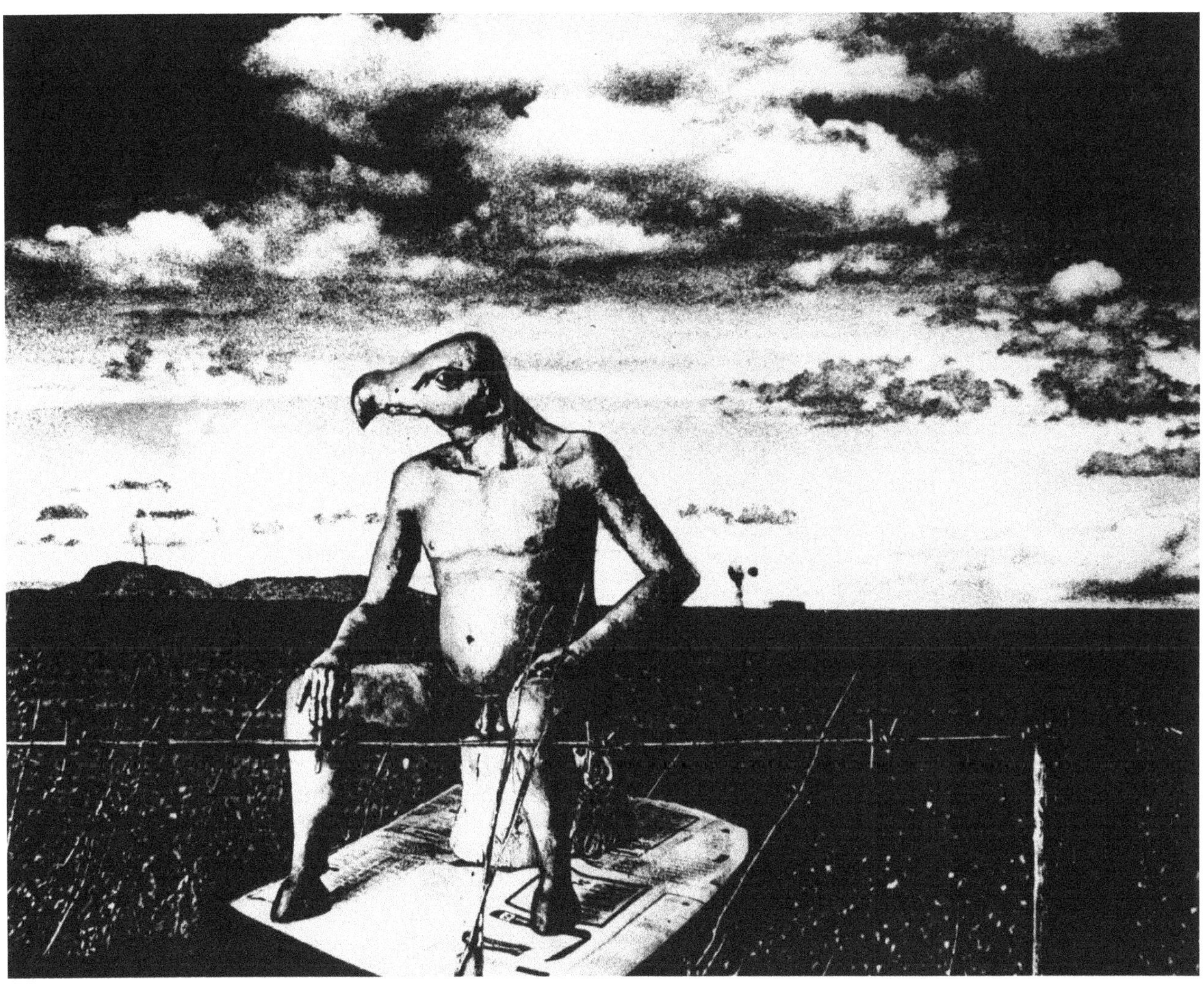

Landowner

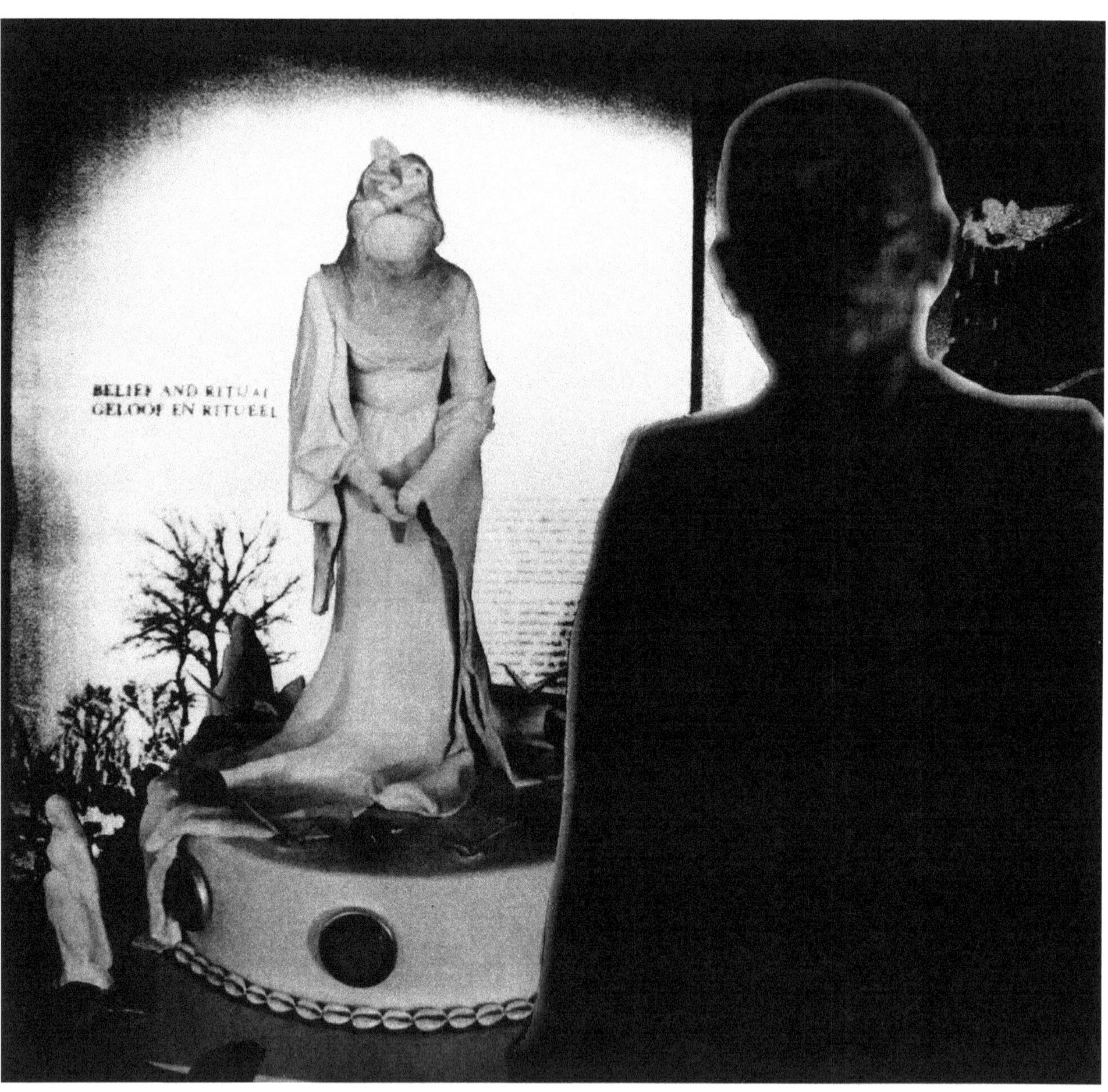

Belief and Ritual / Geloof en Ritueel:
Respecting

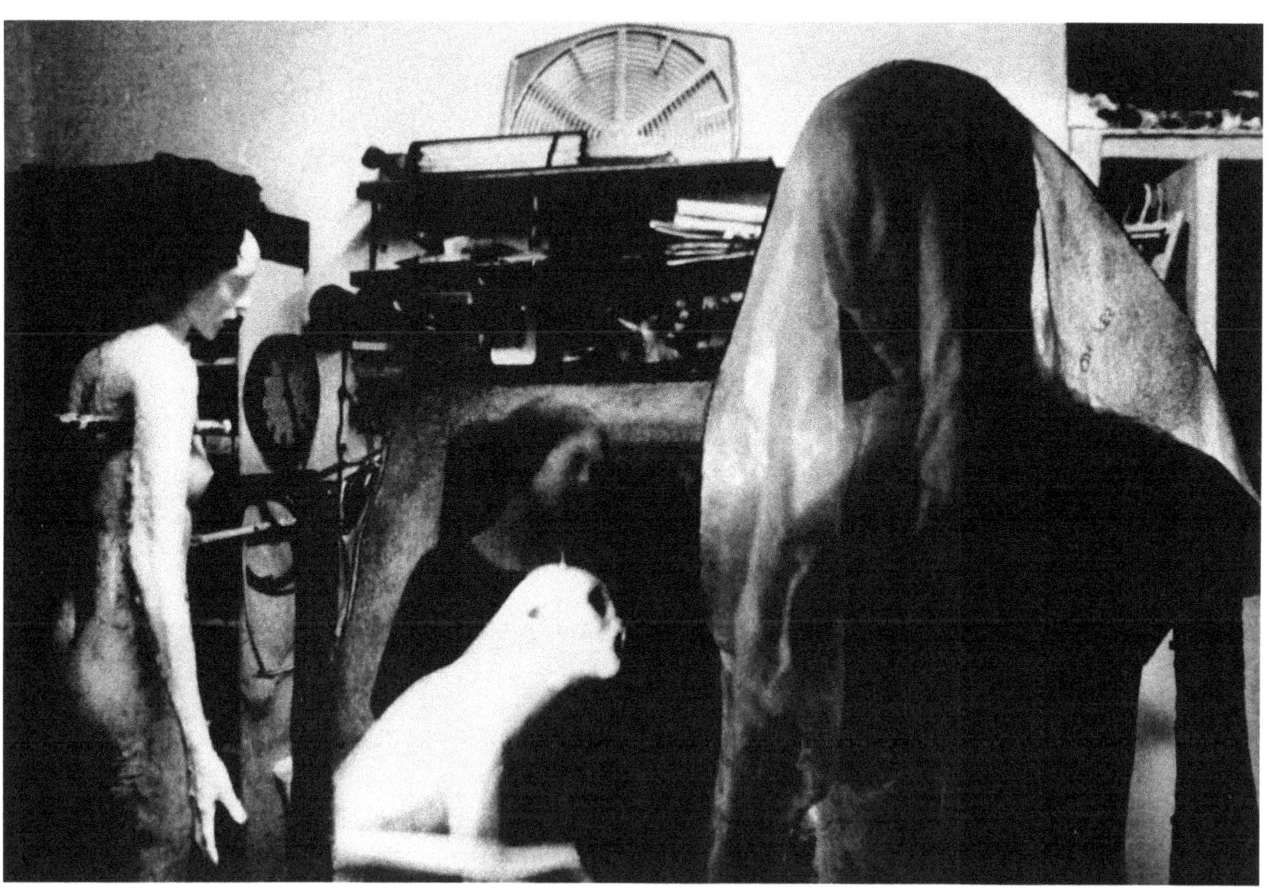

Convention

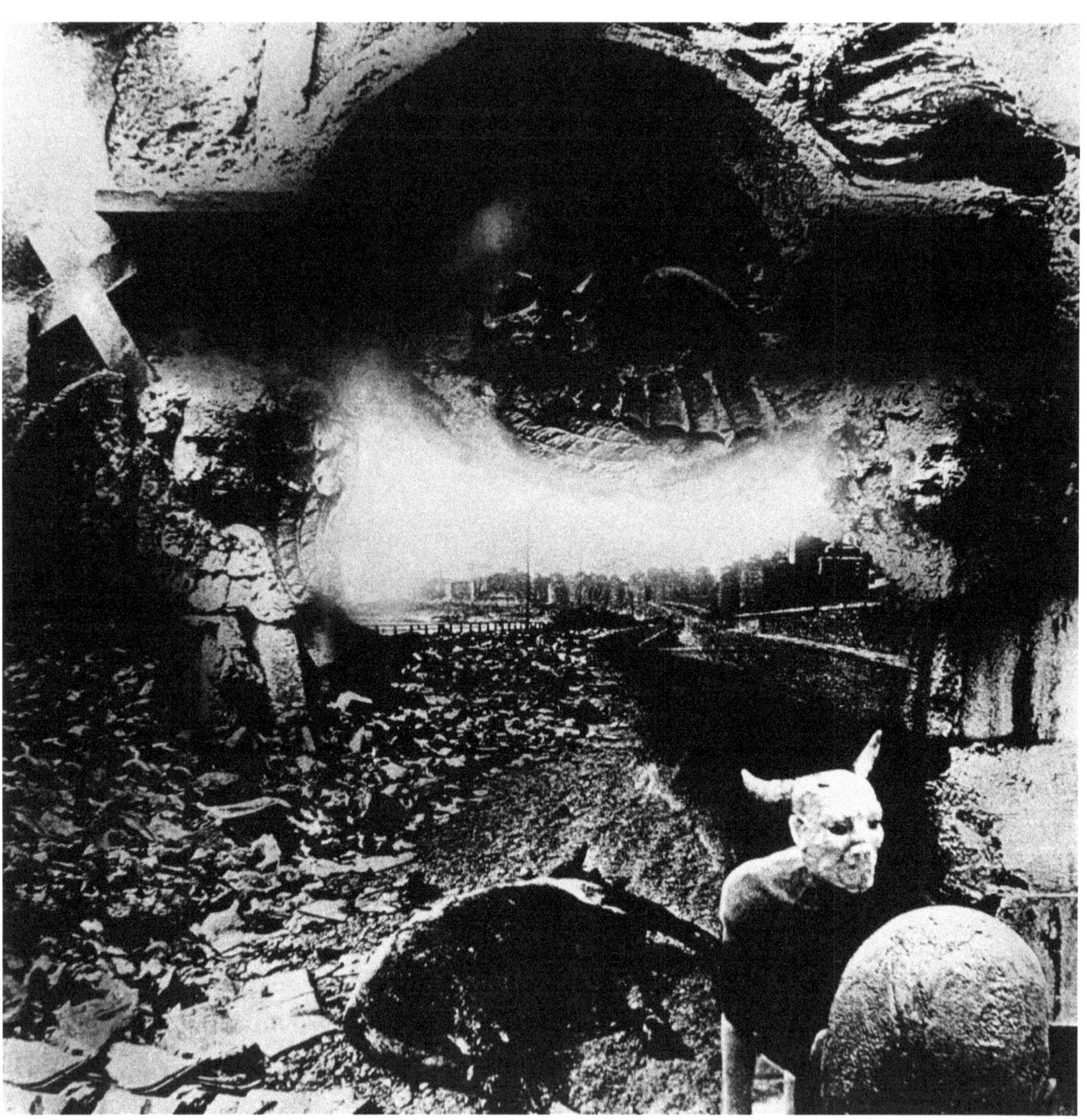

Landscape

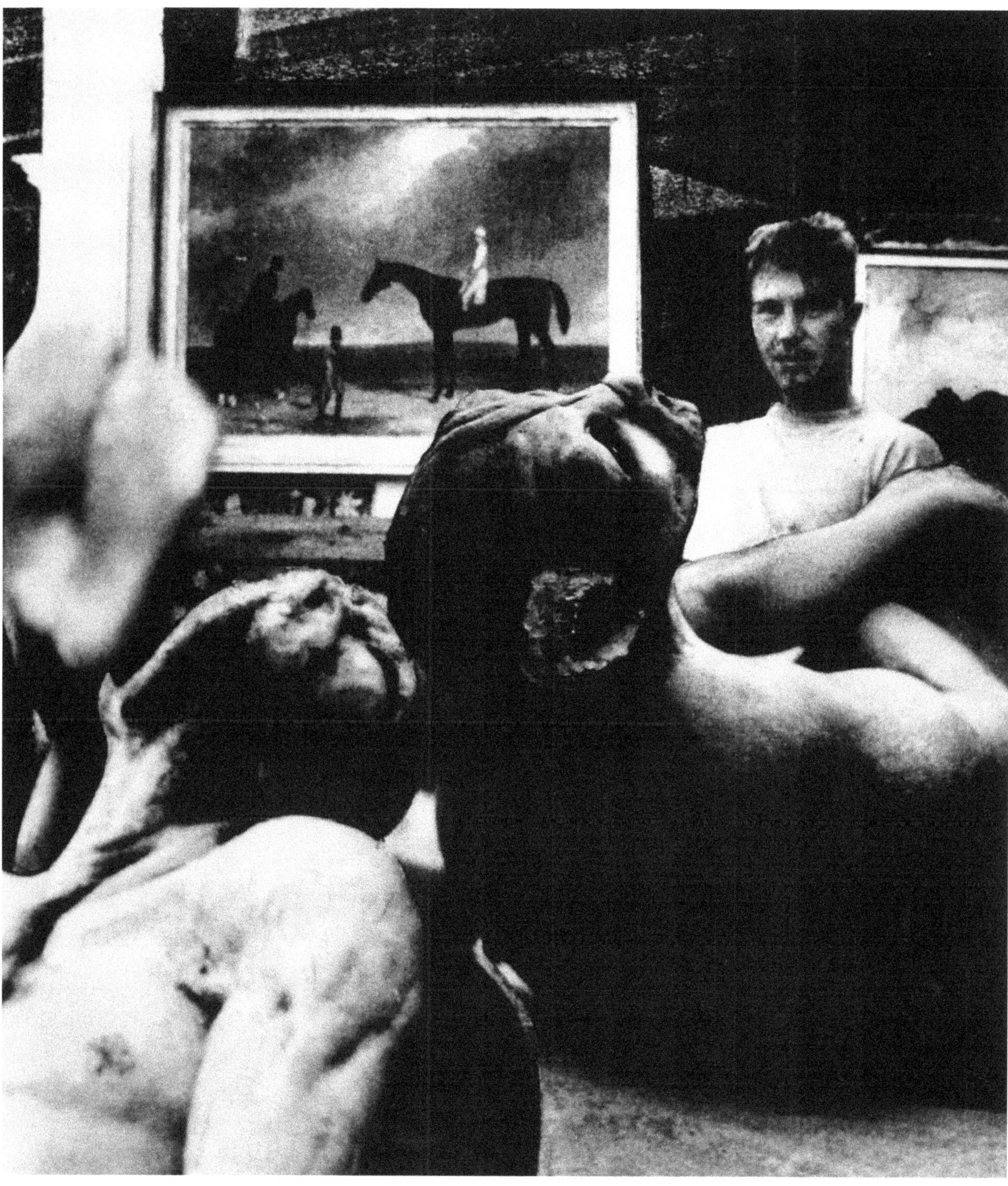

At the restorer

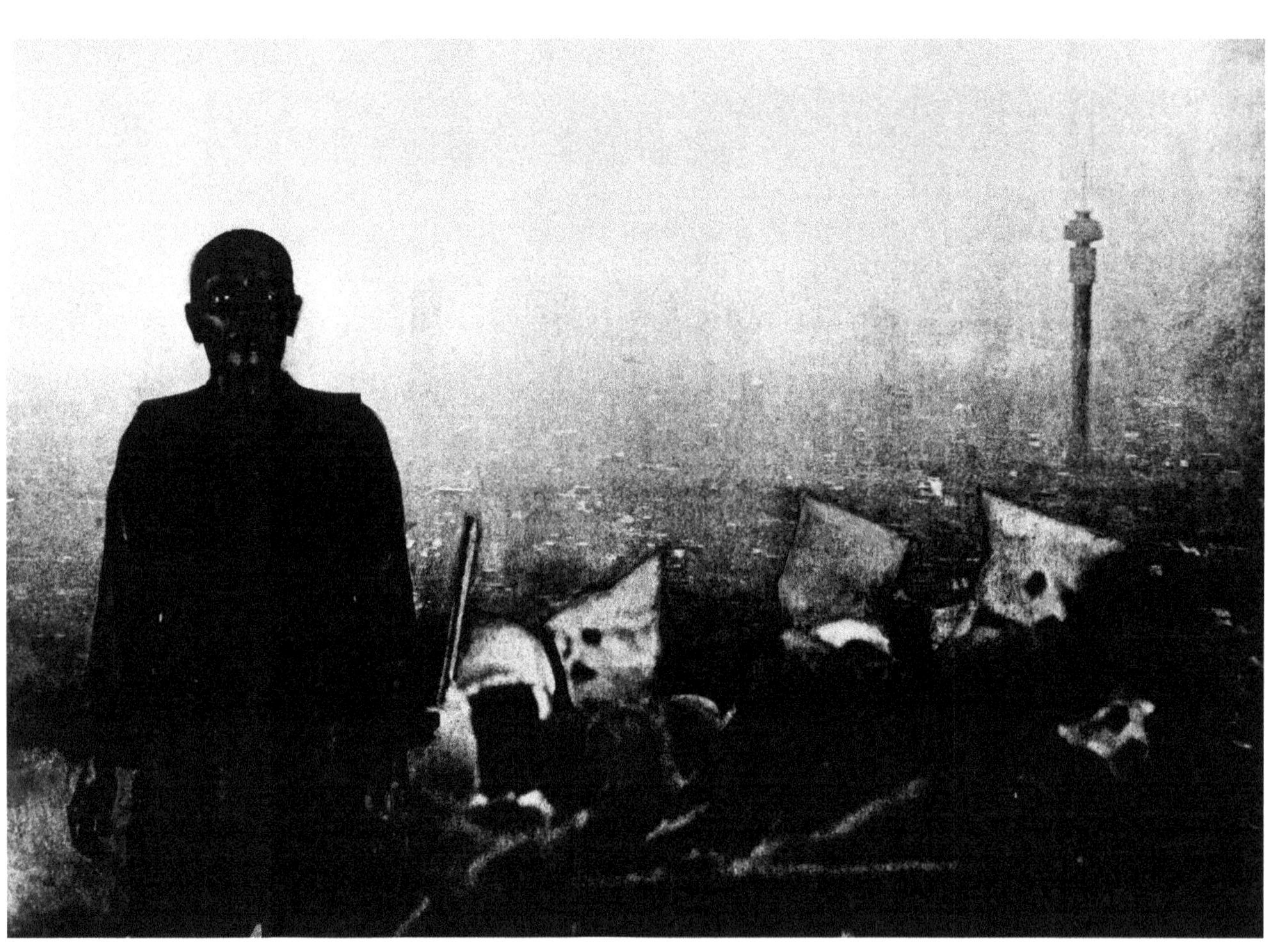

Man with Stability Unit and tower

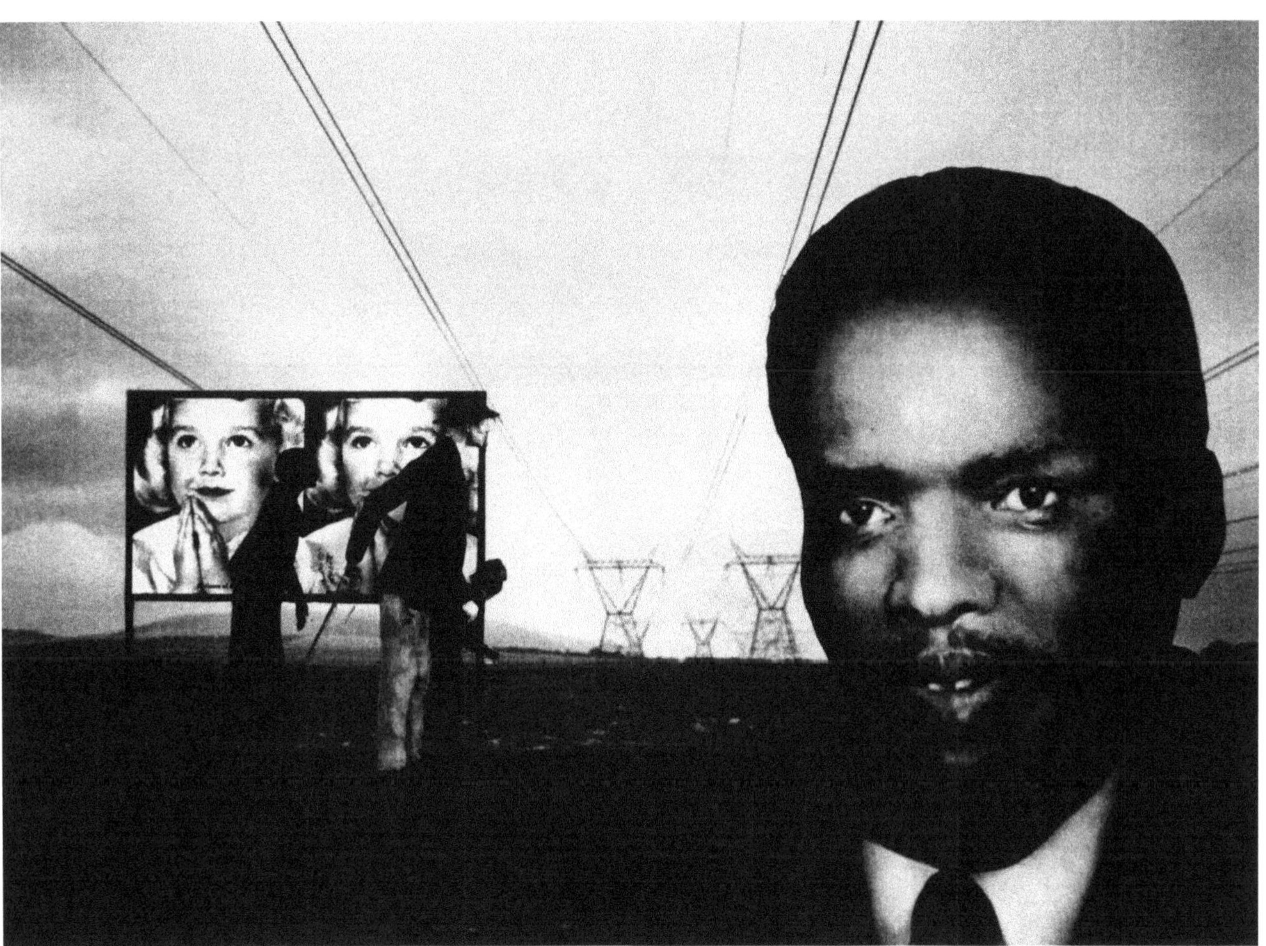

Portrait of a man with landscape and
procession (Bantu Stephen Biko 1946-1977)

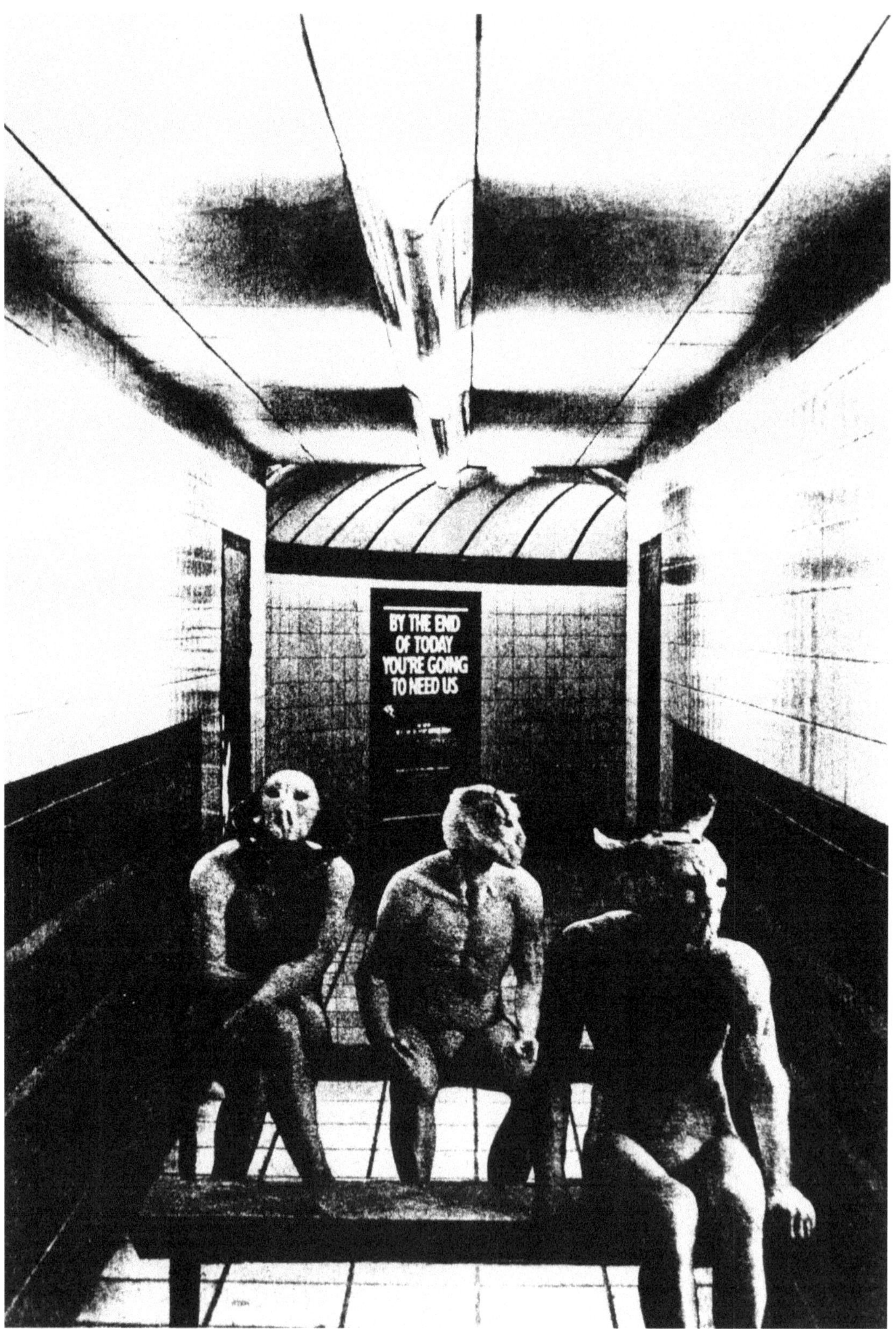

BY THE END OF TODAY YOU'RE
GOING TO NEED US

PHOTOMONTAGES 1981-1995

Portrait of a man (adventurer) by
J A Pamilton and J Alexander
1995, 15 × 25.5cm

Phone me for secret
1995, 14.5 × 23cm

In the arcade
1995, 16.5 × 20.5cm

Woman in a two piece
1984, 36 × 29.5cm

Sleeping man
1984, 27 × 21cm

The Cow House
1985, 24.5 × 21cm

This is Television
1984, 25 x 24.5cm

Jane discovers famine
1981, 16 × 20.5cm

Warehouse
1985, 31 x 19.5cm

Search
1981, 25.5 × 14cm

"Purge me with hyssop, and I shall be
clean: Wash me, and I shall be whiter
than snow."
Psalm 51, v 7
1986, 19.5 × 23.5cm

Delivery
1981, 20 × 15cm

Demonstration with wrapped man
1981, 20.5 × 16cm

Ford
1986, 32 × 24cm

Trading was listless
1986, 29.5 × 21.5cm

Confinement
1981, 24 × 17cm

Interior
1981, 20.5 × 18cm

Shepherd
1986, 30 x 21cm

Service
1983, 21.5 × 16.5cm

Gannet
1985, 28.5 × 23.5cm

Lost child
1985, 24.5 × 24cm

Chernobyl medical aid rally,
Leningrad
1986, 29 x 19.5cm

Museum boy
1986, 30 × 21.5cm

Triumph over capitalism: Für
Deutsche Geschichte
1995, 25 × 17cm

"Sauberkeit ist Gesundheit": ancestor
1995, 25 × 15.5cm

Gesellschaft Waren: Merchandise for
society
1995, 29 × 19.5cm

Triumph over capitalism: "Die Ewige
Flamme"
1995, 19.5 × 24.5cm

Triumph over capitalism:
Lustgarten
1995, 19.5 x 22cm

Reconstruction
1995, 18 x 27.5cm

Volk
1986, 33.5 x 24.5cm

Jamboree
1986, 26 × 27.5cm

Belief and Ritual / Geloof en Ritueel:
Portrait of a Man
1995, 16.5 × 24.5cm

Fragmented Group
1995, 23 x 18cm

Beauty in a landscape: born Aliwal
North 19-?, died Boksburg 1992
1995, 22 × 20cm

Landowner
1995, 17.5 × 22.5cm

Belief and Ritual / Geloof en Ritueel:
Respecting
1995, 22 × 23.5cm

Convention
1995, 18 × 27cm

Landscape
1985, 26.5 × 27.5cm

At the restorer
1995, 20 × 18cm

Man with Stability Unit and tower
1994, 20.5 x 29.5cm

Portrait of a man with landscape and
procession (Bantu Stephen Biko 1946-
1977)
1995, 18 × 25cm

BY THE END OF TODAY YOU'RE GOING
TO NEED US
1986, 29 x 20cm

© Jane Alexander, DALRO

FACES OF HISTORY

If you are seeking to make an intervention in visual history, I suggest you start by locating a figurative statue of a controversial person. Focus on the face and especially the nose if within reach. Noses matter because they are literally central to the face, offering a focal point for any viewer at middle to close range, while at the same time being the most structurally vulnerable part of a figurative bust or statue. When, for example, during the Hungarian Revolution of late 1956, the Stalin Monument, a colossal bronze statue, was toppled in Budapest, its nose became the first target of the blowtorches brought by the protesting students and workers.[1] Only once the enormous statue had fallen did the face come within physical reach of ordinary persons participating in the protest. One of the executed leaders of the short-lived revolution, Imre Nagy (1896–1958), was honored in a major anti-communist protest event in 1989; seven years later, the government erected a life-size statue of Nagy standing on a bridge and gazing upon the Hungarian parliament. However, its move to a less politically sensitive location in 2018 was a sign of the times: Viktor Orban's government was busy reinstating Soviet-era symbols unannounced and under cover of darkness.[2] In such cases, statues render changing political fortunes visible via the highly charged photo opportunities they present: mutatis mutandis, comparable examples can be in found in South Africa, the Southern United States, the Middle East, and any other country that has undergone a sudden political transition.[3] As a rule of thumb, the more authoritarian the government involved, the larger the statue is likely to be; by the same token, the larger the statue, the likelier it is to be mutilated, destroyed, or removed in the event of a regime change or other political upheaval.[4]

Such well-known dynamics raise this question: Does history need a face? What is at stake in conceiving the past in relation to individuals? While the first question admits no easy response but rather suggests rich

lines of inquiry, the latter, more specific one certainly received affirmative answers in Greco-Roman times, insofar as it was asked at all. A strong biographical element is visible in authors from the start to finish of antiquity, not merely the writers of biography and history.[5] The exception is Polybius, whose account of Rome's ascendancy in the third and second centuries BCE gave the starring role to the Roman constitution rather than to individual commanders and statesmen. The sixth book of his *Histories* would have an impact on Enlightenment thinkers and on the framers of the US Constitution. The first question posed is intended to prompt a broad inquiry into perceptions of the past, even as the focus of this essay will be on case studies from South Africa. At issue is the intersection of public art and public history, to the extent that specific artistic creations may be considered interpretations of the past for present and future consumption. The use or avoidance of faces is the criterion linking several South African creative works discussed here.

Nonetheless faces have no monopoly of political statements via art. In Johannesburg in 2012, Brett Murray's portrayal of then-President Jacob Zuma in his painting *The Spear* (2010) was disfigured by two persons of different political persuasions on the same day once his exhibit had begun to gain public attention via news and social media. Paint was applied to the president's face and exposed genitals.[6] In the case of the polygamous and progenitive Zuma, private parts are a recurrent satirical theme. The paintings in question were not public art in the same sense as, say, Marion Walgate's bronze statue of Cecil Rhodes (1934), which was famously removed from the University of Cape Town campus in 2015. But they did gain public fame via video footage and photographs that went viral.

First, a word about definitions. "Public history" is a term that has gained currency in the United States, marked by the establishment of the National Council on Public History in 1980. Its charter statement defined public history as an outward-oriented branch of archivally based "guild" history.[7] In South Africa, heritage has been the key concept.[8] Its purview has been large and, from the perspective of some, has effectively absorbed history, which nonetheless remains entrenched in school and university curricula. "Heritage" by any definition encompasses *public* history. Heritage has been institutionalized by the government under the Department of Sport, Arts and Culture, and implemented via that department's organs, especially the National Heritage Council (NHC), the South African Heritage Resource Agency (SAHRA), and SAHRA's provincial branches.[9]

By contrast, public art is less institutionally and more circumstantially defined. In practice, its manifestations "are most often site-specific works triggered by public construction and development projects."[10] The usual characterization of three-dimensional art, aimed at durability, can no longer be meaningful at a time when social media publicize an event such as the disfiguring of Murray's *The Spear*. Whereas the role of the public is often limited to the passive consumption of the finished artwork, "[m]ore public art agencies are turning to participatory approaches that increase involvement and make public art more reflective of the communities in which it is located."[11] This might involve a combination of design (planning, selection), creation, installation, upkeep, and shared appreciation. With these more inclusive and participatory inflections, public art has been central to Richard Florida's influential idea of a "creative class" that is supposedly or potentially at the forefront of urban renewal.[12] Admittedly, Florida's focus is on the global north, and the relevance of his approach to South Africa may be considered an open question. In general, it is fair to say that the difference between an artist's public and other works is determined by commissions received or not received; or art may become public if someone decides on their own initiative to use a public (often ephemeral) medium, which often takes place as a gesture of resistance.

If both public history and public art express particular goals, it is especially the former that is directly articulated. Thus, there is a strong element of

intentionality in the erection of statues honoring a figure such as Imre Nagy or Nelson Mandela. In each case, the political authorities made a conscious decision to celebrate a leader. Both history and art are put to political service, and the government or other leaders have made a calculation, not necessarily explicit, that the public gesture favors their own agendas. In fact, public artwork are often implicit power claims on the part of their originators. Such political dimensions are clearest at the photo opportunities at the public unveiling. Thus, when Zuma unveiled the nine-meter statue outside the Union Building in Pretoria on December 16, 2013, his life-size proportions were literally dwarfed by the colossal bronze statue. Political cartoonists of the time had their work done for them, as the gap between the government's aggrandizing intention and its demeaning realization was apparent for all to see in the press coverage.

For the purposes of this essay, faces are the theme through which to explore the overlap between public art and public history. The face is at once a subset of the body and yet, as suggested by its Romance etymology going back to the Latin *faciēs* (appearance), simultaneously offers itself as a direct index of character (Greek *ēthos*).[13] Needless to say, faces are directly subject to the identity politics that, in South Africa, have revolved around race first and foremost. On a broader view, other elements of identity have come into play in terms of what has more recently been called intersectionality. We will also have to deal with individuality, a critical issue throughout the history of figurative representation. Are they to be considered portraits or not? If faces mark the point between individuality and communalism, they also mark the point between private and public existence. The following case studies have been selected to display a wide range of work. Though painted portraits were prominent in Europe of the 18th and 19th centuries, a fashion that has since considerably waned, the emphasis here falls on three-dimensional statuary, starting with the National Heritage Monument, which seems to represent a certain kind of politically defined and celebratory personalization of the heritage sphere (section I). Critique of the triumphalism implied in such statues has been made by Sethembile Msezane in her performative art, including *Chapangu—the day Rhodes fell* (2015), which is a direct comment on Walgate's bronze statue of Cecil Rhodes at the point of its removal (section II). The spectacular

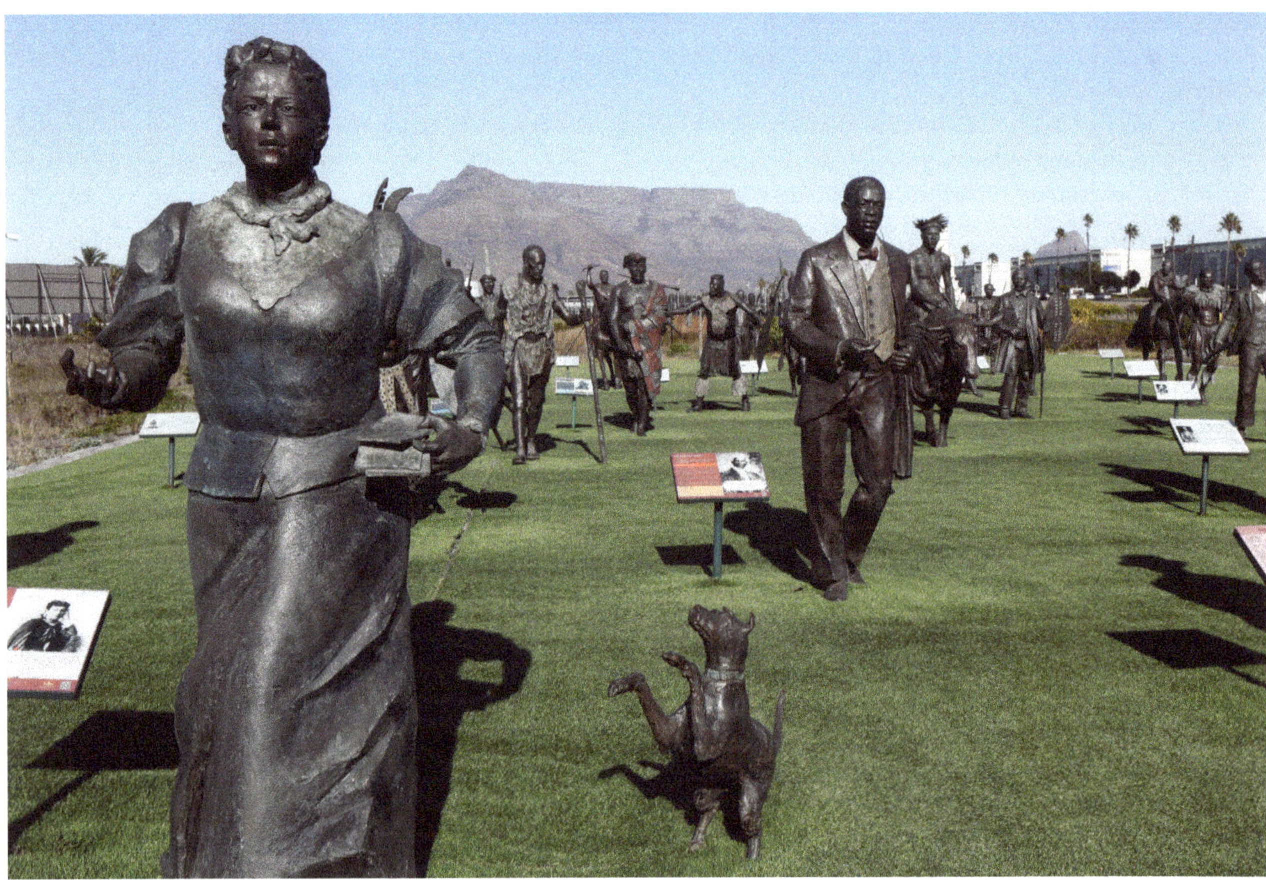

Figure 1. National Heritage Monument, Cape Town. Photograph by Paul Weinberg.

element of such histories is put in relief by a brief survey of South Africa's slave memorials, which, unlike many of their equivalents elsewhere, sometimes eschew figurative representation (section III). A different kind of facelessness occurs in Simon Gush's video essay, *Iseeyou* (2013), which explores Johannesburg's statues and other monuments to mineworkers in relation to the visibility of labor, or rather its invisibility (section IV). By way of a conclusion, a final section evaluates the role and capacity of faces as one key ingredient, along with location, in historically oriented public art (section V).

I. SMILING HEROISM

These heroes of the liberation struggle are being honored in the Long March to Freedom—a procession of 400 individuals who struggled against oppression in South Africa from the early 1700s to Freedom Day in April 1994. From the rebel chiefs and revered kings to

the more well-known activists of the 1980s and 1990s, each figure is poised in walking motion, symbolically fighting for the liberation of South Africa while marching forward to the inevitable advent of democracy.[14]

Faces define the 100 or so statues that have thus far seen the light of day in the Long March to Freedom project at the center of the National Heritage Monument (NHM). The brainchild of Dali Tambo, a media celebrity and the son of the long-serving ANC president, Oliver Tambo, it is run as a nonprofit by Tambo's organization, Koketso Growth, which advertises itself as "cultural heritage and tourism specialists."[15] The project began in 2010 and was unveiled in Groenkloof, a suburb of Pretoria, in 2015 with 55 statues. That number nearly doubled in the next five years but was still well short of its ambitious goal of 400–500. Thus far, 45 artists have been involved, none with more than three statues. It was initially funded by the Department of Arts and Culture, the National Lotteries Commission, and the City of Tshwane (Pretoria), but ongoing funding became an issue. Location has also been a challenge for this project, given that its previous Groenkloof locality is ecologically sensitive, and the envisaged development of the site as an outdoor entertainment center, with an amphitheater and water feature, would, if realized, generate a high degree of petrochemical runoff into the Apies River.[16]

In December 2018 the statues were moved to the Cradle of Humankind in Maropeng, a World Heritage site,[17] and again in November 2019 to Century City, on the fringes of a shopping mall complex in the Cape Town metropolitan area. For all the ambition around the original conception, the NHM Project clearly struggled for a sustainable funding source and location, even as it sought to integrate itself into school programs and local tourism.[18] Even as the NHM Project continues seeking to secure its future, it was nonetheless able to unveil a statue of Archbishop Desmond Mpilo Tutu on March 23, 2023. Tutu had died on December 26, 2021, at the age of 90, following a lengthy illness. Cristina Savoldi and Tania Lee created the work, and the Loup Fine Art Foundry in White River, Mpumalanga, cast it. In attendance were representatives of both the ANC-led national government and the DA-led provincial and municipal government, along with family members.

The symbolism of triumph predominates, and smiles abound. Nelson Mandela, in a bronze statue cast by Barry Jackson and Xhanti Mpakama, leads the way, his right arm held aloft in the gesture that accompanied the end of his lengthy imprisonment in 1990. Followed by Walter and Albertina Sisulu as well as Oliver and Adelaide Tambo,[19] Mandela leads a process that celebrates the end of oppression and the arrival of democracy. This kind of victory procession has its distant origins in the Roman triumph and more proximate ones in ticker-tape parades of the 20th century.[20] But there is another historical reference that makes Mandela the key figure: his memoir *Long Walk to Freedom* (1994). In 1965, a collection of his speeches and essays was published under the title *No Easy Walk to Freedom*. The collection was banned in South Africa but was widely read elsewhere. The phrase "no easy

walk" is itself adapted from a speech by Jawaharlal Nehru, the first Prime Minister of India.[21] Many of the earliest mass protests against the apartheid state took the form of walking, in keeping with US civil rights protests in the same era and Indian anti-colonial protests a generation earlier. The NHM thus creates a pageant of the history of struggle that presents itself as nation building and articulates a "long twentieth century" in which the Mandela generation of leaders is the fulfillment of South African history. In these terms, the Long March to Freedom offers a tightly choreographed march that invokes and expands the struggle and follows it to a gloriously positive outcome. Via the first statue, this history is freeze-framed at the time of Mandela's release, the apogee of the ANC's symbolic power, power that has waned amid deepening corruption, cronyism, and nonfeasance on the part of the party once it came to power. This subsequent dysfunction has caused many younger people especially to become disillusioned and disaffected with the political establishment. Whereas Mandela himself expressed a conciliatory attitude toward statues from the old regime,[22] the student protests that boiled over in 2015–2016 were often directly critical of the man.

Any gesture as grandiose as the NHM will be open to detailed questions of conception and realization. Winnie Mandela, who was at Madiba's side at the Drakenstein release and held his hand for some of that time, was omitted from the original installation but was added later, thus aligning the Mandelas with the Tambos and Sisulus. Winnie's role has been highly controversial.[23] Whereas Helen Suzman (1917–2009), veteran leader of the white parliamentary opposition, received no recognition in the extensive displays of the Apartheid Museum, here she is one of 14 white South Africans to be included in the first 100 figures. In more practical terms, beyond the question of location already described, the collection has also been subject to theft. Despite 24-hour security, a statue of the Khoe leader Damon was removed between installation and inauguration.[24] The thieves' choice added an ironic turn, given the ANC government's ongoing unwillingness to recognize Khoesan as traditional leaders under the new constitution of 1996. In this historical Hall of Fame are several international leaders who have been commemorated for supporting the liberation movement in exile: Fidel Castro (cast by Ruhan Janse van Vuuren), Julius

Nyerere (Otto du Plessis), Olof Palme (Maureen Quinn), and Haile Selassie (Izidro Duarte). The earlier colonial period is represented by traditional leaders such as the baSotho leader Moshoeshoe. Such choices expose the project to the criticism that every inclusion is an exclusion. It is not clear whether any panel of historians was asked to provide scholarly input on the choices, let alone decide them. What is more, the concept of human rights seems creatively interpreted in many cases without being subject to detailed explanation and questioning.

The project is in several ways a blast from the past: a response in kind to statuary from the colonial and apartheid eras and a response especially to the long-term exclusion of Black persons from that visual lexicon. It is hardly a response to stylistic evolution. It represents the desire of a new political elite to be represented in the visual language of the old, even though that language lost a great deal of its communicative capacity between 1910 and 2020.[25] Many post–World War I monuments in South Africa and other British colonies centered on figurative representations, including variants on the Unknown Soldier motif. The apparent monopoly of Koketso Growth has seen the figurative approach of the Long March replicated in other projects it has carried out, including the Women's Living Heritage Monument at Lilian Ngoyi Square in Pretoria, unveiled on August 9, 2016, to commemorate the Women's March via statues of four of its leaders (Lilian Ngoyi, Helen Joseph, Sophia Williams-de Bruyn, and Rahima Moosa). The addition of 20 plaques in 2017 furthered the commemorative agenda that started with the renaming of the square. The opportunity for redevelopment arose following the collapse (2001) of a colossal bronze head of Prime Minister J. G. Strijdom and its soaring semicircular dome as a result of an insufficient foundation. Even nature, it seems, was joining in a politics of spectacle. Alongside the collapsed structure, Danie de Jager's elevated bronze statue of horses at the head of a tall but narrow fountain survived, which has subsequently been moved to the University of Pretoria.

There is an irony in my criticism of the *conventional* nature of the women's statues of 2016, when an earlier commemoration of the same event, in the same city, was criticized for its failure to communicate with popular audiences as a result of the artists' attempts at the kind of *innovation* that is valued by artists and scholars. Wilma Cruise and Marcus Holmes' *Imbokodo* (2002) quotes the chant from the Women's March, "*Wathint' Abafazi, wathint' imbokodo!*" ("If you strike the women, you strike the rock.") Cruise's installation is conceptual, realizing the grinding stone of the chant as its central feature. One scholar has condemned this elaborate conceptual artwork as "belaboured" and a "patronising attempt…to speak on behalf of those less advantaged, whose voices remain silent."[26] David Goldblatt's unpeopled photography of the memorial seems to substantiate the criticism.[27] This focused comparison of two Pretoria commemorations suggests that faces are the distinctive marker of figurative art. The smiles that characterize the Long March to Freedom are a feature of the ANC's claims to historically based legitimacy surrounding the struggle, the politically focused variant on an ancient tradition linking faces and power.[28]

II. CONCEALED FACES

If the Long March to Freedom presents monumental history, performative art offers pointedly different options. One artist whose work is expressly anti-monumental is Sethembile Msezane. In 2014, her work in the Public Holiday series brought the ephemeral medium of performance art into dialogue with the conventional statuary.[29] The first of these was on Heritage Day, which she staged by standing as a quasi-statue in front of Cape Town city hall. Her back to its elaborate classical façade, she faced a statue of King Edward VII that was in the center of the Grand Parade. (2) She marked Workers' Day with a piece that, with a rolled-up sleeve, a flexed bicep, and clenched fist turned inward recalled the World War II poster "We can do it" (1943). That image, made by Howard Miller for Westinghouse Electric, was intended to inspire morale in female workers. It would gain new significance in the feminist movement of the 1980s. Msezane's version, clad in the blue work suit characteristic of South African men, is staged on a pedestrian bridge overlooking a Cape Town freeway, which locates it both temporally and geographically. Her red headscarf (*doek*) closely matches Miller's poster. (3) Freedom Day is marked at Greenmarket Square, Cape Town, with the intricate Gothic Revival spires of the Central Methodist Mission (1876) in the background.[30]

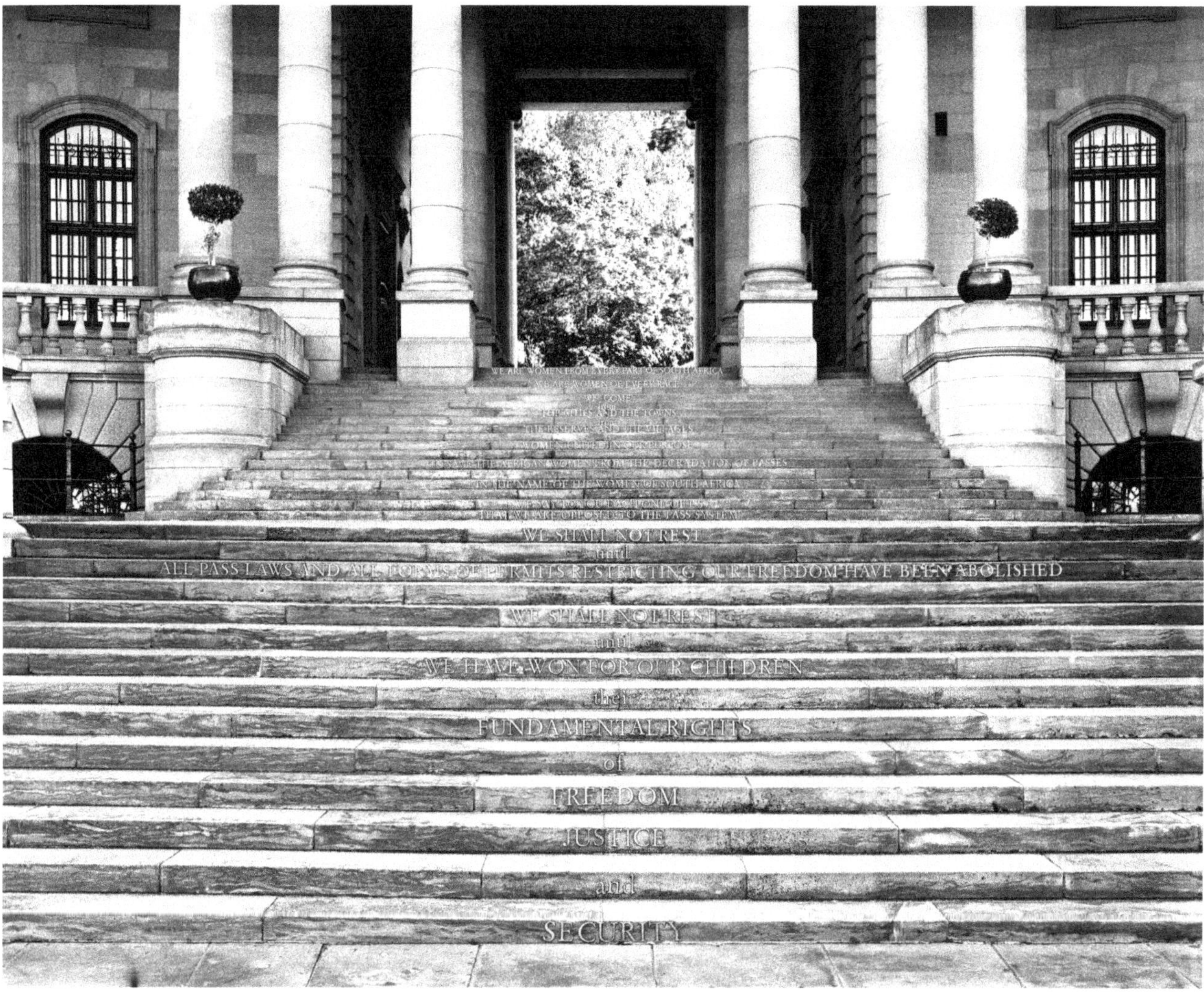

Figure 2. Photograph by David Goldblatt. The Women's Monument at the Union Buildings, Pretoria. It commemorates the march by some 20,000 women on 9 August 1956, through Pretoria to the Union Buildings, where they attempted to present a letter to Prime Minister J.G. Strijdom, protesting the "pass laws" and in particular, the law requiring African women to carry "passes." Neither Strijdom nor anyone else in the government accepted the letter. In 2006, this memorial to the march was unveiled. It is in the amphitheater where the women gathered. The artists were Wilma Cruise and Marcus Holmes. It is not accessible to the public. 1 November 2013 (4_A1141)

She carries a burning torch in her right hand and a slim book in her left, presumably the new constitution of 1996. Her costume is traditional, comprising an animal skin and large conical headgear. Given that Freedom Day celebrates the country's first democratic election on April 27, 1994, this combination suggests that her performance is a muted African version of the Statue of Liberty in New Jersey.

(4) In her piece for Women's Day, Msezane stands elevated on a high platform at Freedom Square located near the busy taxi rank of Langa township on the outskirts of Cape Town. The location is the site of a 1953 protest against the pass laws, in which the Federation of South African Women (FEDSAW) played a leading role. Msezane wears a large blanket, gathered at her waist and extending far down as a result of the narrow base, as a tribute to her great-grandmother, yet anomalously, her upper body is uncovered but for intricate beadwork suspended from her neck. This combination is a tribute to earlier generations and simultaneously the rejection of a passive

role for women. (5) For Youth Day she is dressed as a schoolboy, with blazer, shirt, tie, shorts, and white socks. The location in Soweto is a reference to the 1976 uprising, the origin of the holiday. The books balanced on her head are presumably intended to contradict the gender of the schoolboy by referencing the rural female practice of carrying water. (6) Msezane's Day of Reconciliation is staged at Freedom Park, with a distant view of the Voortrekker Monument in the background. The South African flag brandished in her raised right hand perhaps recalls Delacroix's *Liberty Leading the People* (1831), which celebrates the July Revolution of 1830. These combinations reflect Msezane's agenda of "respond[ing] to geographical spaces, acknowledging the relationship between history, mythmaking, and commemorative practice."[31]

Despite divergences in headgear, in each case Msezane's face is covered with a triangular beaded mask. This feature is shared with other work, including most famously *Chapungu—the Day Rhodes Fell*, but not all. At one level it is an assertion of Nguni tradition, in which modesty might require a young woman to keep her face concealed outside of a safe domestic setting. At another level, the beaded mask answers her "deep sense of dislocation and invisibility. I couldn't see myself represented anywhere."[32] It inverts the gaze. Given her protest against gender-based violence, some of her performances seem designed to titillate and accuse in equal measure.

Whereas Steve McCurry's photograph of the "Afghan girl" in 1984 seems to have been intrusive and taken without the subject's consent,[33] and likewise the same photographer's eventual tracking down on Sharbat Gula in a Pakistan refugee camp 2002,[34] Msezane is fully complicit with the camera. Far from Susan Sontag's characterization of the camera as a predatory weapon,"[35] photography does Msezane's bidding by fulfilling her stated goal of "us[ing] performance art as a form of social commentary to draw people's attention to certain issues as well as addressing the absence of the Black female body in memorialized public spaces, especially on public holidays." Even if Msezane is using photography to achieve these aims, the mask is a gesture that allows her to constrain the viewer's gaze. It

allows her to control the balance between female strength and fragility, between privacy and public appearance.

Given that there are sanctions on the exposure of a young woman's face in Nguni tradition, the issue of gender deserves consideration. In one case, the gender of the performance is overdetermined: her Women's Day work, as both a sexualized young woman and simultaneously a traditional matron. In others, it is transgressively challenged: when she dresses as a schoolboy or manual laborer. These are examples of a critical stance toward gendered roles and expectations. It is fair to say that her use of her body is more confrontational than celebratory. Her particular recipe of "remembrance as resistance,"[36] brings a radical questioning of history itself.[37]

Throughout the Public Holiday series, location is of great importance, offering site-specific reminders of the meaning of specific holidays. These reminders become more necessary when the historical past the holidays are supposed to commemorate are by no means as sacred to South Africans as the Mandela government, which instituted most of them, might have liked. Intergenerational tension came to the fore in the student protests of 2010s and was explicitly expressed in the Rhodes Must Fall and Fees Must Fall protests of 2015–2016.

III. FACELESS HISTORIES

By contrast, slavery involves acute and specific problems to the question of depicting faces. It is slavery that tinges South Africa's colonial origins. The first Dutch colonists made use of enslaved persons from Batavia and other Indian Ocean colonies from the time of their settlement in the 1650s. In 1658, the first free burghers were granted land for agriculture. From that time, slaves were imported for farm labor, starting with those arriving on board the *Amersfoort*, having been captured from a Portuguese slaver heading from Angola to Brazil. By the time of the *Amersfoort*'s arrival, many had died on board. This was the first of several deliveries of enslaved persons to the Cape. Between this time and the British abolition of the slave trade in 1807, persons arrived in roughly equal proportions from the Indonesian archipelago, southern India and Sri Lanka, Madagascar, and from the east coast of Africa. Their diverse origins, further compounded by intermarriage with settlers and with local people, brought enormous diversity. This newly created creole community would be known by various names, including Malay. Cape slavery officially ended on December 1, 1834, but continued for four further years of apprenticeship.

If bondage has been central to the colonial order, how has it been commemorated? As Nigel Worden has shown,[38] many factors have led to amnesia concerning slavery, including taboos around legitimacy, the desire for social advancement, and (in the struggle against apartheid) non-racialism. Despite political changes, many of these factors still prevail. Many of the slaves' descendants are also connected with the indigenous Khoesan groups. And whereas Khoesan heritage offered some hope of recognition to people under the post-1994 constitution, there has been little incentive to claim enslaved pasts. Add to this, the ANC-led government, via the Department of Arts and Culture, the NHC, and other organizations, has actively resisted funding projects commemorating slave histories, claiming that the topic was racially divisive since it applied only to the Coloured group, which is based mainly in the Western Cape, rather than the nation as a whole. At the same time, much of the rhetoric of the NHC focused on liberation as a transcendent signifier for the struggle of oppressed people against colonialism and apartheid, a struggle in which the African National Council took a leading role. Histories of Dutch slavery at the Cape thus seemed to undermine the nation-building project of the ANC government. For this reason, the government blocked participation of Iziko and its other heritage organizations in international projects, such as the UNESCO's multinational Slave Route Project.[39]

Given such a combination of popular and official resistance, it is not surprising that the commemoration of slavery at the Cape has been so limited. One exception is the Slave Lodge in the heart of Cape Town, which was used by the Dutch East India Company (VOC) from 1679 to 1811 to house the people they enslaved. Though its post-slavery use was for official and often grandiose purposes, it was only after the end of apartheid that the Lodge became a museum of slavery and more. Since 1998, in its reframed form as the Iziko

Slave Lodge, its motto has been "From human wrongs to human rights." Here and elsewhere, metaphors have displaced histories, and the broader focus on human rights seen in temporary exhibits has answered the government's demand for a broader definition of slavery. The Slave Lodge has continued to be part of an intricate tug-of-war between different stakeholders.

Within this complex dynamic, the means for commemorating slavery are as underdetermined as the motives for doing so. Heroism is not an option. When the names of enslaved people are known at all from the historical record, it is often in a generic form, as derived from cargo, sale, or other official documents. Louis van Mauritius (d. 1808) is an exception. In October 1808, two years after Dutch rule ended, he led a group of around 340 enslaved people southward from the Zwartland to Cape Town. En route, the rebels attacked farms and destroyed any paper documents they found. Louis brandished in his hand a document that he claimed conferred freedom to the slaves.[40] The NHM commissioned Barry Jackson to create a life-size statue of Louis, thereby commemorating also the slave rebellion he led.[41] It now stands as part of the NHM, the only enslaved person represented among the 100 or so completed statues. It is hard to imagine that such a statue would have been commissioned, certainly in such a conventional and heroic form, in a setting other than the NHM, where, by association, he takes on the mantle of a human rights activist.

The bicentenary of the abolition of the slave trade was marked by a competition to design a memorial for display on Church Square. The City of Cape Town funded the competition. Gavin Younge and Wilma Cruise won with a highly conceptual design consisting of 11 blocks, nine in a three by three formation with two larger ones to the side. All were made of black Zimbabwe granite that had been polished to the point that the viewer's reflection was clearly visible, reminiscent of the material (though not the scale or shape) of Maya Lin's Vietnam Memorial. The larger blocks contained names drawn from the archives, and the smaller ones contained keywords from enslaved histories and legacies. The use of names is also a link with the Vietnam Memorial, which has provided an iconic form of counter-monument, aimed at commemorating loss and grief rather than triumph.[42]

The terms of the commission required the bronze statue of

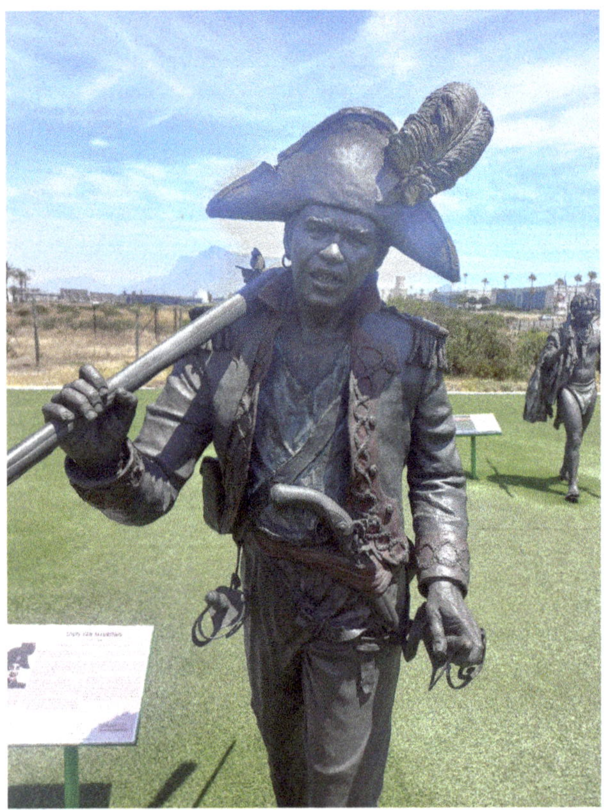

Figure 3. Barry Jackson, Louis van Mauritius statue. Photograph courtesy of Barry Jackson

Onze Jan Hofmeyr, made by Anton van Wouw in 1920, to be left in place at the center of the square. Lifted all of four meters by its sandstone base, the towering figure of Hofmeyr looks toward the entrance of the Moederkerk, home of the Dutch Reformed Church (NG Kerk). The Younge/Cruise design seeks connection with the imposing Old Mutual Building (1863, now housing Iziko's Social History Center) located right behind it,[43] and to a lesser extent with the Slave Lodge,[44] off indirectly to the side and separated by the four lanes of Spin Street. There is a further proximity that is as historically significant as it is publicly inconspicuous: the fir tree under which slaves were auctioned, removed in 1916. A circular marker no more than one meter in diameter, slightly raised from pedestrian level, reads in unassuming bronze letters: "On this spot stood the old slave tree," and in Afrikaans *"Op hierdie plek het die ou slaweboom gestaan."* It was installed in 1953 as part of the median in the middle of Spin Street, which divides Church Square and the Old Mutual Building

from the Slave Lodge.[45] It functions as a kind of footnote to the baleful history of the place, legible only to those who may have sought it out in advance. The low elevation of this memorial, whose inscribed center is approximately the size of a manhole, could not form a greater contrast with the elevated statue of Hofmeyr. These two coexist with the Memorial to the Enslaved in a grossly unequal competition of height. Whether intentionally or not, both the memorial and the place-marker of the old slave tree are integrated into the everyday life of the city, walked over or used as a table or seat by people going about their business in the middle of the city. Hofmeyr's statue towers above, but it remains to be seen whether the resulting prominence, like that of Van Wouw's statue of President M. T. Steyn at the University of the Free State, will precipitate its removal, though in this case the location is less charged than a university campus.[46]

This design was the unanimous winner of a competition, yet even after the decision, the selection committee warned Younge and Cruise that the design might have difficulty winning popular acceptance. Members of the public, the artists were told, might have preferred a "more documentary approach."[47] In fact, most of the competing submissions had been figurative designs. In his tactful account, Younge does not mention a political factor that has grown in intensity in recent years. In an age of identity

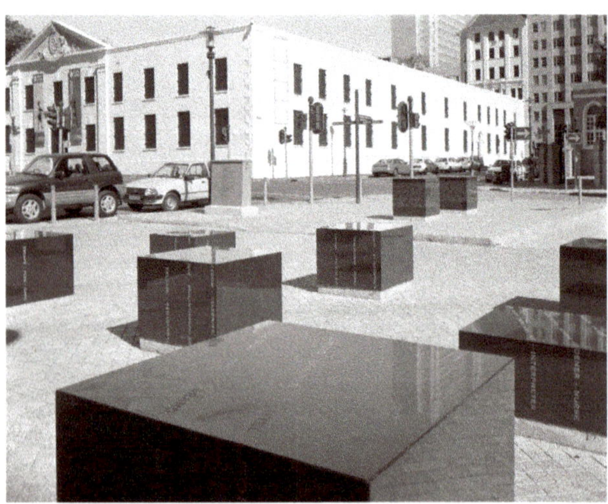

Figure 4. Photograph by David Goldblatt. Memorial to the Enslaved by Wilma Cruise and Gavin Young. The white building was the Dutch East India Company's slave lodge in the center of Cape Town. Some 9,000 slaves, convicts, and mentally disturbed people are thought to have been confined within it between 1679 and 1811. It is now a museum. 11 March 2012 (4_A0894)

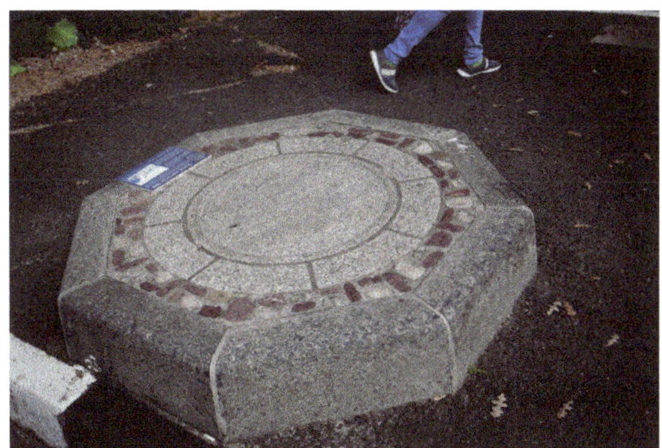

Figure 5. Old Slave Tree Memorial, Spin Street, Cape Town. The Octagonal place-marker, located close to foot level and inscribed in English and Afrikaans, was erected in 1953. It marks the spot where enslaved persons were sold underneath a fir tree. The stump of the tree was cut down by the city of Cape Town in 1916. Photograph by Paul Weinberg.

politics, the commissioned artists were not themselves descended from the oppressed group depicted, which likely exacerbated the discomfort some community members felt about the winning design.

A daring commemoration was designed by Marco Cianfanelli for display at Spier Wine Estate outside Stellenbosch.[48] Its point of departure is Michelangelo's famous marble sculpture known as *The Dying Slave* (1513–1515), which stands some 2.15 meters tall in the Louvre Museum in Paris. Cianfanelli's composition expands this already large design by focusing on the face alone and expanding it to the full height of 4.1 meters. This design contends with and highlights the death throes of the slave—the final ecstatic moment of a life of bondage—and thus intensified pathos. The artist created a highly pixelated version of a photograph of the statue's head, and then worked with the artists of the Spier Art Academy to realize the design in mosaic form. The eight irregularly placed columns It can be viewed from either side, recreating both the positive and negative elements of photography. The work stands an imposing 42 square meters and covers an installation of nearly 30 square meters. Viewers are invited to walk among the pillars, thus inhabiting its physical space. As with Cianfanelli's *Release*, the work suggestively recreates a face of great historical and symbolic significance. The combination of mosaic and pixilation,

or an early modern statue form with a fragmented contemporary form, suggests a juxtaposition of innovation and tradition. Located at a pedestrian crossroads between the luxury Spier Hotel and the conference center, the work is confronting and unmissable. It conveys its own version of *Et in Arcadia ego*, the idea that the wine farms, for all their contemporary elegance, are products of slave labor going back to the Dutch occupation, and perhaps even that the legacies of bondage are visible to anyone looking beyond the tourist and business amenities of the estate. The use of a face, conveying pathos in ecstatic form, is, not surprisingly, the emotional core of the piece in an alarmingly explicit sense. The figurative quality of the image is a direct index of distressing human histories around bondage, yet its disrupted realization heightens its claim on the viewer's attention. In this way, the design may be an unexpected antidote to compassion fatigue, a questioning of its own social setting.

To move further back in time is to find slim pickings. At Elim, one of the mission stations that sustained the lives of formerly enslaved persons, stands a simple monument commemorating the official end of slavery on December 1, 1838 (in keeping with the Slavery Abolition Act of 1833). It was inaugurated a century later on the same date in 1938. It appears to have been set up by the Moravian

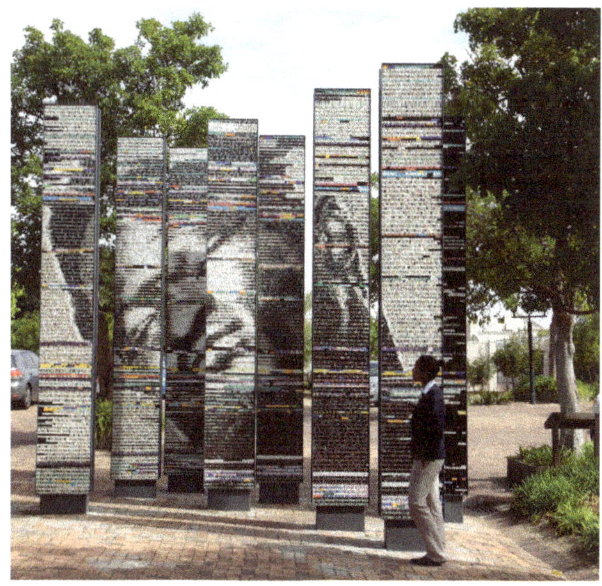

Figure 6. Marco Cianfanelli, The Dying Slave. Photograph courtesy of Marco Cianfanelli.

church. The design could not be simpler: a solid white cube topped by a pyramid-like shape, creating an obelisk-like structure. The inscription reads, *"Aandenking aan die vrylating van slawe. 1 Des[ember] 1838. Offer dank aan God."* ("Commemoration of the emancipation of enslaved people. 1 December 1838. Give thanks to God.") The repetition of the December 1 date is in keeping with the collective memory around slavery. The simplicity of its gestures is striking in its own way. Its abstract design should, in this case, be no surprise. Any figurative design would have been far too strident a statement for the political establishment at the time of J. B. M. Hertzog's premiership. In any case, this design in its outer form rhymes with Afrikaner cairns and obelisks that were used in the 1930s to mark the centenary of the Great Trek. Whereas the shape and proportions are comparable, the flat whitewashed surfaces at Elim could not be more different than the sandstone of Afrikanerdom's monuments. The sandstone cairns and obelisks match the brown Karoo rocks of the hinterland, but the capacious whitewashed obelisk at Elim matches the humble cottages of the Moravian mission station.

Unlike Jackson's Louis and the granite blocks of Younge and Cruise, the Elim monument is in a remote location in the Overstrand. Agulhas, the southernmost point of Africa, is a mere 46 kilometers away, but the road network there lacks a high-speed freeway, which means that Elim has little ability to lure tourists away from the circuit linking Cape Town, the elegant winelands, and the resort town of Hermanus. There is little evidence that the Elim monument was intended for anyone other than the community members. Its restoration in 2004, unveiled by the CEO of the Iziko Museums, Professor Jatti Bredekamp, was marked by a modest event. Quite possibly, the simple poignancy of the monument suggests that it has the unusual potential of holding meaning for local people, rather than for tourists,

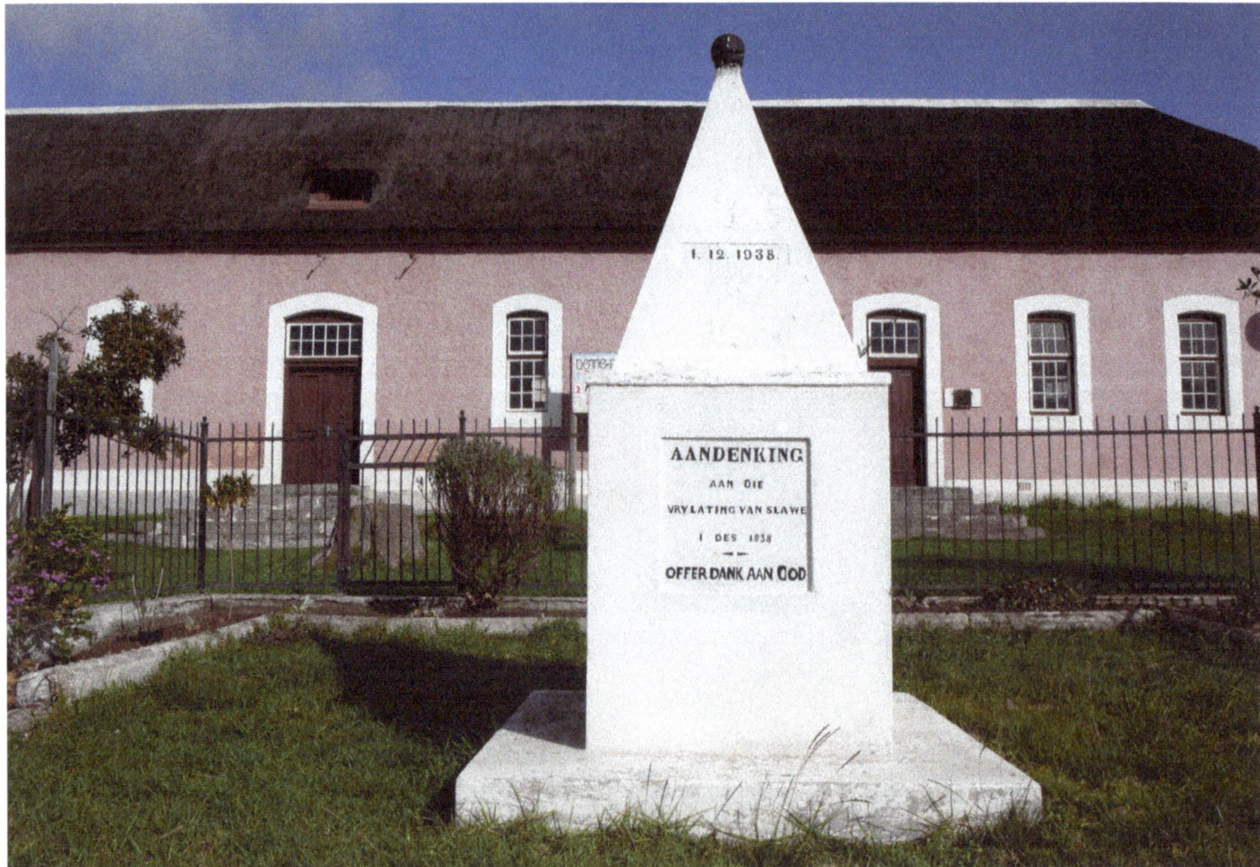

Figure 7. Elim memorial to emancipation. Photograph by Paul Weinberg.

and was intended principally for the locals.

Even if this sample set is too small to allow conclusions to be drawn, this overview of South African slave monuments suggests that faces have had no natural role to play. A key potential difference is between those commemorations aimed at the tourists, as is the case in so many African contexts, and those that appear to have more local resonance.

It is unclear what international comparisons can bring to the question beyond showing that both figurative and conceptual designs have been used in the past three decades. Certainly, some memorials are site-specific. The Gateway of No Return, at Ouidah, Benin, is linked to the route of the Middle Passage. This concrete, cement, and copper structure is decorated with etchings depicting groups of chained men heading toward the ocean and, by implication, to slavery in the Americas. It was inaugurated in 1995, funded by the government of Benin and UNESCO as part of its Slave Route.[49] At Lancaster, a former slave port in the UK, *Captured Africans* (2005) by Kevin Dalton-Johnson focuses on the slave trade in a complex abstract design. Dominated by a stainless-steel frame, this work also involved mosaic artists and youth art programs. With its many features, it aims to attract viewers and hold their attention in a reflective spirit. It contains some small human figures in gestures of distress, on the ground, positioned on a map of the Atlantic Middle Passage.[50] In both cases, the matter of faces is obviated by the small scale and generic nature of the depicted bodies.

Nonetheless, figurative memorials are by no means unknown, as we see in two examples from 1998, marking the 150th anniversary of abolition. At the slave market in Stone Town, Zanzibar, which was a major location for the slave trade, Clara Sörnäs' Memorial for the Slaves depicts five concrete figures in a submerged enclosure. The figures have expressions that are sullen and dejected but also quietly dignified. All five face outward without mutual connection other than the chain binding their necks, as if awaiting purchase. Here, faces are vehicles of pathos. By contrast, those at the Anse Cafard Slavery Memorial in Martinique are rough-hewn and lacking in detail. Twenty slumped figures, without facial distinctiveness and with their heads slumped, look toward the ocean to a point where a slave ship sank in 1830. The overall impression here is of uniformity shaped by their dismal shared fate. In both the Zanzibar and Martinique installations, the price of the depicting pathos is the removal of any sense of agency on the part of the enslaved figures.

If faces sit awkwardly with the commemoration of slavery, the same is true regarding the Holocaust. Herman Wald's *Memorial to the Six Million* was completed in 1959 in Johannesburg's Westpark Cemetery. It included hands instead as a synecdoche for the large number of victims. Each of the fists is 1.5 meters high, as if bursting out of the ground, and holds a ram's horn (5.1 meters high) to form a series of three arches. The feature in the center constitutes a flame articulating the sixth commandment, "Thou shalt not kill." This is a living monument, rededicated on April 27, 1995, on the 50th anniversary of the liberation of the camps and still used by the Jewish community for regular remembrance rituals. Wald (1906–1970) was born in Hungary and came to Johannesburg in 1937, where he became famous for his large-scale sculptures. In this case, the use of faces would have violated Jewish aniconism, expressed in the second commandment (Exodus 20: 3–6), whereas the exaggerated hands contribute to a symbolic design.

IV. FACES FROM UNDERGROUND

The next example takes us from statues in the usual sense to video art focused on statues and other site-specific public art. In his video essay of 13 minutes and 51 seconds entitled *Iseeyou* (2013), Simon Gush trains his camera on representations of mining in Johannesburg in order to consider what is at stake in the visibility and invisibility of labor.[51] The nature of work itself in its political and ideological dimensions comes into question, including a good deal of self-reflection on the filmmaker's part. Gush references several of his own works as a photographer, including the process that went into creating the film. For the purposes of this essay, *Iseeyou* is a secondary frame of commemoration in that it engages with preexisting statues to consider underlying social phenomena.

Gush's survey begins with the bronze colossus, *The Miner*.

At four times life size, it greets everyone entering the city on what is now Albertina Sisulu Road from the direction of the airport. At 9 meters tall including the base, it is one of the country's tallest monuments. Commissioned by the Johannesburg City Council to mark the centenary of the city in 1988, and designed by Tienie Pritchard, it depicts George Harrison, who was supposedly the first discoverer of gold on the farm Langlaagte.[52] The gesture is extravagant. The male figure, with his right foot far forward and slightly raised, is naked above the waist and wears the long trousers and boots of a miner. With a pickaxe in his left hand and a knapsack on his right hip, the figure looks upward with a sharply tilted head at a rock triumphantly held in his right hand: gold, "a monument to aspiration" (00:39). Its bulking size has protected the statue from the kind of neglect and destruction that has befallen the Langlaagte site itself, which has been curated as George Harrison Park.[53] The overdetermined visibility of the monument gives it a Statue of Liberty quality, but the face itself is out of view, pointed upward at a considerable height. Conceivably, this invisibility of the face deracializes the monument as seen from the ground, thus giving it a chance of surviving the current impetus to decolonize the commemorative landscape.

This is merely the first of six main statues canvased by Gush, complemented by other monumental features of the built environment, whether architectural (e.g., the Chamber of Mines building, with the decorative roundels on its façade depicting miners) or else the large-scale mining equipment redeployed in the CBD as urban adornment (including Kumba, a retired iron ore truck of Gulliverian proportions, and the Langlaagte Stamp Mill).[54] At Gold Reef City, a former mine turned amusement park, the life-threatening dangers of mining are sugar-coated as the banal thrills of a visit to the Tower of Terror, as announced by a painted sign at the top of the headgear.

Statues from before and after the end of apartheid predominate in the film, creating a sense of continuity that implicitly questions the political transition of the 1990s. David McGregor's *Monument to the Miners* (1964), which includes a trio of bronze male miner figures—one white foreman and two black workers—was intended to represent a typical underground scene from 1936. It is located outside the Johannesburg Civic Center (1963). The installation of the three bronze miners, which face west toward Langlaagte, thus marked the 50th anniversary of the discovery of gold as a belated commemoration that also celebrated the high modernism of the newly built Civic Center.[55] The installation was a combined gift from the chambers of mines of the Orange Free State and the Transvaal. In its realism, the installation gives the miners a heroic status that would not have been out of keeping with Soviet public art of the same period. In the high noon of Verwoerdian segregation, at a time when apartheid laws sought to prevent racial groups from mixing not only in marriage and sexual relations but even on the theatrical stage, mining was somehow exempt from these strictures. This monument, by the same token, was located in the country's financial headquarters, a place of physical proximity of mining capital and unskilled labor. Presumably the status disparities implicit in the statue group were supposed to be obvious enough to viewers. In any case, the economic importance of mining trumped other social mores.

Whatever the political sea changes since the 1960s, mining monuments continue to be, in Gush's presentation, a telling window to the country's economy and social attitudes. Johannesburg's transition from mining to manufacturing to a service economy is emblematic of much larger trends, and monuments are an index of the changes that have occurred from the origins of Johannesburg through the 21st century. In the final scene of his video essay, Gush films the digging of a hole alongside a suburban arterial road he repeatedly traveled in making the film. In the context of mineworking, this everyday moment of suburban life is subject to defamiliarization, particularly because no worker is shown. There is merely sand emerging from the deepening hole. Gush reflects, "[B]ecause we see less and less work directly, images of work have become nostalgic." Images, both photographs and his photograph-like films, "capture something about a simpler time"—that is, from a different economic regime.

On the pavement outside the Chamber of Mines is Andile Msongelwa's statue of a solitary miner who kneels while drilling (02:00). Inaugurated on May 7, 2013, it reflects the agreement between the Chamber and trade unions

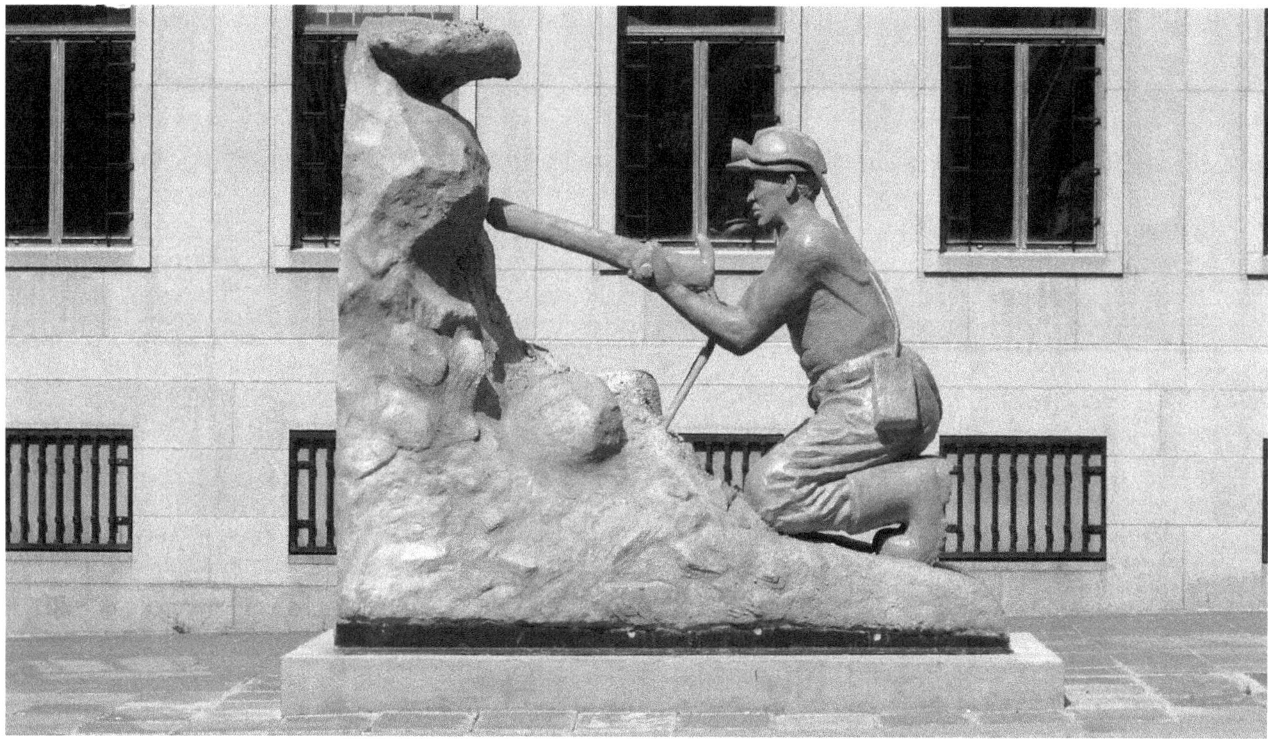

Figure 8. Andile Msongelwa, Statue of a miner kneeling. Still from Simon Gush's film, *Iseeyou*. Image courtesy of Simon Gush.

(National Union of Mineworkers, UASA, and Solidarity) at the end of wage negotiations in 2007. The statue itself expresses their agreement to "recognize the role played by mineworkers in developing the economy" of the country, including mining towns and areas providing labor:

> We salute these economic heroes who rushed their lives to make Johannesburg on the most economically vibrant cities of the continent. We value their contribution to the economy and will strive for quality education for our children and the development of skills of mine workers to enable them to play their rightful role in the continuing economic development of mining communities, labour sending areas and of the country as a whole.

If the inscription itself is a testament to the politics of recognition, its detailed coverage allows Gush to explain the wordplay of the title: *Iseeyou* invokes the name of

the Industrial and Commercial Workers (ICU) founded by the Malawi-born Clements Kadalie (1896–1951) in 1919. Visibility is not an unqualified good. It can mean political recognition. On the other hand, invisibility can mark collective bargaining power and with it an individual's ability to gain safety by hiding in the crowd.

> *I see you* is an idea that highlights an interesting ambiguity about visibility and representation. To the unrepresented worker, the union might be saying "I see you, I see how you are treated, you are not invisible to us." But the power of invisibility is also part of the power of the unions. You are no longer an individual who can be singled out, but part of a unified voice, a crowd. Because of the power of the collective, invisibility can be as valuable as visibility.

Several of Gush's works from around this time explore the idea of work in different aspects. *Red* (2014, created in collaboration with James Cairns) is a full-length documentary on the extended wildcat strike at the Mercedes-Benz plant in East London in 1990. During the strike, workers took it upon themselves to build a red Mercedes-Benz 500SE for the newly freed Nelson Mandela. *Calvin and Holiday* (2014) explores Geneva's urban landscape in order to reframe the Protestant work ethic. The architecture of John Calvin's city gives clues about values. *Lazy Nigel* (2015) involves the mining town of Nigel on the East Rand. Via warehouses, amusement parks, and other scenes from everyday life, Gush measures the dynamics of work and leisure. Here especially, he reveals a photographic technique that is reminiscent of Goldblatt: a black-and-white larger landscape with a static outer frame that circumscribes tightly controlled internal movement. These video essays make use of white noise: inconspicuous circumambient sound emanating from traffic, wind, and other sources that are typically not visible in the frame itself.

Iseeyou canvases monumental faces as indexes of social and economic relations around work. Faces are how Gush's camera can offer an angle on practices of economic life and the thinking that underlies them. As a variant on South Africa's rich tradition of documentary photography and photojournalism, which typically focuses on human subjects as directly as possible, *Iseeyou* exploits the different rhythms of static black-and-white photography, in which the representation itself is part of the equation. There is a paradox in this scenario: as Gush puts it, "[i]mages of work are created through its public representation to ennoble the act of labour." Thus, there may be something deceitful in public art, a phenomenon akin to Pierre Nora's famous distinction between "places of memory" and "milieux of memory," where the former are more arbitrary and the latter are more organic, continuous, and deeply rooted.[56] Explicit commemorative acts can be a response to an overwhelming implicit amnesia and even a continuation of them. Paradoxically, then, monuments mark society's oversights. The question thus raised by Gush is a radical one: that monuments may be considered dead on arrival, their unveiling in unintended effect absolving and blocking communities from more meaningful ongoing acknowledgement.

The faces in the film express recognition in a starkly political sense. Ostensibly they bestow individuality on humans thus imagined. Faces are how Gush urges his viewers to take a humane view of the hard, physical work that has underpinned Johannesburg from its beginnings to the present. Yet he also shows the limits of such a vision by referring to the Protestant work ethic, with its troubling assumptions about the redemptive nature of labor. The faces also raise a political question concerning trade unions and political parties that claim to represent the interests of mining and other labor. Statuary faces make it possible for Gush to question the degree to which viewers connect with public commemorations. All told, statues in Gush's vision cast doubt on the relationship between individuals and collectives.

Via the videographic medium, Gush adds an interpretive layer between the statues and the viewer. The statues are flattened into the two dimensions of Golblattian photography, with their distinctive frames based around geometrical shapes. Gush's use of sound enhances the contexts of the statues, both physical and social. Statuary faces, or the pointed lack thereof, allow Gush to illustrate the evanescence of labor in the neoliberal economy. The is increasing disappearance of labor from view leaves face-bearing statues as an anomalous reminder of earlier times. The use of black and white, harking back to Goldblatt's heyday, itself adds a "nostalgic" touch, to use Gush's own word.

V. FACE + PLACE = PUBLIC HISTORY?

 If the guiding question is whether history needs a face, then the simple equation hypothesized here by way of a conclusion would be too extreme, even though it surely contains some measure of truth. Faces bestow vividness on locations, animating what might otherwise be a standard, simple plaque of the kind erected by the Historical Monuments Commission (1923–1969), the National Monuments Council (1969–2000), and, in this millennium, SAHRA and its provincial organs. In some of the examples canvased here, the location involved can become clogged with a profusion of commemorations. Consider the uneasy combination of the Afrikaner leader Onze Jan Hofmeyr in Church Square with two different memorials to slavery, installed some 50 years apart. Or the Grand Parade, where Nelson Mandela looks out from the balcony where he first addressed the world following his release. He is facing King

Edward VII—on an axis briefly occupied by Msezane for a few hours on Heritage Day 2014. Pretoria's Lilian Ngoyi Square, a renamed and redesigned form of what had been Strijdom Square, epitomizes the commemorative implications of political transition.

The formula hypothesized here requires artists, communities, and governmental organizations to have the opportunity to make creative use of particular places with some sense of assurance that their voices count. In the case of authoritarian states, this is not an issue. To take an extreme example, 20th-century totalitarian monumentality lives on in one of its most grandiose relics: the Mansudae Grand Monument in Pyongyang, North Korea. At its center are bronze statues of former leaders Kim Il-sung (r. 1948–94) and Kim Jong-il (1994–2011). Standing 20 meters tall, they would dwarf even the Union Building Mandela. These statues present a highly personalized ideology of power, which also provides legitimacy and authority to the incumbent, Kim Jong-un. The individuality of this duo contrasts with the 50-meter-long bronze panel of figures on either side, 228 in total, representing the Korean War or, as the North Korean government would have it, the Fatherland Liberation War. In between these large groups is the Korean Revolution Museum, its vast façade of concrete pillars and mosaics constituting the background to the leaders' colossal statues.

When, in a parliamentary presentation on September 3, 2020, Arts and Culture Minister Nathi Mthethwa mentioned the possibility of creating a theme park for statues from the colonial and apartheid periods, the "Budapest option" was raised. The idea does not come as a surprise.[57] While the idea of theme park makes sense from the point of view of safety and security, it subjects the resulting installation to a fundamental objection. Nora's point that curated "places of memory" are counterproductive to the more organic "milieux of memory" is all the more apt. If, by Nora's reckoning, monuments have the paradoxical ability to absolve societies from the need to remember the past, then statue parks represent a further marginalization of the collective memory and its objects. Any meaningful solution to the problem of commemoration has to be much wider ranging than a statue or memorial itself,

and the solution must address memory, especially traumatic memory, in ways that are more closely connected with the people who are supposed to do the remembering. On these lines, James Young has praised commemorations like Gunter Demnig's small, ground-level *Stolpersteine* (stumbling stones) precisely because these are unobtrusively integrated into everyday life.[58] Such measures, which are at the farthest possible point on the continuum from triumphalist, figurative statues, are a solution, but one that only works in conjunction with the fuller social range of a "milieu of memory," which, in the case of South Africa, would have to address place names and the historical content of school curricula. Such measures have much less to do with the spectacle of the kind that statues have attracted and much more to do with deeply held ideologies, identities, and values in subtler ways—what Bourdieu called *habitus.*

The faces we have seen here are sometimes about individual heroism and power, in keeping with Greco-Roman tradition.[59] In a South African setting, they convey the implication that human history, and particularly national identity, may be perceived in human terms. Monuments, especially when colossal, can thus be considered three-dimensional instantiations of charisma. The placement of such statues at places of historical significance can be a way of naturalizing them. In the post-apartheid era, the question of nation building has, to a considerable extent, been publicly presented in terms of individuals, especially Mandela and Archbishop Tutu in the 1990s. One token of the politics of personality was the 1994 election, in which each party on the ballot sheet was represented by the face of the leader along with the party name and emblem. This feature, followed in several but certainly not all countries, was a concession to first-time voters and very likely benefited Mandela, who had star quality his rivals could not match. Statues seem like the logical consequence of this development. Yet the matter is far from simple. The supposedly mature democracy of the United States has seen, if anything, an extraordinary escalation in the politics of personality that is especially visible in the election season, and perhaps exponentially so in the Trump era. This overdetermined individuality presents many problems of historical vision. For one thing, processes are short-changed. In a South African context, this is a very real question around the struggle against apartheid. Though it might suit the ruling ANC to celebrate its freedom-fighting heroes as the true founders of the republic, a more scholarly approach would canvas other factors beyond the domestic and continental resistance. Proximate causes such as economic sanctions and the end of the Cold War do not lend themselves to representation in a historical pageant. To what degree should they be represented, and by what means? These are questions that are fully deserving of a multilateral conversation, which they did not necessarily receive before the sprawling NHM got underway.

The case of Archbishop Tutu is instructive. His appearance in the NHM's Long March to Freedom in March 2023 seems retrograde in view of the earlier commemoration in the Arch for Arch, unveiled outside St. George's Cathedral on October 7, 2017, to mark his 86th birthday. At the earlier event, Tutu himself was in attendance, having apparently given his approval to the design in advance. By contrast, his outspoken criticism of the ANC in his later years, not to mention his irreverent manner, raise the question of whether he would have accepted a place within the triumphalist frame of the NHM.

The faces we have seen here also express physical vulnerability. If physical violence is an imminent danger to South African statues, then it is a danger to persons. One obvious feature shared by public history and public art is the notion of the public per se. If public protests are a new norm, it is simply not feasible to erect monumental artworks with an assumption of eternity. Ephemeral media such as Msezane's anti-monumental performance pieces are much more suited to a world in which change and uncertainty are, paradoxically, the only certainty. If bodies are vulnerable, then even such pop-up works require some kind of public that allows the performance to take place. This issue is not easily discussed and its terminology far from agreed. No self-respecting progressive-minded scholar wants to use the "law and order" rhetoric of authoritarian leaders such as Mussolini, Bolzonaro, or Trump. Some designs invite viewers' interventions and thus obviate the question of

what is sometimes called vandalism. But the question remains: What version of "public" will allow public art to be created and viewed, and public history to be taught and learned? For reasons both abstract and concrete, no monument can be expected to articulate consensus that does not exist socially.

Constitution Hill in Braamfontein offers one model for public art but hardly in the sense of statuary discussed in this essay.[60] On the contrary, it offers an alternative paradigm. Once the Old Fort Prison that held Gandhi and Mandela for short spells, the complex has been entirely redesigned to house the highest court in the land within an extended human rights–themed precinct that contains several museums. The design—an unexpected combination of lawcourt and living museum with a strong commitment to the creative arts—is the brainchild of Albie Sachs, a freedom fighter turned judge. The complex also contains a revolving art exhibit in different media, though not necessarily performative. The overwhelming message emerging from the design is inclusiveness and open-endedness.[61] Key features of relevance to the current discussion include the significance of place, going back to the time of Paul Kruger's South African Republic; architecture per se, in this case an intentional combination of rebuilding and historic preservation; and the idea of reuse as political and even ethical transformation. This may not be public art in the usual sense, yet it, too, has the impact of historically inflected art in the public domain—not a town square but a complex to which access is carefully controlled by security personnel. The model of public space is different to a university campus or a public park such as the Company's Gardens in Cape Town. Far from being safe spaces for public art, campuses have become places of heightened vulnerability in South Africa and elsewhere. Whereas many other locations rely on figurative statuary to obtain an aura of historical significance, the design and scale of Constitution Hill make it the exception that proves the rule.

— **Grant Parker**

BIBLIOGRAPHY

Beard, Mary. *The Roman Triumph.* Belknap, 2007.

Brennan, Jan. "Public Art and the Art of Public Participation." *National Civic Review* 108, no. 3 (2019): 34–44. https://www.nationalcivicleague.org/ncr-article/public-art-and-the-art-of-public-participation/.

Bridgland, Fred. *Truth, Lies and Alibis: A Winnie Mandela Story.* Tafelberg, 2018.

Edwards, Mark and Simon Swain, eds. *Portraits: Biographical Representation in the Greek and Latin Literature of the Roman Empire.* Clarendon, 1997.

Fejfer, Jane and Kristine Bøggild Johannsen, eds. *Face to Face: Thorvaldsen & Portraiture.* Thorvaldsen's Museum, 2020.

Florida, Richard L. *Cities and the Creative Class.* Routledge, 2005.

Florida, Richard L. *The New Urban Crisis: How Our Cities Are Increasing Inequality, Deepening Segregation, and Failing the Middle Class—And What We Can Do About It.* Basic Books, 2017.

Freschi, Federico. "Postapartheid Publics and the Politics of Ornament: Nationalism, Identity, and the Rhetoric of Community in the Decorative Program of the New Constitutional Court, Johannesburg," *Africa Today* 54. 2 (2007): 27-49

Jansen, Jonathan D. "'It is Not Even Past': Dealing with Monuments and Memorials on Divided Campuses." In *Troubling Images: Visual Culture and the Politics of Afrikaner Nationalism,* edited by Federico Freschi, Brenda Schmahmann and Lize Van Robbroeck. Wits University Press, 2020.

Lodge, Tom. *Mandela: A Critical Life.* Oxford University Press, 2006.

Marschall, Sabine. *Landscape of Memory: Commemorative Monuments, Memorials and Public Statuary in Post-Apartheid South Africa.* Brill, 2010.

Msimang, Sisonke. *The Resurrection of Winnie Mandela: A Biography of Survival.* Jonathan Ball Publishers, 2018.

Nora, Pierre. "Between Memory and History: Les Lieux De Mémoire." *Representations* 26, 1 (1989): 7–24. https://doi.org/10.2307/2928520.

Pauwels, Matthias. "Agonistic Entanglements of Art and Activism: #RhodesMustFall and Sethembile Msezane's Chapangu Performances." De Arte 54, 3 (2019): 1–19. https://doi.org/10.1080/00043389.2019.1612540.

Rankin, Elizabeth. "Creating/Curating Cultural Capital: Monuments and Museums for Post-Apartheid South Africa." Humanities 2, 1 (2013): 72–98. https://doi.org/10.3390/h2010072.

Schmahmann, Brenda. *Picturing Change: Curating Visual Culture at Post-Apartheid Universities.* Wits University Press, 2013.

Sontag, Susan. *On Photography.* Picador, 1977.

Shepherd, Nick and Steven L. Robins, eds. *New South African Keywords.* Jacana, 2008.

Steinberg, Jonny. *Nelson and Winnie: A Portrait of Marriage.* Jonathan Ball Publishers, 2023.

Stewart, Andrew F. *Faces of Power: Alexander's Image and Hellenistic Politics.* University of California Press, 1993.

Way, Lucan A. "The Authoritarian Threat: Weaknesses of Autocracy Promotion," *Journal of Democracy,* 27. 1 (2016): 64-75.

Wedeen, Lisa. *Authoritarian Apprehensions: Ideology, Judgment and Mourning in Syria.* University of Chicago Press, 2019.

Worden, Nigel. "Cape Slaves in the Paper Empire of the VOC." *Kronos* 40 (2009): 23–44. http://www.scielo.org.za/scielo.php?script=sci_arttext&pid=S0259-01902014000100002&lng=en&nrm=iso.

Worden, Nigel. "The Changing Politics of Slave Heritage in the Western Cape, South Africa." *Journal of African History* 50, 1 (2009). https://www.jstor.org/stable/40206696.

Worden, Nigel. "Armed with Swords and Ostrich Feathers: Militarism and Cultural Revolution in the Cape Slave Uprising of 1808." In *War, Empire and Slavery, 1770-1830,* edited by Richard Bessel, Nicholas Guyatt, and Jane Rendall. Palgrave Macmillan, 2010.

Worden, Nigel. "Cape Slaves in the Paper Empire of the VOC," *Kronos* 40 (2014): 23-44.

Young, James Edward. *The Texture of Memory: Holocaust Memorials and Meaning.* Yale University Press, 1993.

Younge, Gavin. "The Mirror and the Square—Old Ideological Conflicts in Motion: Church Square Slavery Memorial." In *Public Art in South Africa: Bronze Warriors and Plastic Presidents,* edited by Kim Miller and Brenda Schmahmann. Indiana University Press, 2017.

ENDNOTES

1 Jacey Fortin, "Toppling Monuments, A Visual History," *New York Times*, August 17, 2017, https://www.nytimes.com/2017/08/17/world/controversial-statues-monuments-destroyed.html. A South African example is the bust of Cecil Rhodes in the Rhodes Memorial, the nose of which was sawn off in September 2015, five months after his statue had been removed from the University of Cape Town's upper campus: https://www.iol.co.za/news/mystery-of-rhodes-missing-nose-1918649.

2 "Hungary Removes Statue of Anti-Soviet Hero Imre Nagy," BBC, December 28, 2028, https://www.bbc.com/news/world-europe-46704111. Ironically, Orban spoke in Nagy's honor at the 1989 event.

3 Max Fisher, "The Truth About Iconic 2003 Saddam Statue-Toppling," The Atlantic, January 3, 2011, https://www.theatlantic.com/international/archive/2011/01/the-truth-about-iconic-2003-saddam-statue-toppling/342802/. To take a more recent example, the toppling of Saddam Hussein's statue at Firdos Square, Baghdad, on April 9, 2003, was shown to have been staged by US forces to project an exaggerated sense of their support among the Iraqi population.

4 Lucan A. Way, "The Authoritarian Threat: Weaknesses of Autocracy Promotion," *Journal of Democracy*, 27. 1 (2016): 64-75; Lisa Wedeen, *Authoritarian Apprehensions: Ideology, Judgment and Mourning in Syria*, (University of Chicago Press, 2019).

5 Mark Edwards and Simon Swain, eds., *Portraits: Biographical Representation in the Greek and Latin Literature of the Roman Empire* (Clarendon, 1997).

6 "Brett Murray/Hail to the Thief II/2012," Goodman Gallery, access date November 14, 2024, https://www.goodman-gallery.com/exhibitions/johannesburg-gallery-brett-murray-hail-to-the-thief-ii-2012. The painting—acrylic on canvas, 185 cm by 140 cm—riffed directly on Semyonovich Ivanov's famous depiction of Lenin. It was part of Murray's exhibit, *Hail to the Thief II*, held at the Goodman Gallery in Johannesburg.

7 National Council on Public History, access date November 14, 2024, https://ncph.org/what-is-public-history/about-the-field/.

8 Nick Shepherd and Steven L. Robins, eds, *New South African Keywords*, (Jacana, 2008).

9 Department of Sport, Arts and Culture, access date November 14, 2024, https://www.dsac.gov.za/; National Heritage Council, access date November 14, 2024, http://www.nhc.org.za/; South Africa Heritage Resources Agency, access date November 14, 2024, https://www.sahra.org.za/.

10 Jan Brennan, "Public Art and the Art of Public Participation," *National Civic Review* 108, no. 3 (2019): 34, https://www.nationalcivicleague.org/ncr-article/public-art-and-the-art-of-public-participation/.

11 Brennan, "Public Art," 35.

12 Richard L. Florida, *Cities and the Creative Class*, (Routledge, 2005). The concept of the creative class has generated much interest but also critique. In later work, Florida shows how certain cities have become less affordable because of urban renewal and ironically owing partly to the role of the creative class.

13 The work of Stewart (1993) on the image of Alexander the Great remains influential; see now Marest-Caffey (2017) concerning faces on smaller media.

14 National Heritage Monument, accessed August 17, 2021, link inactive February 11, 2024, https://www.nhmsa.co.za/march.html#!Introduction.

15 http://www.koketso.co.za/

16 Sheree Bega, "Dali's Dream Memorial Under Fire," *IOL*, February 27, 2016, https://www.iol.co.za/news/south-africa/gauteng/dalis-dream-memorial-under-fire-1990707.

17 "Fossil Hominid Sites of South Africa," UNESCO World Heritage Convention, access date November 14, 2024, https://whc.unesco.org/en/list/915/. While the need to vacate the initial Groenkloof site was urgent, the Maropeng site was a nonstarter in at least two ways. Located at least an hour's drive out of Johannesburg, this relatively remote spot was at odds with the mostly urban-based activities of most of the heroes. In addition, the Cradle of Humankind exhibits early hominids rather than modern history.

18 "National Heritage Monument Project; Department of Tourism Implementation of BRRR & Oversight Reports; with Deputy Minister," Parliamentary Monitory Group, September 19, 2023, https://pmg.org.za/committee-meeting/37526/.

19 These were cast by Zelda Stroud (Oliver Tambo) and the rest by Tania Lee.

20 Mary Beard, *The Roman Triumph*, (Belknap, 2007).

21 Tom Lodge, *Mandela: A Critical Life*, (Oxford University Press, 2006), 69.

22 Elizabeth Rankin, "Creating/Curating Cultural Capital: Monuments and Museums for Post-Apartheid South Africa," *Humanities* 2, 1 (2013): 73–74. https://doi.org/10.3390/h2010072.

23 Fred Bridgland, *Truth, Lies and Alibis: A Winnie Mandela Story*, (Tafelberg, 2018); Sisonke Msimang, *The Resurrection of Winnie Mandela: A Biography of Survival*, (Jonathan Ball Publishers, 2018); Jonny Steinberg, *Nelson and Winnie: A Portrait of Marriage*, (Jonathan Ball Publishers, 2023).

24 Rapula Moatshe, "55 new struggle icon statues unveiled," *IOL*, September 16, 2015. https://www.iol.co.za/news/south-africa/gauteng/55-new-struggle-icon-statues-unveiled-1917081.

25 Jane Fejfer and Kristine Bøggild Johannsen, eds., *Portraits: Biographical Representation in the Greek and Latin Literature of the Roman Empire*, (Clarendon, 1997), 219.

26 Sabine Marschall, *Landscape of Memory: Commemorative Monuments, Memorials and Public Statuary in Post-Apartheid South Africa*, (Brill, 2010), 258.

27 Goldblatt's critique is implicit in his laconic note concerning the physical setting of this supposedly public monument: "It is not accessible to the public."

28 Andrew F. Stewart, *Faces of Power: The Image of Alexander and Hellenistic Politics*, (University of California Press, 1993).

29 https://www.sethembile-msezane.com/public-holiday-series, access date December 4, 2024.

30 "Metropolitan Methodist Church," Artefacts, access date November 14, 2024, https://www.artefacts.co.za/main/Buildings/bldgframes.php?bldgid=4139.

31 "Sethembile Msezane" Zeitz Museum of Contemporary Art Africa, access date November 14, 2024, https://zeitzmocaa.museum/artists/sethembile-msezane/.

32 Sethembile Msezane, "We Don't Need Statues—We Can Preserve Our History in More Memorable Ways," *TED*, July 17, 2020, https://ideas.ted.com/we-dont-need-statues-we-can-preserve-our-history-in-more-memorable-ways/.

33 The photograph appeared in the June 1985 edition of *National Geographic* amid enormous public interest in the United States.

34 Ribhu Karnad and Raghu Karnad, "You'll Never See the Iconic Photo of the 'Afghan Girl' the Same Way Again," *The Wire*, March 12, 2019, https://thewire.in/media/afghan-girl-steve-mccurry-national-geographic. The financial gain of McCurry and *National Geographic* contrasts with the consequences faced by Gula because of the media exposure, including arrest and ongoing precarity.

35 Susan Sontag, *On Photography*, (Picador, 1977), 14.

36 Kopano Maroga, "The Poetics of Remembrance as Resistance: The Works of Sethembile Msezane" *ArtTrob*, February 27, 2017. https://artthrob.

co.za/2017/02/27/the-poetics-of-remembrance-as-resistance-the-work-of-sethembile-msezane/.

[37] Matthias Pauwels, "Agonistic Entanglements of Art and Activism: #RhodesMustFall and Sethembile Msezane's Chapangu Performances," *De Arte* 54, 3 (2019): 1–19, https://doi.org/10.1080/00043389.2019.1612540.

[38] Nigel Worden, "Changing Politics."

[39] "Routes of Enslaved Peoples," UNESCO, access date November 14, 2024, https://en.unesco.org/themes/fostering-rights-inclusion/slave-route.

[40] Nigel Worden, "Cape Slaves in the Paper Empire of the VOC," *Kronos* 40 (2014), 37 Nigel Worden, "Armed with Swords and Ostrich Feathers: Militarism and Cultural Revolution in the Cape Slave Uprising of 1808," in *War, Empire and Slavery, 1770-1830*, edited by Richard Bessel, Nicholas Guyatt, and Jane Rendall (Palgrave Macmillan, 2010).

[41] https://www.nhmsa.co.za/sculpture.html?tag=louis_van_mauritius. This website offers moderate detail (but no references) that would help anyone wishing to research the biography of Louis van Mauritius in greater depth; "Louis. Van Mauritius and the Slave Revolt of 1808," South African History Online, access date November 14, 2024, https://www.sahistory.org.za/article/louis-van-mauritius-and-slave-revolt-1808#endnote-1-ref. More popular history (with references) can be found on the South African History Online website.

[42] James Edward Young, *The Texture of Memory: Holocaust Memorials and Meaning*, (Yale University Press, 1993).

[43] "Old Mutual," ArteFacts, access date November 14, 2024, https://www.artefacts.co.za/main/Buildings/bldgframes.php?bldgid=14299.

[44] "Iziko Museum–Slave Lodge–Supreme Court," ArteFacts, access date November 14, 2024, https://www.artefacts.co.za/main/Buildings/bldgframes.php?bldgid=157.

[45] https://digitalcollections.lib.uct.ac.za/islandora/object/islandora%3A17486/print_object

[46] Brenda Schmahmann, *Picturing Change: Curating Visual Culture at Post-Apartheid Universities*, (Wits University Press, 2013); Jonathan D Jansen, "'It Is Not Even Past'. Dealing with Monuments and Memorials on Divided Campuses," in *Troubling Images: Visual Culture and the Politics of Afrikaner Nationalism*, edited by Federico Freschi, Brenda Schmahmann and Lize Van Robbroeck, (Wits University Press, 2020).

[47] Gavin Younge, "The Mirror and the Square—Old Ideological Conflicts in Motion: Church Square Slavery Memorial," in *Public Art in South Africa: Bronze Warriors and Plastic Presidents*, edited by Kim Miller and Brenda Schmahmann (Indiana University Press, 2017), 61.

[48] "Cianfanelli Brings Dying Slave to Life," Spier, September 4, 2012, https://www.spier.co.za/blog/cianfanelli-brings-dying-slave-to-life.

[49] "La porte du non retour (The Gate of No Return) (Ouidah, Benin)," Contemporary Monuments to the Past, access date November 14, 2024, https://www.slaverymonuments.org/items/show/1147.

[50] "Captured African," Kevin Dalton-Johnson, access date November 14, 2024, http://www.kevindaltonjohnson.com/Commissions.php.

[51] "Films and Exhibitions," Simon Gush, access date November 14, 2024, https://simongush.net/simongush/; Simon Gush, "Iseeyou," Vimeo, November 3, 2013, https://vimeo.com/78477616. *Iseeyou* and other films are to be found on Gush's own website. Timings are in keeping with the Vimeo version.

[52] Tienie Pritchard Sculptor, access date November 14, 2024, http://tieniepritchard.co.za/. Pritchard's bronze work had gained fame by the 1980s, winning him many government and corporate commissions for portrait statues.

[53] James Ball, "A Depressing Visit to George Harrison Park," The Heritage Portal, October 14, 2015, http://www.theheritageportal.co.za/article/depressing-visit-george-harrison-park.

[54] Chipkin (1993: 16, 130); Bunn (1998).

[55] "Johannesburg Civic Center," ArteFacts, access date November 14, 2024, https://www.artefacts.co.za/main/Buildings/bldgframes.php?bldgid=8765.

[56] Pierre Nora, "Between Memory and History: Les Lieux De Mémoire," *Representations* 26, 1 (1989): 7, https://doi.org/10.2307/2928520.

[57] Marschall, *Landscape of Memory*, 148, 151.

[58] Stolpersteine, access date November 14, 2024, http://www.stolpersteine.eu/en/home/.

[59] Stewart, *Faces of Power*.

[60] "About Constitution Hill," Constitution Hill, access date November 14, 2024, https://www.constitutionhill.org.za/pages/about-constitution-hill

[61] Federico Freschi, "Postapartheid Publics and the Politics of Ornament: Nationalism, Identity, and the Rhetoric of Community in the Decorative Program of the New Constitutional Court, Johannesburg," *Africa Today* 54. 2 (2007): 27-49.